D1190928

DEMOCRACY ABROAD, LYNCHING AT HOME

UNIVERSITY PRESS OF FLORIDA

Florida A&M University, Tallahassee
Florida Atlantic University, Boca Raton
Florida Gulf Coast University, Ft. Myers
Florida International University, Miami
Florida State University, Tallahassee
New College of Florida, Sarasota
University of Central Florida, Orlando
University of Florida, Gainesville
University of North Florida, Jacksonville
University of South Florida, Tampa
University of West Florida, Pensacola

To the Florida Book Awards —

June 3, 2016

DEMOCRACY ABROAD, LYNCHING AT HOME

RACIAL VIOLENCE IN FLORIDA

TAMEKA BRADLEY HOBBS

Tameka Bradley Hobbs

University Press of Florida

Gainesville · Tallahassee · Tampa · Boca Raton

Pensacola · Orlando · Miami · Jacksonville · Ft. Myers · Sarasota

VIVA FLORIDA 500.
1513-2013

A Florida Quincentennial Book

20 19 18 17 16 15   6 5 4 3 2 1

Library of Congress Cataloging-in-Publication Data
Hobbs, Tameka B., author.
Democracy abroad, lynching at home : racial violence in Florida / Tameka
Bradley Hobbs.
pages cm
Includes bibliographical references and index.
ISBN 978-0-8130-6104-7
1. Lynching—Florida. 2. Florida—Race relations—History. 3. African
Americans—Crimes against—Florida. I. Title.
HV6465.F6H63 2015
364.1'34—dc23
2015006606

The University Press of Florida is the scholarly publishing agency for the
State University System of Florida, comprising Florida A&M University,
Florida Atlantic University, Florida Gulf Coast University, Florida
International University, Florida State University, New College of Florida,
University of Central Florida, University of Florida, University of North
Florida, University of South Florida, and University of West Florida.

University Press of Florida
15 Northwest 15th Street
Gainesville, FL 32611-2079
http://www.upf.com

To my family

CONTENTS

List of Figures / ix

Acknowledgments / xi

Introduction / 1

1. Lynched Twice: Arthur C. Williams, Gadsden County, 1941 / 33

2. A Degree of Restraint: The Trials of Cellos Harrison, 1940–1943 / 68

3. The Failure of Forbearance: The Lynching of Cellos Harrison, Jackson County, 1943 / 88

4. "A Very Cheap Article": The Lynching of Willie James Howard, Suwannee County, 1944 / 121

5. Still at It: The Lynching of Jesse James Payne, Madison County, 1945 / 156

Conclusion / 189

Epilogue. Strange Fruit, Bitter Seeds: The Echoes of Lynching Violence / 213

Notes / 221

Bibliography / 251

Index / 265

FIGURES

I.1. Claude Neal 30

1.1. Arthur C. Williams 63

2.1. W. Barkley Gause 77

2.2. William "Buddy" Gasque 80

2.3. Benjamin F. Barnes 85

5.1. Jesse James Payne 159

5.2. International Labor Defense (ILD) antilynching flyer (1945)
(*front*) 175

5.3. International Labor Defense (ILD) antilynching flyer (1945)
(*back*) 176

5.4. Cartoon, "Right forever on the scaffold, Wrong forever on
the throne" 180

5.5. Cartoon, "Still at It" 185

C.1. Cartoon, "Hitler Is Here" 193

C.2. Governor Spessard Holland and Governor-elect
Millard Caldwell 197

ACKNOWLEDGMENTS

This work has come to fruition as a result of much encouragement along a winding path over the last twenty years. My passion for African American history was sparked first by Elizabeth Murell Dawson at Florida A&M University (FAMU). Her enthusiasm for her craft changed the course of my life, and she remains one of my most trusted advisers. The seed she planted in me was watered and cultivated by my time in the Meeks-Eaton Southeastern Regional Black Archives Research Center and Museum under the tutelage of the late James N. Eaton.

There are a few of many instructors, colleagues, and former students at FAMU who encouraged and supported me over the years, including Barbara Cotton, Kyle Eidahl, Titus Brown, William Guzmán, Yanela Gordon McLeod, Anthony Dixon, Shirletta Kitchen, Darius Young, Reginald Ellis, and Goliath Davis. David Jackson in particular has helped to shape this work over these years and has remained a source of inspiration with his example of scholarship and his generous guidance. I am also deeply appreciative for the feedback from Derrick White and Irvin D. S. Winsboro on my manuscript. Their input helped to improve the final work considerably.

The seeds of this project were cultivated during my time at Florida State University under the tutelage of Maxine D. Jones, James P. Jones, Matt Childs, and Darryl Dixon-Carr. I owe a special debt of thanks to Joe M. Richardson for his many reviews of this work, as well as my colleague at Florida Memorial University, Anthony Fraser, for his keen eye and sharp criticism. My sincere thanks to my colleague Russell Motley for his review of an early version of this work.

I would also like to thank my former boss and mentor, Althemese P. Barnes, for her support and encouragement over the years, as well as her tireless efforts to promote historians and historic preservation in the state of Florida. Two of my sister-scholars, Andrea Howard Oliver and Dawn Herd-Clarke, have been steadfast in their walk along this road with me. I thank you for your friendship and your examples.

The Florida Education Fund (FEF) was instrumental to my education, providing invaluable resources and training. I am especially thankful for the influence of the late Israel Tribble, Betty Parker Smith, Larry More-house, Charles Jackson, and all the FEF fellows.

My professional career took me on what I initially believed to be a de-tour to Richmond, Virginia, but it was an experience that proved to be incredibly formative to my development as a historian. I am grateful to have had the opportunity to learn from the example of my former colleagues at the Library of Virginia, Brent Tarter and Gregg Kimball, who both read early drafts of this work and encouraged me to pursue publication. I also benefited from the rich community of historians and preservationists in the Richmond area. Special thanks are due to Lauranett Lee (Virginia Historical Society) and Andrea Simpson (University of Richmond).

Two of my students from Florida Memorial University, Ashia Riley and Wilmede Charles, provided helpful assistance in updating my research database.

I offer a special thanks to all of my interview subjects and community gatekeepers, too numerous to list here individually, for being willing to share their stories, facilitate introduction, and point out resources along the way, especially Larry and Ruth Kinsolving, Sue Tindel, the late Roy Roulhac, Shelly Ann Payne, and Rosa Worth Payne.

I would be remiss if I did not acknowledge the reference staff at the Florida State Archives for all of their help over the years, as well as James Cusick and the staff at the Smathers Special Collection Library at the University of Florida.

Last but not least, I would also like to thank my loving parents, Lawrence and Dorothy Bradley, for their enduring support and for creating a space for me to research and write during my summer visits; my sons, "Will" and Amiri, for their love, patience, humor, and understanding; and my rock and my support, Billy, for holding down the front line while I was away on research trips and for tolerating my "process." I am so grateful for your presence. Thank you.

*   *   *

My initial interest in the topic of racial violence in Florida was sparked by the late Theodore "Ted" Hemmingway at Florida A&M University. It was at his direction that I conducted some of the earliest oral histories that inform this work. For a time, the Suwannee River seemed to have wholly and completely swallowed Willie James Howard and the story of his lynching. Growing up in Live Oak, Florida, I had never heard of him. It was during my sophomore year as an undergraduate student at Florida A&M University in Tallahassee that I first heard Howard's name. As he discussed the legacy of racial violence in America, Dr. Hemmingway turned to me and said in his deep baritone voice, "I bet you didn't know they lynched a boy in Live Oak." I stared at him blankly, and shook my head. No, I had not heard of Willie James Howard, or anyone else, being lynched in Live Oak. Part of my reaction was incredulity. Surely if something as terrible as that had taken place in my hometown, I would have heard something about it. Reading my expression, Dr. Hemmingway laughed and said, "Well, they did. And I can show you the proof."

That exchange set my life on a different course. After class that day, Dr. Hemmingway told me more details about Howard's murder and the fact that he was forced to jump into the Suwannee River. My next trip home, I made a point to visit my grandfather, the late Rev. Freeman Grimmage Jr., to ask him about all this. When I mentioned Howard's name, his eyes became distant, his demeanor, somber. "Yeah, baby, I remember when they killed that boy," he said, looking off into the distance. "I remember in those days, when I'd go into town, if I even saw a white woman walking my way, I'd turn around and go home."

I was stunned. Part of me wanted him to deny it, to prove my professor wrong. I was also shocked because this was the first time that I can remember discussing with my grandfather his life during segregation.

As I continued to learn more about African American history, particularly those parts that my grandfather lived through, I began to understand and appreciate more about him and his life than I ever had before. His previous silence on the topic, and his sadness on that day, made sense.

Likewise, other aspects of his personality began to make sense as well. His seemingly prideful determination to accumulate wealth. His sometimes explosive anger. His forceful command of his household, his church, his neighborhood, and everyone he encountered within them. He demanded respect from everyone, perhaps in order to compensate for the habitual disrespect of his humanity, his manhood that he had experienced during his life. Growing up as a black boy in the segregated South, my grandfather swallowed many a bitter pill, and that bitterness shaped the man he eventually became. He survived the same society that killed Willie James Howard and lived to tell the story. He was not, however, without scars. I would like to dedicate this work to his memory.

INTRODUCTION

On the morning of May 28, 2003, in Belle Glade, Florida—a rural farming community situated near the southern tip of Lake Okeechobee in the southern part of the state—Bernice Golden made a horrifying discovery in her mother's yard. She arrived to find the body of her son, thirty-two-year-old Feraris "Ray" Golden, suspended fifteen feet off the ground, hanging from a schefflera "umbrella" tree. Ray's hands, witnesses said, were bound behind his back. It had rained the night before, but, strangely, there was no mud on his shoes. Bernice was convinced that her son had been lynched, and she was determined to tell the world.[1]

Over the next few days, word of Ray Golden's death spread through the town, accompanied by troubling rumors. People whispered that Golden had been lynched by whites for being romantically involved with a white woman named Judi Stambaugh, the daughter of the local sheriff. Nevertheless, two days after the body was discovered, the medical examiner ruled Golden's death a suicide, a claim, law enforcement officials argued, that was supported not only by the physical evidence but also by how those close to Golden described his state of mind in the days before his death. The divorced and recently unemployed man felt he was a burden to his family and had spoken to loved ones about ending his life. Law enforcement officials, as they later admitted, never considered investigating the death as a homicide.

While the majority of the white community accepted the ruling, blacks in Belle Glade remained unconvinced. Deep suspicion of white law enforcement officials overrode the evidence pointing to Golden's state of mind. Many blacks in Belle Glade did not believe law enforcement officials were above tampering with the evidence.[2] For African Americans in Palm Beach County, as well as in the rest of the state and nation, the circumstances of Golden's death were painfully familiar: a black man who had been romantically linked to a white woman in violation of conventions of southern society was found hanging in a tree from the end of a makeshift noose. The circumstances immediately raised concerns, not only in Belle Glade but around the state and nation, that the horrors of lynching had spread into the twenty-first century.

The National Association for the Advancement of Colored People (NAACP) quickly stepped in as representatives for the Golden family, demanding a coroner's inquest, the first in Palm Beach County in eighteen years. Later that month, Bernice Golden traveled to Memphis, Tennessee, for the forty-fifth annual convention of the Southern Christian Leadership Conference (SCLC) to commence her campaign for justice on behalf of her son. There she shared the stage with Martin Luther King III, the son of the slain civil rights leader Martin Luther King Jr. and president of the SCLC, to bring attention to the circumstances of her son's death. For those who were alive during the advent of the modern civil rights movement, it was a scene eerily reminiscent of pleas for justice made nearly fifty years earlier, in 1955, by Mamie Till on behalf of her own murdered son, Emmett. King urged the conference participants to pass a resolution seeking further investigation into Golden's death. "Black folks don't hang themselves," he said, repudiating the claim that the death was a suicide.[3]

As July 28—the day of the inquest—approached, public interest in the Golden case grew. National news agencies, including *USA Today* and CNN, and journalists from as far away as India and Australia came to the small town to report from the Belle Glade courtroom. Officials expected an overflow crowd and prepared to have the proceedings broadcast to other rooms in the building to accommodate the spectators. As the session began in the Belle Glade courtroom, the historical legacy of racial distrust unfolded. As participants entered the courtroom, they segregated themselves, whites sitting on one side, blacks on the other. The tension was thick.[4]

During the inquest, Judge Harold Cohen heard testimony from police, investigators, and the medical examiners. One officer took the stand and presented to the court the green bed sheet from which they found Golden's body hanging. Family members confirmed it had come from the bed where Golden slept in his grandmother's home. They also showed pictures of the decedent's body to prove that the only marks were around his neck. Next, Christopher Wilson, the medical examiner, who happened to be an African American, introduced evidence that, at the time of Golden's death, his alcohol level was four times over the legal limit for driving, and there were traces of cocaine in his system. Even after listening to this testimony, many of the blacks in the courtroom remained skeptical of the claim of suicide. They sent questions to the judge asking if Golden was drunk, how did he manage to climb into a tree and hang himself? Many still doubted that the police had done enough to investigate the possibility of murder.[5]

The inquest ended two days later, on July 30, when Judge Cohen handed down his decision: he had heard no evidence that convinced him that Ray Golden's death was the result of anything other than suicide. Aside from the case at hand, Cohen also commented on the anger and division that had gripped the community since Golden's body was found. "It's a sad commentary on our culture," Judge Cohen announced to the courtroom.[6]

Many people, Judge Cohen included, were shocked by the radical differences in opinion that seemed to divide the community along racial lines. Any person familiar with the history of race relations in the United States, however, would not have been surprised. Golden's death brought to the surface the historical distrust that still exists in the hearts and minds of many African Americans in Florida. Stories of lynching and racial violence have been passed down through generations in black families, becoming a part of communal lore. At their core, they serve as warnings against unseen dangers. Despite progress, in places like Belle Glade and other rural areas throughout the South, there were certain things that white people still would not accept from black people. A black man dating a white woman was one of those things.[7]

The circumstances surrounding Ray Golden's death triggered the historical memory of the black community in Belle Glade and elicited all-too-familiar recollections of extralegal violence that resulted in the tragic deaths of black citizens, without the guilty parties being brought to justice. For blacks in Belle Glade, Golden's death had all the markers of a lynching, and many could not be convinced that he did not die any other way. Despite the physical evidence and the innuendo, the situation in Belle Glade illustrated a deep and painful truth: while lynching is no longer a prominent part of American life in the way that it once was, the legacy of suspicion, distrust, and an inherent lack of faith in the legal and judicial system remains embedded in the collective consciousness of the city's African American population. Extralegal executions and high-level conspiracies are still plausible in the minds of many blacks because of the painful experiences of the past. The legacy of lynching continued to haunt this Florida community.

Although Golden's death took place in the twenty-first century, the practice of lynching in America had been most common during the late nineteenth and early twentieth centuries. From the time that such incidents began to be regularly reported after 1882 by the nation's newspapers, civil rights organizations, and sociologists, the record shows that, by the 1950s, nearly 5,000 people, primarily black men living in the South, lost their lives at the hands of white vigilantes. While rates of lynching gradually subsided, the practice did not go away completely. Lynch law continued its rule in Florida during the 1940s.

The focus of this study is to provide a detailed analysis of four lynchings that took place during that decade—Arthur C. Williams in Quincy in 1941, Cellos Harrison in Marianna in 1943, Willie James Howard in Live Oak in 1944, and Jesse James Payne in Madison in 1945—and to connect them to the continuum of lynching violence in Florida. Besides the investigational aspect of these incidents, this book seeks to analyze the responses of state and federal officials to these lynchings with special consideration of the significant political, economic, and social changes engendered by the New Deal and the impending crises of the Second World War. By couching these incidents within this expanded framework, it becomes clear that the new international aims of the U.S. government dramatically impacted the ability of vigilantes in the South to continue to abuse and subjugate African Americans with impunity. The nation, and the world, was watching, and these realities demanded change if America was to claim the mantle of the world's greatest democracy.

*   *   *

Lynching as a form of antiblack violence has its origins in the racial strife that bloomed in the post–Civil War South, as blacks and whites competed for economic resources and political inclusion. In the aftermath and upheaval of the Civil War and emancipation, the questions at the center of Reconstruction debates revolved around the degree of civil participation and constitutional protection that would be allowed to newly freed men, women, and children. Whites, specifically liberal Republicans, who sympathized with them and were concerned with their future prospects, realized that blacks needed the power of civil participation, the protection of the law, and the authority of the judicial system in order to ensure that the gains established during Reconstruction would be protected in the future. The passage of the Thirteenth, Fourteenth, and Fifteenth Amendments offered the promise of constitutional protection by officially ending the practice of slavery, providing the full rights of citizenship to African Americans, and granting adult black men the right to vote. While these amendments provided significant securities for black Americans in principle, the protections they offered, without appropriate enforcement, were simply words on paper.[8]

Blacks in Florida, after enjoying a brief period of political inclusion, social independence, and educational access, watched their dreams of creating a peaceful, interracial society crash down around them during the last decades of the nineteenth century. After suffering the sting of military defeat and years of "carpetbag" rule, white southerners eagerly reasserted their own sense of social and political order. The withdrawal of federal troops from the South in 1877, the result of a political deal between Republicans and Democrats after the controversial presidential election of 1876, signaled the end of federal protection for African Americans in the South. During this period of "Redemption," southern whites worked to reestablish and reinstitutionalize the authority they had previously exercised over their former slaves. Southern whites accomplished this end through the implementation of "Black Codes" that legislated economic oppression, social segregation, and political exclusion.

Violence was the consequence for anyone who dared to openly resist the forces of white dominance. Four years after the end of the Civil War, one of the most dramatic examples of this viciousness played out in Florida's panhandle. Between 1869 and 1870, as many as 150 people lost their lives in gun battles, assassination attempts, and retaliations fueled by political and racial strife during a period that historians refer to as the Jackson County War. Similar clashes occurred throughout the state, though less violent, but with similar results. Deprived of political power and protection, African Americans were left without effective recourse to the injustices being perpetrated against them.[9]

As a result, during the late nineteenth and early twentieth centuries, white supremacy and the concomitant subjugation of blacks became the key themes of race relations in Florida as well as in other southern states. Jim Crow laws reinstituted white social control over African Americans, keeping the framework of preemancipation race relations as the norm.[10] The policies of segregation and discrimination meant limited economic and educational opportunities, low-paying jobs, and a life of abject poverty for most blacks. Within this system, white paternalistic and racist attitudes justified the abuse of African Americans, whether verbal or physical, as necessary for the maintenance of southern social structure.[11] The passage of a new state constitution in 1885 all but eliminated the ability of African Americans to participate in government in any meaningful way. The document instituted a poll tax, eliminated blacks from juries, and stripped people accused of petty crimes of their right to vote. Further, state legislators segregated public schools and then dismantled funding for black education. The Florida state constitution even took the additional step of banning interracial marriage.[12]

Despite the disappointments and political reversals embodied in the 1885 state constitution, African Americans in Florida remained vigilant in their determination to combat the inequities they faced, making the most of the limited opportunities and relying on, as the historian Paul Ortiz describes, "mutual aid, labor struggle, historical memory, armed self-defense, and independent voting as cultural and political acts of survival and resistance."[13] For example, in 1888 the National Anti-Mob and Lynch Law Association ran an announcement in a newspaper in Bartow, a small central Florida town located in Polk County, offering a reward for information leading to the perpetrators responsible for burning a black man at the stake. Farther north, in Marion County, members of the Anti-Mob and Lynch Club earned the ire of local whites when they attempted to solve the lynching of a black man facing trial for murder in June 1899. Hostilities in Dunnellon, also in Marion County, reached a peak in October when members of the group participated in a deadly gun battle with local law enforcement officers and other deputized whites.[14] While ultimately unsuccessful, these incidents demonstrate the self-determined stance taken by blacks in Florida, fostered perhaps by the self-confidence gained through military experience in the Civil War and the Spanish-American War, as well as a sense of unity and manhood rooted in the fraternal tradition. Neither would be enough to stem the tide of antiblack violence in Florida over the coming decades as mobs continued their gruesome work. In November 1893, whites in Columbia County in North Florida lynched three black men accused of murder. Another heinous triple lynching of black men accused of rape occurred two years later in Madison County, also in the north-central region of the state. The lynchers tortured the victims, cutting off their scalps, ears, and tongues before carving into their flesh. Their lives finally came to an end when their tormentors burned them alive at the stake. In March 1897, eight black men were lynched within a span of ten days in Marion County in a stunning display; the county would go on to accumulate the bloodiest record of lynching violence in the entire state.[15]

As the gruesome tally of black lynching victims continued to climb, African American journalists around the nation used their talents to draw attention to the injustice of the extralegal murder. Chief among this cadre of writer-activists was Ida B. Wells, whose publications *Southern Horrors* in 1892 and *A Red Record* in 1894 used investigative journalism to quantify and convincingly refute claims by white southerners that lynching was their only recourse to combat rampant black criminality. Using her own accounting of data, Wells demonstrated that less than a quarter of lynching victims had been accused of rape or attempted rape. Her studies revealed the true function of the extralegal violence—as attacks on "race manhood" that used violence to eliminate blacks as economic competition and to maintain white supremacy when it was perceived as being threatened by black advancement. Slavery's whip had been exchanged for the noose and the gun. Lashing was no longer sufficient punishment, as it was replaced by burning, hanging, shooting, castration, and mutilation, usually resulting in death. Blacks throughout the South lived in fear of the indiscriminate and torturous violence that whites could carry out against them at any given moment for the slightest of reasons, without legal indictments or prosecution.[16] Wells's trailblazing work made her a target for violence, forcing her to abandon her home and her work in Memphis,

Tennessee, for the safety of the North.[17] Building on her investigative reporting, other black journalists drew attention to the brutal injustice represented by lynching, including Florida-native T. Thomas Fortune, editor of the *New York Age*, and William Monroe Trotter, of the *Boston Guardian*.[18]

Continued lynching and racial violence against blacks throughout the nation demonstrated the need for a coordinated campaign to combat such attacks. The NAACP offered hope as a new, nationwide vehicle through which antilynching and civil rights activists could direct their efforts. W. E. B. DuBois, the renowned scholar and intellectual who edited the NAACP's *Crisis* magazine, continued to raise awareness of lynching as a threat to the civil rights of blacks with regular reporting of lynching violence. The ascension of one of Florida's native sons, Jacksonville's James Weldon Johnson, within the ranks of the organization generated interest throughout the state. By 1915, the first NAACP branches in Florida were established in Key West and Tampa. Another wave of enrollment occurred when Johnson, in his new role as NAACP field secretary, toured the state in 1917 and 1918. Johnson's visits and speeches added new branches in St. Augustine to the NAACP's rolls.

Noticeably, the NAACP's successes during this period were limited to the state's metropolitan areas, underscoring the difficulty blacks living in Florida's rural counties faced in confronting the white power structure. It was also during these years that the organization began to focus its energies on combating the scourge of lynching, a fight that Johnson would lead in the early 1920s.[19] The NAACP faced an uphill journey in Florida. The state's leading politician, Governor Sidney J. Catts, actively inflamed antiblack sentiment in the state. In response to a query about a recent lynching in Florida, Catts not only refused to condemn lynching violence but complained that if the NAACP would teach "your people not to kill our white officers and disgrace our white women, you would keep down a thousand times greater disgrace."[20]

Spectators outside of the South were not so willing, however, to turn a blind eye toward the violence. Continued lynchings throughout the nation and the race riots that scarred the country during the "Red Summer" of 1919 fueled support for a federal solution to the bloodletting. Many white southerners were no doubt alarmed by Congressman Leonidas Dyer's (R-MO) introduction of federal antilynching legislation in the U.S. House of

Representatives in 1918 and 1919. For many southerners, it was a spectacle too reminiscent of the "horrors" of the Reconstruction era when, in their interpretation, African Americans, with the help of northern Republicans, interfered in the South's domestic affairs to the detriment of whites in the region. The proposal of a federal antilynching law was, in effect, a warning to the South: either end the racial violence that plagued the region or risk outside intervention.[21]

The threat of federal interference into state matters was not powerful enough to deter the forces for white supremacy in Florida. The year 1920 ushered in what would prove to be a showdown of enormous magnitude between African Americans determined to exercise their right to vote and those whites hell-bent on keeping them from it. Throughout the state, a reorganized and reinvigorated Ku Klux Klan (KKK) terrorized potential black voters. "Fortified by the determination to defend white supremacy in its gravest hour yet," notes Paul Ortiz, "the KKK in Florida became the most formidable paramilitary force in the United States." In the summer of 1920, members of the Klan bombed the black neighborhood of Coconut Grove in Miami.[22] After blacks attempted to participate in the political process by voting in November 2, 1920, whites destroyed the black section of Ocoee in Orange County in central Florida, burning black churches, the local lodge, and several homes. One man, July Perry, was lynched, and another was savagely beaten and castrated. The final death toll is unknown, but the violence led to the permanent dislocation of Ocoee's black population, an estimated 500 people, and the destruction of several homes, schools, and buildings, which completely eradicated the black population in that town. Numerous violent confrontations occurred at polling places around the state that same day, marking one of the most widespread instances of massive racial violence in Florida's history.[23] While African American voters in Jacksonville, Daytona, and Miami, finding strength in numbers, boldly stood up to the intimidation, blacks in rural areas like Suwannee, Madison, Gadsden, and Orange Counties fared poorly in the face of unbridled vigilante terror. Three years later, in 1923, during another brazen act of extralegal violence, whites completely destroyed the all-black township of Rosewood in Levy County, resulting in the death of six blacks and two whites, after a white woman falsely claimed a black man assaulted her. The brutal lessons taught by the events at Ocoee and Rosewood haunted black Floridians for generations.[24]

Despite the violence, African Americans continued their protest against lynching violence, both from within and outside of the state of Florida. Following in the footsteps of longtime activist Ida B. Wells, other black women lent their voices in opposition to lynching violence. Activist and organizer Mary Talbert helped to create the Anti-Lynching Crusaders, a women's organization under the auspices of the NAACP. Founded in 1922 and operating under the mantra "A Million Women United to Stop Lynching," Talbert and the Crusaders raised money, primarily through the sale of buttons, in support of the effort to pass the Dyer Anti-Lynching Bill. During its years in existence, the organization did much to publicize the atrocities committed against blacks, and Talbert was rewarded with the 1922 Spingarn Medal for her leadership in the antilynching campaign.[25] Businesswoman and philanthropist Eartha M. M. White, of Jacksonville, coordinated the activities of the Anti-Lynching Crusaders in Florida.[26] Mary McLeod Bethune also lent her talents and voice to the fight against lynching. A civil rights leader and founder of Bethune-Cookman College in Daytona, she publicly spoke against the practice in the state of Florida and across the nation.[27]

While working to combat lynchers in the state, blacks in Florida were also forced to contend with the economic decline that characterized the late 1920s and 1930s. The stock market crash of 1929 was the capstone of nearly a decade of unfortunate fiscal events. The Florida land boom had gone bust, only to be followed by the environmental and structural damage created by the monster hurricanes that visited the state in 1926 and 1928. Add to that a host of bank closures and an invasion by the Mediterranean fruit fly that practically destroyed the state's orange groves, and it was a perfect storm of pecuniary misfortune. Florida entered the 1930s economically devastated; it had the highest unemployment rate in the South, and nearly one-fourth of its population was on the dole. At the same time, Florida's population expanded at a rate quadruple the national average, with the influx of people leading to the state becoming the first in the region to transition from a predominantly rural to a predominantly urban residential pattern. These realities—combined with the continuing decline of the Old South agricultural system and increased political competition with population centers farther south—resulted in the increasing isolation of the northern panhandle areas of the state.[28] These factors only served to exacerbate what were already tense race relations within the state.

Beginning in the first decade of the twentieth century, a new cadre of actors entered the antilynching debate in earnest: white southern liberals. Recognizing the scope of the South's unique "Negro problem" and believing that the people in the region would have to come up with their own solutions, they used their power as opinion-makers, researchers, educators, and community leaders to move white southerners away from the tacit acceptance of extralegal activity toward a position of equal protection under the law for all citizens. The Committee for Interracial Cooperation (CIC) became the channel for these goals. Founded by Will W. Alexander in 1919, the organization sought to create a dialogue between the "better" classes of whites and blacks in the South in order to seek solutions to the problems of lynching and mob violence.[29] Based in Atlanta, the CIC gathered statistics on lynching and published them with the hope that the organization could educate southerners away from their casual acceptance of lynching violence. While the group opposed a federal antilynching law, the CIC encouraged individual states to adopt their own versions of such laws. They also targeted effective law enforcement as the best deterrent against mob violence. These reformers' progressive views, however, did not extend pass the color line, as they couched their advocacy within a firm dedication to the principle of racial segregation.[30]

The CIC spawned other initiatives that specifically targeted the issue of lynching violence. At the invitation of Alexander, George Fort Milton, editor of the *Chattanooga News*, became the chair of the Southern Commission for the Study of Lynching (SCSL) in 1929. He was joined by other liberals, black and white, including Julian Harris, editor of the *Atlanta Constitution*; sociologist Howard Odum, of the University of North Carolina; John Hope, president of Atlanta University; sociologist Charles S. Johnson, from Fisk University; and President R. R. Moton and Monroe N. Work, both from Tuskegee Institute. Under their guidance the SCSL published two important studies on lynching in the region: *Lynchings and What They Mean* in 1931, followed two years later by Arthur F. Raper's *The Tragedy of Lynching*. Stylistically, the works borrowed heavily from the models of antilynching journalism instituted by Ida B. Wells, as well as the NAACP's 1918 publication, *Thirty Years of Lynching*. That framework was enhanced with rigorous sociologic documentation and statistics resulting in an authoritative condemnation of southern lawlessness. Perhaps the most powerful feature of these and later SCSL-commissioned works was the fact that they were produced at the direction of white southerners, not

African Americans or northerners. The medicine proved effective; both publications were warmly received and well considered throughout the region, achieving a key point of the CIC's mission. The discussions they inspired marked an important shift in the attitudes of the leading whites in the South on the matter of race.[31]

Another by-product of the CIC was the Association of Southern Women for the Prevention of Lynching (ASWPL). Founded in 1930 by Jessie Daniel Ames, who had served as the head of the Committee on Woman's Work within the CIC, this group of primarily upper-class white women amplified an important set of voices within the antilynching struggle. The ASWPL's mission was to dispel the classic myth used by southern white men to justify lynching: that it was necessary to protect white women from lurking black predators who would otherwise rape them. According to sexual legend in the region, black men were animalistic, were sexually uninhibited, and possessed an unquenchable desire for white women. As the historian Jacquelyn Dowd Hall pointed out, this guise of white male chivalry became the unshakeable foundation upon which southern race relations were reconstructed after the Civil War. This myth preoccupied southern social thought, and having created this "monster," white men who would carry out lynching lived "in constant fear of [their] own creation."[32] It was the requirement of caste rules that

> any Negro man who makes advances toward a white woman, even though she be a professional prostitute, has broken the strongest taboo of the system and risks a terrible punishment. . . . Since he is regarded as a primitive being, emotionally unrestrained and sexually uncontrolled, the Negro man is thought by the whites to be always a potential rapist.[33]

As a result of this dynamic, black men could be lynched for committing an array of minor offenses that caused any slight discomfort for a white woman: winking, looking directly into the face or eyes, failing to distance himself, touching or brushing against a white woman, or whistling at a white woman. Statistically, however, one-third of lynching victims killed between the 1880s and 1930s were falsely accused of such crimes. In one infamous case, Rubin Stacey was lynched in Fort Lauderdale in 1935 for allegedly frightening a white woman.[34]

Using statistical data to refute claims about the prevalence of sexual assault by black men against white women, and urging adherence to the law instead of vigilante action, the ASWPL hoped to turn public sentiment in the South against lynch mobs, thereby ending the violent practice of lynching. Using the social tools available to them—their cultural status as a protected class within the social structure of the South, and their positions as privileged spouses—the women of the ASWPL proved to be very influential in changing the nature of the discourse about lynching. By charming the leading white men of the region—legislators, ministers, newspaper editors, judges, and law enforcement officers—members of the ASWPL encouraged adherence to due process under the law and the exercise of preventative measures to thwart attempts at lynchings.[35]

Indicative, at least in part, of efforts by both black and white antilynching activists, extralegal violence began to wane in the South over the course of several decades. Their diverse efforts—research, publication, and letter writing—were successful in changing the attitudes in the South regarding lynching.[36] After the 1930s, lynchings occurred less frequently than they had at the turn of the century, something Jessie Daniel Ames pointed out in her 1942 publication, *The Changing Character of Lynching*.[37] Not only did the number of lynchings decrease, she noted, but they had changed in methods as well. Attendance decreased from crowds of thousands to small mobs, then to a handful of individuals carrying out secretive kidnappings and executions, reflecting a seeming decline in the popularity of lynching as sport or entertainment. At the same time, state and local officials came under increasing pressure to act or intervene on occasions of racial strife—due in no small part to the efforts of antilynching activists—and because stories about lynchings were being published more frequently by the national press. Aware of this, some community leaders, especially newspaper editors, became openly critical of lynching, shunning the disgrace and unwanted attention national and international news of lynching brought to their communities. Negative publicity had other deleterious effects, most notably in discouraging outside business and industry leaders, worried about the impact of such violence, from investing in the region. Ames credited the ASWPL and the pressure it exerted on southern newspaper editors for this positive change.[38]

Ironically, this decrease in the number of lynchings in the South created a dilemma for the two main antilynching groups—the ASWPL and the NAACP. The crux of the issue lay in the varied missions of these organizations. The ASWPL was interested in solving the problem of lynching, and took any sign of improvement as a pretext to declare victory over the mob. In its view, the decline reflected the fact that white southerners were mending their ways, indicating that the South's lynching crisis had been resolved. However, the leadership of the NAACP disagreed. Instead of open violence, NAACP officials argued that lynchers were becoming more clandestine and less carnivalesque with the same grim results: the death and intimidation of black people. The journalist Jonathan Daniels, writing for the *Nation* in 1940, spoke to this metamorphosis toward private killings and secrecy in the South. Lynchings still took place but

> what has happened is that lynchings have gone "underground." The Underground Railroad now, they say, is operated by white Southerners, and it runs in killing quietness to the river, the buzzards, and the grave too deep for the dogs to dig up.
>
> Obviously there is no reason for a federal antilynching bill if the lynchings no longer occur. But those who still advocate the legislation strenuously insist that a "new technique" has been worked out to "kill the niggers" and yet keep the killings, which are expressions of white group bitterness and not of mere individual murderousness, out of the statistics and the newspapers. That keeps them also off the conscience of the South and the nation. Cases of such killings have been investigated and reported by Negroes and by white men, too. The pattern of violence, they say, has changed. Even country towns have learned that lynchings are bad for business. Indignation, near and far, has made many people more sensitive than they were a few years ago.[39]

Furthermore, the NAACP had a vested interest in continuing to beat the antilynching drum, as it had become the mainstay of its operations over the previous decades. The organization used its reporting of lynchings to draw attention to its campaign to improve the lives of blacks, not only by ending the practice of lynching but also by fighting for political and civil rights.

These differences came to a head in 1940, when the ASWPL declared a "lynchless year"—dating between May 8, 1939, and May 9, 1940.[40] Leaders in the NAACP quickly took exception. The difference of opinion was largely based on motive. Defining what constituted a lynch mob created difficulties for those tracking and protesting the practice. The ASWPL, in particular, opposed including incidents that involved law enforcement officers. Under these changing circumstances, the NAACP, ASWPL, and Tuskegee Institute, which had been systematically tracking lynching statistics since 1882, could no longer agree on what characterized a lynching. To settle this dispute, the groups agreed to meet at Tuskegee in December 1940. As a result of compromise, they settled on a definition of lynching that temporarily satisfied all parties. These parameters prescribed that there had to be a dead body; the death had to be a result of extralegal action, meaning it occurred outside of the normal legal process of arrest, trial, sentencing, and execution by the state or federal government; the murder had to be carried out by a group (the number of which was not settled); and the motivation for the killing had to serve justice, tradition, or race.[41] The truce, however, proved fragile, with Ames later rejecting the definition proposed at the Tuskegee conference. Despite this technical quandary, the truth was that the extralegal murder of black people still occurred without legal repercussions, albeit in fewer numbers, and that these continued civil rights violations significantly hampered the aspirations of African Americans throughout the South.

*   *   *

While a good deal of the credit for the decline in lynching violence during the 1920s and 1930s can be attributed to antilynching activity, a combination of domestic and international issues complicated race relations in the United States during this same period, also contributing to a change in the way Americans perceived lynching violence. This phenomenon, in part, can be credited to several developments in the first two decades of the twentieth century. First, as black Americans "closed ranks" with their white countrymen and women during World War I, they nurtured expectations that the sacrifices they made in Europe, and their contributions on the home front, would help to ameliorate their condition as second-class citizens. African Americans, primarily black soldiers, gained a sense of confidence and worldliness as a result of their experiences. When black soldiers serving in Europe were treated with respect and admiration, especially by the French people, as opposed to the general scorn and distain they received in America, the experience gave them hope that one day they could live in their native land unencumbered by racism. Second, on the home front, millions of African Americans were transformed by the experience of the Great Migration, exercising a measure of self-determination by leaving the poverty and abuse that often characterized their lives in the South and seeking the promise of better opportunities for themselves and their families in the North and West.[42]

These positive experiences, however, were dampened by the reality of continued racism and racial violence as World War I came to a close in 1919. Despite hopes that their wartime sacrifices would translate into an improvement in their domestic situation at the end of the conflict, African Americans were horrified by an increase in lynching violence and a spate of race riots throughout the country, earning the moniker of the "Red Summer" of 1919.[43] Tempered by the flames of war, however, black Americans boldly met these challenges with reinvigorated resolve. The NAACP's *Crisis* magazine fervently criticized the U.S. government for its failure to ensure blacks' civil rights. The Jamaican Marcus Garvey and his Universal Negro Improvement Association (UNIA) also empowered black Americans with his militant vision of a united African diasporic community, linked by common ties to Africa. His preachings broadened the psyches of blacks around the world and inspired them with dreams of self-determination and liberty.[44]

In the aftermath of World War I, many African American leaders embraced a global view of themselves as members of the international community of colored people—brown, black, and yellow—united in a struggle against white supremacy in the form of colonialism, exploitation, racism, and oppression.[45] Inspired by this international perspective, and envisioning black Americans in the vanguard of this emerging multinational populace, W. E. B. DuBois, William Monroe Trotter, Madame C. J. Walker, and other leaders organized the International League of Darker People to raise awareness of the collective plight of nonwhite people around the globe during the Paris Peace Conference in 1919.[46] The group, like antilynching crusader Ida B. Wells earlier, hoped to use the international spotlight both to draw attention to the brutality faced by black Americans and to expose the hypocrisy of the United States' failure to fulfill its proclaimed democratic values for all citizens, regardless of race or creed. These activists developed alliances with the Japanese, whom many saw as the group best empowered to be the spokespersons for "the colored citizens of the world." Their delegation sought to have a resolution introduced before the body recognizing the principle of racial equality, which, if passed, would have given black Americans grounds for an international challenge to their treatment by the U.S. government. In return, the Japanese agreed to present DuBois's petition outlining the oppression of blacks in the United States before the group.[47]

The Japanese were not the only source of inspiration on the global scene for black Americans. The ripples of the Communist revolution in Russia reached the United States in the 1920s, offering a unique appeal to downtrodden African Americans throughout the nation. In the North, Communists sided with blacks against the worst aspects of labor, housing, and economic exploitation. In the South, they sought to organize farm workers against the crushing hand of the plantation class, factory owners, and textile mill operators. In what was perhaps its most convincing demonstration of a commitment to blacks' rights, the legal arm of the Communist Party of America, the International Labor Defense (ILD), won the respect of many blacks with its vigorous defense of the "Scottsboro Boys" in the 1930s. For any African American looking for an alternative to America's racist capitalism, members of the Communist Party upheld the vision of a raceless Communist utopia that was being developed in the U.S.S.R. but that could also come to exist in America.[48]

Conversely, Communists in the U.S.S.R. took full advantage of the opportunity for political propaganda that was presented by American racism. The Soviet press frequently referenced lynching violence against blacks in the United States as an incriminatory contrast to their own government, which they promoted as antiracist, and their society, which they claimed was a raceless civilization where people of all ethnicities could enjoy equality.[49] Articles describing lynchings, along with photographs of charred and hanging black male bodies, appeared frequently in the Russian press in the 1920s and 1930s. The symbols of the noose and the swastika were used in Russian political cartoons criticizing the United States for its brutal treatment of its black citizens. As Meredith Roman notes about the international perspective on race relations during the 1930s, "Before the Nazis came to power in Germany, U.S. racism was identified in the Soviet Union as the most egregiously horrific aspect of capitalism, and the United States was represented as the most racist country in the world."[50] The African American press, in turn, held up examples of the

Soviets' liberal attitude on race to further expose racial inequities in the United States, and especially in the South. The U.S.S.R.'s widely publicized trial of two white Americans (hailing from the South) for an attack on a black American at a tractor factory in Stalingrad served as a public example of the Communists' commitment to the ideology of true brotherhood. Further, during the Sixth World Comintern Congress in 1928 in Moscow, officials took the unprecedented step of recognizing people of African descent in America as an oppressed nation within a nation, and entitled to the right of self-government and self-determination in the same way as other colonized nations.[51]

Global events during the 1930s became a source of comment and comparison for African Americans who interpreted international events in the terms of their own domestic agendas. The realities of colonialism and independence struggles around the globe intrigued black American observers, who could see within these conflicts the influence of Jim Crow and white supremacy writ large. They watched with keen interest the convulsions against British colonialism in India, as well as the outbreak of civil war in Spain. Ethiopia, too, became a lightning rod when the League of Nations refused to rebuke Italy's invasion of that sovereign nation in 1935. The black press kept their readership abreast of these global developments, helping their readers to cultivate a more cosmic understanding of racism that stretched beyond the boundaries of the United States. The *Pittsburgh Courier* went so far as to station a reporter, J. A. Rogers, in Ethiopia to provide updates on the struggle. The failure of the League of Nations to act to protect Ethiopia from Italy's aggression served as bitter confirmation of the power of white supremacy and racism internationally.[52]

In the same way that African Americans turned their gaze to the international front, foreign powers used race relations in America both as a gauge of the nation's level of dedication to its professed democratic principles and as evidence of the failure of the nation's capitalist policies. Nothing illustrated the failure of America's commitment to civil rights for its black citizens more vividly than the gruesome images and descriptions of lynchings. Both Russia and Japan, for a time, found value in undermining America's democratic chest-beating, and race relations was the nation's Achilles' heel. Reports of lynching appeared in the foreign press frequently enough that both the Russians and the Japanese added words to their vocabularies, "*linchevat*," and "*shikei*" or "*rinchi*," respectively, in order to identify the phenomenon. Walter White's *Fire in the Flint*, originally published in the United States in 1924, was translated into Japanese and published in 1935 and 1937 under the title *Lynching*. The Japanese version of the novel met with great acclaim, due in no small part to promotion by Japanese government agents eager to embarrass the United States.[53]

In 1933, the polemics of race on the international scene changed dramatically with the rise of Adolf Hitler and the National Socialist Party in Germany. Hitler's philosophies of Aryan supremacy and race purity mirrored ideas that had been championed by the KKK and other white supremacists in the United States for decades. As news of increasing discrimination against and abuse of Jewish people in Europe reached America, African Americans eagerly pointed out the parallels between Nazi Germany and the Jim Crow South. Germany's institution of the Nuremberg Laws in 1935, curtailing the civil rights of Jews, preventing their intermarriage with Germans, and penalizing interracial sex, as well as boycotting Jewish businesses, only confirmed the validity of blacks' criticism of similar Jim Crow policies in America. Black thinkers and activists painted the South as "a region of the United States that seemed to have more in common with the Führer than with the Founders."[54] The black press frequently used the crisis with Germany as a rhetorical weapon with which to attack racist policies and ongoing racial violence in their own country. Race reformers were particularly vexed by the double standard that allowed an outpouring of sympathetic media attention on the plight of European Jews, while the suffering of black Americans went virtually ignored by the mainstream press. "When the only 'inferior' peoples were 'niggers' it was hard to get the attention of *The New York Times* for little matters of race, lynching and mobs," W. E. B. DuBois bitterly wrote. "But now that the damned included the owner of the *Times*, moral indignation is perking up."[55] The editors of the *Washington Tribune* also noted the irony of the situation:

> Despite the mistreatment of the Negroes in America and the recent disgraceful scene in Congress when a bill to give some measure of protection to Negroes was introduced and filibustered to death without a word from the President who now extends a hand to Jews in Europe, this same Chief Executive has the effrontery to reach his hand across the Atlantic in the face of conditions and make this

grand gesture. . . . The American Negro has nothing but the deepest sympathy for Jews in Europe, but Hitler and Mussolini certainly must be tickled.[56]

In the mid-1930s, Florida governor Fred Cone experienced early tremors along these emerging global and political fault lines. On December 9, 1935, white Tampa resident and socialist leader Joseph Shoemaker died after a brutal attack, which was widely believed to have been orchestrated and carried out by Klansmen, along with other local whites angered by his attempts to disrupt the city's dominant political machine. This was not a run-of-the-mill lynching. The viciousness of the attack (of the three victims, Shoemaker received the worst of the punishment, which included severe beatings with hoses and chains as well as tarring and feathering), the race of the victim (white), and the nature of his "offense" (political as opposed to criminal) combined to create a particularly irksome situation for those interested in protecting the state's reputation.[57] The American Civil Liberties Union (ACLU) offered a reward to anyone who could identify Shoemaker's assailants. A group of New York–based civil rights and labor organizations, including the ILD and the NAACP, banned together under the umbrella of the Committee for the Defense of Civil Rights in Tampa. The group closely monitored and reported on the case and campaigned for federal intervention in Florida.[58]

After the indictments and successful convictions of six of the attackers in 1936, the Florida Supreme Court ordered a new trial for the defendants. Predictably, the men were acquitted after the second round of trials in 1937. The decision came as a disappointment not only to those who had spent two years advocating for justice in the case but also to the state and national media. The *Miami Herald* characterized the verdicts as "a source of profound disgrace for this state." The anxiety over the impact of the case nationally and internationally foreshadowed a new consciousness that would challenge the nation, and especially the South. Whether Floridians acknowledged it or not, they had a role to play in protecting America's international reputation. "The Shoemaker case would be understandable under a reign of terror in Russia," reasoned the editors of the *Miami Herald*, "but not in the United States."[59]

Governor Cone, traveling in New York City on business shortly after news of the lynching broke in October 1937, was put in the awkward position of defending his state's reputation while protecting the right of Florida's citizens to resort to extralegal violence. He did his best to straddle a thorny ideological fence, on the one hand acknowledging the justifiable condemnation from outside the state, and at the same time protecting what had become a way of life in Florida. He admitted he was "ashamed of Florida," but added he believed anyone advocating political unrest "ought to be hung on a tree."[60] His comments set off another round of criticism, this time specifically aimed at Cone's vocalized support of lynching. New York mayor Fiorello La Guardia refused to meet with Cone, and the city's newspapers roundly condemned Cone personally and Florida generally. Continued lynching in Florida, and the failure of the state's government to react appropriately, made the state a national pariah.[61]

Southern attitudes about race, nevertheless, remained unchanged. The region's congressional leaders had already faced down the threat of federal antilynching legislation, which managed to pass in the House of Representatives in 1922 and 1937, before being killed in the Senate. Compounding the problem was the Roosevelt administration's seemingly "soft" (by southern standards) stance on race. As proof, detractors cited Roosevelt's habit of conferring, however symbolically, with select black leaders and scholars in his so-called black cabinet about racial policies, as well as First Lady Eleanor Roosevelt's activism on behalf of blacks. In 1936, Mary McLeod Bethune sponsored an interracial student conference at her institution, Bethune-Cookman College, to discuss solutions to improve black life in Florida, particularly addressing continued racial violence in the state. Her activism, and later her access to the White House via her friend Eleanor Roosevelt, helped bring attention to the suffering and inequality blacks experienced throughout the nation.[62]

Moreover, Roosevelt's New Deal had unintended consequences for southern race relations. During the first three decades of the twentieth century, Florida and other southern states contended with a massive out-migration of blacks from the region in pursuit of better jobs and an improved way of life in the North, destabilizing the South's main source of cheap labor. For those blacks who remained in the South, implementation of the Agricultural Adjustment Act (AAA) negatively impacted many black sharecroppers, displacing them and making them more vulnerable to exploitation. Southern congressmen successfully fought to exclude agricultural and domestic laborers from protections under the National Labor Relations Act (NLRA), including a minimum wage and unemployment benefits.[63] On the other hand, other initiatives like the Civilian Conservation Corps (CCC) and the Works Progress Administration (WPA) gave African Americans a chance to earn better pay than they ever had. This economic empowerment allowed black families to exercise more control over their own labor and the jobs they would and would not take, threatening the traditional control white southerners were accustomed to exercising over them. As one white farmer put it, "Negroes have got to be bossed, and you can't boss them when they make that kind of money and when they can get another job anywhere they want."[64] Similarly, the decision of many black women to refrain from domestic work because they found better-paying work, or perhaps because their spouses were earning more money, led to unfounded rumors that they had formed "Eleanor Clubs" (referencing the First Lady's embrace of black causes) with the goal of punishing southern white women by making them clean their own homes.[65]

President Franklin Roosevelt's address to Congress on January 6, 1941, marked a significant turning point in preparing the nation for the potential of military engagement in World War II. His articulation of the "Four Freedoms"—freedom from want and fear, freedom of worship and speech—encapsulated a broad vision for the nation and the world, operating in contrast to the rising dictatorships around the globe. For African Americans, however, the rhetoric rang hollow. Nevertheless, black leaders seized the opportunity to assert their civil rights agenda into the discourse of the day. A true commitment to expanding the "Four Freedoms" around the world, they argued, would be best demonstrated by their complete achievement in the nation of their origin. "We want the Four Freedoms to apply to black Americans as well as to brutalized peoples of Europe and to the other underprivileged peoples of the world," contended the historian Rayford Logan. "We insist that insofar as the equality asserted in the Declaration of Independence is applicable to all men, it should include us."[66] Confirmation of this assertive posturing was illustrated by the events that led to FDR's issuance of Executive Order #8802 in June 1941, creating the Fair Employment Practices Commission (FEPC). The president's hand had been forced by labor leader A. Philip Randolph, a native of Crescent City,

Florida, whose March on Washington Movement (MOWM) threatened to bring 100,000 black protestors to the nation's capital to demonstrate against discriminatory hiring practices by federal contractors. While the FEPC proved to have a limited ability to effect real change, the episode inspired African American leaders that effective organizing during this international crisis could yield significant benefits in the areas of civil and economic rights.[67]

After the bombing of Pearl Harbor on December 7, 1941, African Americans had to reevaluate and recalibrate the tenor of their protest for their own rights with the needs of a nation heading to war. The mood of the day was captured by James G. Thompson when he wrote to the *Pittsburgh Courier* in January 1942. "The V for victory sign is being displayed prominently in all so-called democratic countries which are fighting for victory over aggression, slavery and tyranny," Thompson noted. "Let we colored Americans adopt the double V for a double victory. The first V for victory over our enemies from without, the second V for victory over our enemies from within."[68] His concept planted the seed of the "Double V" campaign, which became the mantra for African Americans during the war years. Unlike with the previous war when the nation's blacks were encouraged to "close ranks" with their white countrymen and women and put aside their agitation for civil rights in favor of supporting the war effort, this time they were determined to keep their eyes on their prize. "Our aim then must not only be to defeat Nazism, fascism, and militarism on the battlefield," argued Randolph, "but to win the peace, for democracy, for freedom and the Brotherhood of Man without regard to his pigmentation, land of his birth or the God of his fathers."[69]

The war mobilization of 1941 marked a transitional period for most of the South, and Florida was no exception. The war boom profoundly affected the state, as it became a major training center for naval and aviation forces, witnessing an influx of both black and white soldiers. With them came federal money to build training sites and the necessary supporting infrastructure to accompany them. By the end of the war, 172 military bases had been established in Florida, up from just seven before the war. In the private sector, the war meant more defense industry contracts and new job opportunities. The demographic changes were just as radical, with the state's population nearly doubling over the course of the 1940s, as well as the concomitant shift from rural areas to Florida's cities. This was the cusp of the transitional period in the state's history that Gary Mormino coined Florida's "Big Bang."[70]

The United States ironically sought to fight a war for democracy using a Jim Crow army. Military bases became the sites of explosive confrontations between blacks and whites, as African Americans from the North were forced to contend with segregation both on and off base. Examples of wartime racial strife were abundant. In 1941, confrontation in Tampa led to the shooting of two black soldiers by white MPs. In Tallahassee, where black enlistees with the U.S. Army Air Corps were stationed at Dale Mabry Air Field, local police shot Private Wilbur Harris after a confrontation in September 1942. Black troops and white MPs clashed at Camp Gordon Johnston near Carrabelle in October 1944. Off bases, black soldiers tangled with white business owners in Cross City near the U.S. Army Air Corps base in May 1943 after being barred from local restaurants and bars. After an alleged mutiny at MacDill Air Field, located near Tampa, in 1943, ten black soldiers were court-martialed. Even larger confrontations were to come. In April 1945, 250 African American soldiers from Dale Mabry Air Field and Camp Gordon Johnston participated in a major riot in the predominantly black neighborhood of Frenchtown in Tallahassee. The following year, one of the largest riots in air force history occurred again at MacDill Air Field when 300 black soldiers battled against white MPs and civilians.[71]

Nevertheless, for many whites across the nation, issues of race seemed secondary to the nation's focus on World War II, the battle to defeat the Axis powers, and the preservation of democracy in the world. Southerners in particular never lost sight of the importance of preserving white supremacy; for them, the FEPC, along with the National Labor Relations Board (NLRB) and other New Deal programs, represented a step toward the slippery slope of empowering African Americans by undermining the delicate balance of racialized economic exploitation that had been cultivated in the state's agricultural industries. In the mid-1930s, United Citrus Workers found its efforts to unionize laborers in the central part of the state consistently undermined by "the terror initiated by the KKK and the local authorizes [sic], in conjunction with the growers and canners."[72] In September 1942, Florida Klansmen openly intimidated black citrus workers on the eve of a vote for organizing a labor union at the Phillips Citrus packinghouse in Apopka, riding through the black community wearing their hoods. This came after a number of attacks on workers and a massive KKK recruiting drive during the preceding weeks.[73] War industries were not immune from the violence. There was a racial disturbance at the Tampa Shipbuilding Yards in April 1942 after a confrontation between black and white workers that nearly resulted in a melee. This entrenched and sustained resistance to the expansion of the economic and social gains of the New Deal and war mobilization to blacks in Florida is evidence of how deep antiblack sentiment ran among whites and the uphill battle blacks faced in challenging it. Despite the war and the growth that accompanied it, separation and subjugation of blacks remained paramount for whites in the South. Lynching, along with other forms of violence, continued to be tools for the enforcement of the racial status quo even during this time of dramatic economic and political change.[74]

*   *   *

While Florida is geographically the southernmost state within the South, historically and socially it has been portrayed as the least "southern" of all the states in the region—despite the fact that Florida was the third southern state, after South Carolina and Mississippi, to withdraw from the Union during the secession crisis. Florida, however, proved to be very southern in the habit of racial violence. Between 1882 and 1951, 4,730 lynchings were recorded in the United States. Of these, 282 were recorded in Florida.[75] Even though Florida was one of the most sparsely populated of the southern states, between 1882 and 1930 it had the highest rate of lynching per 100,000 of its black citizens at 79.8, followed by Mississippi with 52.8. This meant that African Americans in Florida had the greatest probability of being lynched of any blacks in the nation. Not only were lynching rates higher in Florida, but by the 1940s the state was one of only two in the nation to record lynchings. Measured by the intensity and longevity of antiblack violence, Florida could stand shoulder to shoulder with its peers in the region.[76]

There has been a continued effort to rebut the idea of Florida's exceptionalism erected by political scientists of another generation that claims, among other things, that racial strife was not as severe in the Sunshine State as it was in other, more "traditional" Deep South states. There have been several published studies on the history of race relations in Florida that disavow this viewpoint, and this examination of the four lynchings

in the 1940s aids the effort to debunk this myth.[77] First, the relative late-
ness of these lynchings, compared to the traditional focal range of years
(1882-1930), serves as evidence that antiblack violence had an unusual
stronghold in Florida. Jesse James Payne's killing in 1945 was the only
lynching recorded in the nation that year, an ignominious achievement
for a state viewed as experiencing modest levels of racial strife compared
to the rest of the region.

Beside the lynchings, there were other instances of racial tension, mysterious deaths, and averted lynchings that rounded out the decade. Florida's realm of the KKK was one of the largest and most active in the nation
for most of the early twentieth century. By the late 1920s, KKK leaders estimated that one-third of the Klan's total national membership came from
Florida. Over the next several decades, Grand Wizards of the organization
routinely pointed to Florida with pride as one of the Klan's most faithful
dominions. The presence of a large KKK in the state translated to a high
level of KKK members and sympathizers among the ranks of law enforcement officers and political officeholders in Florida.[78] Ultimately, when
coupled with the well-established fact of the state's high rate of lynching
violence in comparison to other southern states, the breadth and scope of
the extralegal murder of blacks in the state argue for Florida's inclusion
among the ranks of states whose African American citizens experienced a
level of terror among the worst in the South during the Jim Crow era.

In addition to examining the interrelationship between racial violence
and changes wrought by World War II, dissecting these four lynchings
expands what has been a somewhat truncated historiography of lynching violence in the state of Florida and in the region, and helps explain
the transformation and decline of lynchings in the South during the mid-
twentieth century. Previous studies provide context for the change and
transition of lynching violence in Florida over the course of the twentieth
century. In *Urban Vigilantes in the New South*, Robert Ingalls examined the
phenomenon of lynching and how it manifested in Tampa, one of Florida's main urban centers, between 1882 and 1936, and concluded that the
elites of the community either openly supported or participated in various forms of vigilantism as a means to maintain the status quo. The communal backing that Ingalls describes is generally characteristic of lynching
violence, and, in at least one case, adherence to the socioeconomic status
quo trumped traditional racial motivations. This was especially true of the

lynching of whites in Tampa during the 1930s, as the spark for the brutality came from class and labor struggles within the city.[79]

Scholars studying lynchings that occurred during the 1930s and 1940s in Florida point out some trends in the practice as it manifested in the state during these decades. Analyzing lynchings in Florida during this period, Walter Howard found notable differences. First and foremost, the number of victims decreased from fifteen to four, representing a significant downward trend. Furthermore, none of the victims lynched during the 1940s were white, compared with three whites who were killed during the previous decade. There was also an appreciable trend toward a fewer number of participants responsible for carrying out lynching violence. The lynching parties during the 1930s, with the exception of the Claude Neal lynching, were composed of a small number of people acting in relative secrecy; this pattern continued into the next decade. Given their size and intent, the lynchers who were active in Florida during the 1940s fell into the category of private mobs. For the most part, they were a small group of individuals (available descriptions show no more than three or four people who were involved) who acted in secrecy and, in three of the four cases examined, kidnapped their victims from jail.[80]

This change in method is significant, in part because of what it indicates about the attitudes of Florida lynchers and the communities in which they operated. Large crowds, torture, and human bonfires were not a part of the methods used in the four lynchings described in this study. Instead, a few individuals carried them out in secrecy, following the "private mob" model described by W. Fitzhugh Brundage in his work *Lynching in the New South*.[81] Brundage's work broke ground in its dissection of the "lynching bees" in Georgia and Virginia in the late nineteenth and early twentieth centuries. Combining both narrative and empirical approaches to his investigation, Brundage offers a more quantitative interpretation of lynching violence, based on economics and demography as causational factors but also documenting a transition in mob violence in the early twentieth century from large spectacles to increasingly secretive affairs carried out by private mobs.

While there are no records reflecting the thoughts and motivations of the men who participated in lynchings in the 1940s, a careful reading of their actions offers a worthwhile point of comparison. Secrecy is evidence of fear, especially when considered in contrast to the bold and public lynching bees that dotted Florida's past. The deliberate clandestineness surrounding these events signals that, by the 1940s, lynchers somehow felt less confident that they could participate in extralegal activities and evade detection and prosecution. Could vigilantes still rely on the traditional pillars of maintaining white supremacy—the sheriff, the citizens, and the courts—to conceal their identities and prevent their arrest? If the sheriff failed to act, would he be removed from office by a governor eager to assuage negative public opinion emanating from within or outside of the state? While hardly conclusive, there is enough anecdotal evidence that whites in Florida saw the signs that a significant shift in attitudes about race and justice was taking place, and they would not be able to continue to lynch blacks with impunity without risking detection, arrest, and prosecution. James McGovern, in his analysis of the brutal 1934 lynching of Claude Neal in Jackson County, Florida, noted a similar theme, although in the converse. While acknowledging that the evidence and details in the Neal case were too scattered to pinpoint the cause of the lynching to any one factor, McGovern acknowledged that the lynchers were encouraged because it was highly unlikely that they would be prosecuted for murder.[82] This reality is born of a broader cultural phenomenon within the region, specifically the casual acceptance of murder in the service of pride or tradition. Michael J. Pfeifer, when comparing attitudes and behaviors around extralegal violence between New England and the Mid-Atlantic states, pinpoints regional variations in the understanding and implementation of due process. Compared to a northern preference for "law and order," he found that southerners preferred summary "justice" unencumbered by the uncertainties of a slow-moving court system.[83] Such deeply ingrained attitudes and behaviors are not challenged or changed easily in the South.

Another important indicator of changes in the practice of lynching in Florida was the location of the lynchings. Whereas lynchings in the 1930s took place all over the state, with nearly half occurring in urban areas, the lynchings of the next decade were confined to rural north Florida. Unlike other areas of the state, the lynching communities of the 1940s did not have major cities, diversified nonagricultural economies, or, with the exception of Jackson County, the presence of military bases or training camps. Stewart E. Tolnay and E. M. Beck's cliometric study of lynching violence in the South documented the connection between the lynching violence and the need to control black agricultural laborers between the "prime" lynching years of 1882 and 1930. Using statistical data, the work debunks theories of the positive relationship between demographics and lynching rates (the belief that there were higher occurrences in areas where blacks outnumbered whites), in favor of a documentable relationship between the economy (in this case, cotton prices) and racial violence. This socioeconomic trend in lynching violence holds true for lynching in Florida during the 1940s, as the communities that witnessed extralegal murders—Gadsden, Jackson, Suwannee, and Madison Counties—were not directly impacted by the economic changes and military development that did so much to modernize other areas of the state. Overall, these economic and cultural indicators might have predisposed Gadsden, Jackson, Suwannee, and Madison Counties for the production of such strange fruit found there during the 1940s.[84]

There were also outside factors that contributed to the decline of lynching in Florida. Walter Howard attributed the decline of lynching violence, in part, to the increased coverage of instances of vigilante justice in the national press. Communities were not eager to have their townships associated with the sadism that accompanied lynching because outbursts of violence would color white residents with the taint of bestiality. This was especially true in the aftermath of the Neal lynching in 1934, which, through the print media, brought the eyes of the nation upon the state. Howard also noted that the majority of the lynchings during the decade took place in urban areas as opposed to the countryside. This conclusion conflicts with suggestions by some sociologists that rural areas were more prone to lynching violence.[85]

Last, despite the stylistic variations, these four instances had the same outcome as previous lynchings: the incidents traumatized African Americans in the communities where they occurred and devastated the families of the lynching victims, and the perpetrators of these murders were never identified and/or indicted. In sum, as with other lynchings in years past, the violence reinforced the message that whites in Florida were determined to maintain the existing racial boundaries at any cost.

*   *   *

The lynchings of Arthur C. Williams in Quincy in 1941, Cellos Harrison in Marianna in 1943, Willie James Howard in Live Oak in 1944, and Jesse James Payne in Madison in 1945 are a small but important part of the

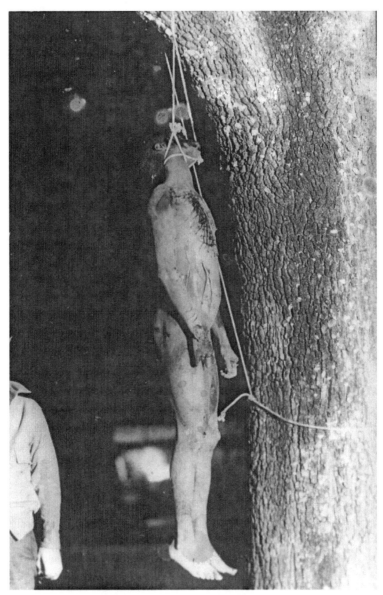

FIGURE I.1. The dead body of Claude Neal, October 17, 1934, hanging at the courthouse square in Marianna, Florida. Courtesy of the State Archives of Florida.

United States' bloody lynching legacy. Each incident elicited varied responses of the local, state, and federal government, as well as the American public. With the onset of World War II, and its portrayal by the Roosevelt administration as a war to preserve democracy in the world, more Americans became keenly aware of the injustice lynching represented and its glaring inconsistency with U.S. war aims. Shifting priorities at the national level, especially achieving the moral authority necessary to command respect abroad, demanded that America directly address the issue of civil rights for all Americans. As a result, public servants and politicians attempted to balance the traditional acceptance of lynching and black oppression with the fascism the United States fought against in World War II. The lynchings examined in this study outline shifting trends in antiblack violence, particularly how the practice of extralegal murder transformed after the 1930s and, perhaps more important, how the response of the American public changed in response to continued lynching violence.

Moreover, these lynchings are significant for what they reveal about the struggles and tensions that characterized the modernization of Florida during the era of World War II, especially within the broader context of international affairs and shifting national priorities. As examined in the pages that follow, public responses to lynchings in Florida during the 1940s flooded into the state from around the nation, manifesting in letter-writing and telegram campaigns as well as blistering newspaper editorials that criticized the state's leaders for not putting a stop to extralegal violence. Elected officials in the state contended with this unwanted attention as they thought best, defending the state's reputation against the criticism while carefully avoiding direct intervention into the jurisdictions where these lynchings took place. The gubernatorial administrations of Spessard Holland (1940–1944) and Millard Caldwell (1944–1948) employed the force of their office, and that of their attorney generals, to give the appearance of pursuing appropriate reactive measures in the aftermath of lynching violence. In some cases, the Federal Bureau of Investigation (FBI) and the Department of Justice also completed their own inquiries. While the results were less than satisfactory—no one was indicted in any of the four cases, and no law enforcement officers were found guilty of malfeasance—taken together, these responses clearly demonstrate a change in the posture, from passive neglect to increased responsiveness, of those responsible for maintaining law and order in the state and the nation. When adjudicating the case of Cellos Harrison, even justices on the Florida Supreme Court seemed to adjust their stance in response to the ideological ground shifting beneath their feet. During the era of World War II, the wall of silence that lynchers in Florida depended on to shield them from being held legally responsible for their extralegal activities steadily eroded in the face of social and political pressure from outside of the state.

LYNCHED TWICE

Arthur C. Williams, Gadsden County, 1941

> As believers in the democratic system, we
> hate tyranny and all its attributions, but
> the fight for freedom can't be won until we
> recognize the fact that democracy in its true
> meaning involves not only the lip-service to
> the doctrine that all men are created equal
> but a real change in our attitude.
>
> **Pearl Buck, December 1941**

The 1941 lynching of Arthur C. Williams in Gadsden County was the first recorded in Florida during the decade, and the fourth to take place in the nation that year. While there had been a general decline in the number of extralegal murders in the state over the previous two decades, and in the nation for that matter, the scourge of lynching continued to be a painful indicator of the intractability of race relations in Florida. Racial violence had blotted the state's record frequently during the previous decade, which witnessed a total of fifteen lynchings, including the gruesome killing of Claude Neal in 1934, which earned Florida notoriety as the scene of the largest mass or "spectacle" lynching in the nation's recent memory. Throughout the 1930s, newspapers across the nation increasingly reported the grisly extralegal murders in the South. The heightened awareness of southern atrocities by people living above the Mason-Dixon Line brought

unwanted criticism and outrage from outside the region. The usual justification for these abominable activities—that white men needed to
protect white women from bestial black men—became increasingly less
convincing, while the details of bloody lynching bees became too much
for many ordinary Americans, black and white, northern and southern,
to tolerate without comment. The circumstances of Williams's lynching
attracted condemnation for two reasons. First, the lynchers demonstrated
an alarming boldness and persistence in the pursuit of their victim—coming after him again when their first attempt to kill him failed—while local law enforcement officials proved either unable or unwilling to protect
Williams's life on either occasion. Second, the reaction to this lynching
by members of the American press, especially nationally syndicated journalist Westbrook Pegler, demonstrated a growing unwillingness on the
part of the American public to continue in their role as silent witnesses
to brutality. This fact evidences a slow cultural evolution around issues of
racial justice that would only become more dramatic as America entered
World War II, informed, in part, by the revulsion many Americans felt
for Adolf Hitler's reign of terror in Europe. This trend toward increased
public criticism became more pronounced with other instances of lynching and racial violence that occurred once the United States entered the
war in December 1941 and throughout the war years. Civil rights activists
capitalized on this powerful wartime rhetoric and international perspective in their attempts to advance the war they were waging against Jim
Crow at home.[1]

The persistence of lynching violence in Florida caused significant crises
for the state's elected officials. Just five months after taking office in January 1937, Governor Fred P. Cone confronted a potential lynching in Franklin County after Robert Hinds was arrested and accused of raping a white
woman. Local law enforcement officers, with support from Cone's office,
protected Hinds from the mob long enough for him to be hustled through
a speedy trial and on to a swift electrocution that July. Technically, Cone
managed to avoid Hinds's murder and the negative press coverage that
would have accompanied it, but only by substituting a "legal lynching"
for an extralegal one. This apparent success, however, proved short-lived
when, three days before Hinds's scheduled execution on July 23, whites
kidnapped and lynched two African American teenagers, Richard Ponder

and Ernest Hawkins, in Tallahassee; the dead bodies of the victims were found just yards away from the home of state supreme court justice William Glenn Terrell.[2]

The lynching of Ponder and Hawkins provided useful leverage for those advocating the passage of a federal antilynching bill. The NAACP, since its founding in 1909, emerged as the leader in the fight against racial violence, and lynching remained its primary focus during its first fifty years of existence. The group seized the opportunity to continue its push for the Wagner-Van Nuys Bill (named for its Democratic sponsors, Rep. Robert Wagner, of New York, and Rep. Frederick Van Nuys, of Indiana), then before the U.S. Senate, using the incidents in Florida as prime examples of why such laws were necessary. Armed with a flood of support from the public, the group faced opposition from the southern bloc in the U.S. Congress, and would not have the backing of the White House, as President Franklin Roosevelt remained unwilling to jeopardize his own legislative priorities.[3] Both of Florida's senators, Claude Pepper and Charlie Andrews, added their voices to the chorus of opposition. As the measure was being considered by the Senate in the winter of 1937–38, Andrews continually expressed his disapproval of the proposed law through nationally broadcast radio speeches, rebuking the idea that there was racism in the South at all, and vilifying the measure as a strike at the sovereignty of the American people.[4] Predictably, southern senators launched a six-weeks-long filibuster against the measure, during which Pepper spoke for a total of eleven hours in opposition to the bill over the course of two days. Citing the example of Reconstruction and the failure of the Fifteenth Amendment to protect the rights of African Americans to vote, Pepper characterized the bill as another well-intended but unenforceable northern intrusion into southern traditions. "The colored race [had not and] will not vote," said Pepper, "because in doing so under present circumstances they endanger the supremacy of a race to which God has committed the destiny of a continent, perhaps the world." He concluded that antilynching legislation would also fail because "mere legislation does not change dynamic social conditions." Pepper's arguments were not original, as they had been echoed by southern politicians for generations, including Florida governors Sidney Catts and Park Trammell. In their view, any advancement in the civil rights of blacks was linked to the destabilization of southern society as a whole, and specifically as a sexual threat to white women. Unable to garner the necessary support, the measure ultimately failed.[5]

Lynching violence continued to blot Florida's record, with the killings of J. C. Evans in 1937, Otis Price in 1938, Miles Brown in 1938, and Lee Snell in 1939.[6] The dawning of a new decade, however, offered an opportunity to turn a corner on the violence of the previous years. In May 1940, the Association of Southern Women for the Prevention of Lynching (ASWPL) eagerly proclaimed the last twelve months as the nation's first "lynch-free year" in decades, citing figures from the Tuskegee Institute, although the NAACP rigorously disputed the claim. A year without a lynching validated the efforts of the ASWPL's educational and letter-writing campaigns, and bolstered the organization's contention that the struggle against racial violence in the South could be won by homegrown solutions, as opposed to federal intervention in local matters. Decreasing instances of reported extralegal murders supported these claims. By extension, this argued against the need for what southerners viewed as invasive federal anti-lynching bills. Tamping down on lynching violence helped to stave off federal intervention, meddling outsiders, and a potential return to federal involvement in southern affairs that, for white southerners, would look too much like Reconstruction. [7]

Coming into the new decade, state officials wanted to redeem Florida's reputation from its embarrassing track record on racial violence. Upon taking office in 1941, Florida's newly elected governor, Polk County native Spessard Holland, was eager to turn the corner on the lynching record of the previous decade and avoid a repeat of the negative attention the state received because of its failure to successfully contend with lynching. If it appeared that racial violence was beyond the control of state officials, the image of raving mobs of white vigilantes roaming the state could frighten potential investors and negatively affect Florida's economic viability.[8] However, maintaining the appearance of racial harmony while preserving the racial status quo proved an increasingly difficult task. Like his predecessor, Governor Holland was only five months into his term when he was forced to confront the fallout from a lynching, this time the lynching of Arthur Williams. The affair represented the beginning of a series of tense confrontations between local, state, and federal officials over the continued racial violence against African Americans in the state. On the one hand, state leaders like Holland wrestled with the national criticism and demands for investigations and prosecutions when lynchings occurred. On the other hand, many locals still excused lynching as a justifiable form of homicide and despised the meddling of outsiders who did not understand the southern way of life or their unique "Negro problem."

This was a serious concern for southerners, especially given the changes brought by President Franklin D. Roosevelt's New Deal programs and by civil rights protests. The ruling class in Florida, like their counterparts throughout the region, were already contending with the effects of the Great Depression and the economic instability brought on by the New Deal policies that affected agriculture and labor. Southern representatives in Congress successfully campaigned to exclude domestic and farm laborers, occupations with high proportions of African Americans, from the protections included in the National Labor Relations Act, denying them the benefits of a minimum wage and unionization. Other programs like the Works Progress Administration (WPA) and the Civilian Conservation Corps (CCC) offered comparatively higher wages and competed successfully for black laborers. Southern lawmakers fought against these measures, fearful that African American workers would be "spoiled" by high-paying federal jobs. Higher incomes, they feared, might translate into ambition for social equality and political participation, undoing the work of decades of white hegemonic practices.[9]

Racial difficulties were one of many social and infrastructural transformations Florida underwent as the necessities of war mobilization turned the state into one of the foremost training grounds for American soldiers headed to fight overseas in World War II. Labor shortages became a problem when what had been a trickle of black immigration out of the South since the 1910s became a flood; scores of African Americans left Florida and headed north and west in search of jobs in the burgeoning war industries, as well as an overall better quality of life. Black workers, however, found that Jim Crow labor practices confined them to low-paying, unskilled jobs. To address this discrimination, in late 1940 and early 1941 native Floridian A. Philip Randolph began planning for a massive demonstration that would bring tens of thousands of African Americans to the nation's capital to protest routine discrimination against black laborers in the war industries and to pressure the Roosevelt administration to address these inequalities.[10] African Americans in Florida, encouraged by national civil rights victories, pursued similar strategies to fight inequality within the state. Battles against lynching, along with campaigns to equalize teacher pay and to contest the all-white primary system, represented some of the early tremors of what would become a full-scale movement for civil rights for African Americans in the 1950s and 1960s. Working on parallel tracks, civil rights activists and black journalists, by the dawn of the 1940s, had managed to link the struggle against fascism abroad to the struggle against racist oppression at home. The conversation about lynching violence, as demonstrated in the aftermath of lynchings in Florida, illustrated the leverage that World War II provided African Americans to aid their domestic struggles for equality, and the limits of its effectiveness.[11]

When it came to addressing lynching violence during the late 1930s and early 1940s, the continued threat of a federal antilynching law, the public campaigns by antilynching activists, and the international attention placed on the many examples of fascist oppression taking place in Europe significantly reshaped the ideological playing field upon which federal officials had to act. In contrast to the rise of oppressive regimes under Hitler and Mussolini in Europe, American leaders sought to present the United States as a democratic "city on a hill," especially its promises of equal protection under the law to its citizens. Roosevelt's administration contextualized the war in Europe as a global contest between "democracies" ("our type of civilization") and "dictatorships." The rhetoric foreshadowed America's desire to assert its influence in a world restructured by colonization and war. As one scholar notes, "this nearly obsessive concern with the nation's *international* image grew out of circumstances specific to the early 1940s. More than anything else, it signaled the widespread acceptance in government circles of the belief that the United States could best advance its own geopolitical position through selling its ideology and its way of life, rather than through costly and disruptive exercises in military conquest."[12]

Lynching and other forms of racial violence, however, highlighted the inability of local law enforcement officials to protect black citizens (or, more often, their willingness to comply with the violent methods used to maintain white supremacy), as well as the inability or lack of interest of state officials in bringing lynchers to justice. These realities created a credibility gap for the United States as it promoted its political and economic ideologies, and the national values of democracy and liberty, especially in the comparison the nation's leaders sought to draw between themselves and the authoritarianism and oppression represented by the Axis powers. Issues of race complicated this equation. The "Negro problem" was the Achilles' heel of America's foreign policy. The State Department was forced to confront the fact "that discrimination against African Americans—because of its sheer scale and brutality—damaged America's global image more than any other single issue." The issue affected more than just America's image, becoming "a significant obstacle to their [the United States's] ability to conduct their business throughout the world in the way that they wanted." The sharp contrast the nation sought to draw softened significantly when forced to reconcile its purported democratic principles with the continuing reality of unchecked racial violence.[13] Giving testimony about lynching violence before the Senate Sub-Committee on the Judiciary in March 1938, NAACP president Arthur Spingarn referenced an editorial in a Nazi-run German newspaper that claimed blacks in the United States were treated worse that Jews in Germany.[14] Such damaging comparisons gained more credence with each instance of extralegal murder, riot, and rampage committed against African Americans.

In the rhetorical skirmishes of the World War II era, black and white activists used the counterbalance of Nazi Germany to draw parallels between the injustices suffered by Jews in Europe and the ongoing atrocities faced by African Americans in the South. Continued instances of racial friction in the military, violence, and lynchings like those that took place in Florida became fodder for the Axis powers' propaganda machine. One prominent example of the distance between America's proclaimed values and its practice involved blacks in the military. "While the United States tried to muffle the sounds of racial conflict within American ranks," Thomas Borstelmann notes in his work *Cold War and the Color Line*, "Germany and Japan strove to amplify it. German and Japanese propagandists eagerly brandished every report of racial discrimination in the United States as evidence of American speciousness and the hollowness of Allied rhetoric about democracy and freedom."[15] The fact that the armed forces mandated racial segregation was clear evidence of hypocrisy, a point that was not lost on the Axis powers or black Americans. Furthermore, the horror stories shared by black men and women as they attempted to volunteer for service or complete their training significantly undermined the morale of both black soldiers and citizens. Phillip McGuire's research on the experience of African American soldiers demonstrates that

> black soldiers were humiliated, despised, denied regular army privileges, insulted by post commanders, subjected to military and civilian police brutality, accused of crimes they did not commit, constrained by traditional mores, unfairly discharged from military service, denied adequate medical services, court-martialed excessively, and denied adequate entertainment. Their treatment often suggested that they were viewed not as American soldiers but as wards of the armed forces. As a result of these practices the *esprit de corps* of black soldiers remained low throughout the war.[16]

Evidence of these troubles abounded. In April 1941, the uniformed body of Private Felix Hall, a native of Montgomery, Alabama, was found hanging from a tree in the woods on the base at Fort Benning, Georgia. Military officials ruled the death a suicide despite the fact that Hall's hands were tied behind his back and his feet were bound.[17] Another soldier, in a desperate but anonymous letter to the *Chicago Defender*, aired his frustration about the routine and demoralizing racism he faced within the military: "Isn't it true we are fighting for the same cause as the white man—for democracy—which is not practiced in the land in which we serve?" He did not feel safe, however, to openly complain about the circumstances that he and the other black troops in his unit faced, closing his letter with a plea that revealed the root of his anxiety: "Don't mention my name in the paper please. For they would lynch me if they knew I was writing to a newspaper about this."[18] Just as significant as the international ramifications of these examples of racism and injustice was the disillusionment they caused among blacks. As one African American college student desolately surmised, "The Army jim crows us. The Navy lets us serve only as mess men. The Red Cross refuses our blood. Employers and labor unions shut us out. Lynching[s] continue. We are disfranchised, jim crowed, spat upon. What more could Hitler do than that?"[19]

The news of the lynching of Arthur Williams in May 1941, as with the other Florida lynchings that occurred in the following years, would be viewed through a prism created by international events that diffused significantly different reactions—intellectual, moral, and political—to instances of extralegal violence against African Americans. The response of the nation, however, demonstrated growing opposition to what had been accepted as the normal pattern of southern race relations. Critics within the state and around the nation forced white residents of Gadsden County to defend their community against claims of barbarity and backwardness, standards that were increasingly being measured against Nazi aggression in Europe in the late 1930s and 1940s. This growing trend toward a vocal rejection of lynching violence as the norm cannot be disassociated from the larger concerns of the international reputation of the United States, as is articulated by many of the correspondents who criticized the events in Quincy, the town in Gadsden County where Williams was lynched.

*   *   *

The history of Gadsden County mirrors that of other locales in the plantation South. Carved out of the Florida frontier and chartered in 1823, Gadsden County offered the allure of new lands and new opportunities, inducing wealthy planters and yeoman farmers to the area. Once there, farmers experimented with several crops, but by 1828 tobacco prevailed as the region's agricultural mainstay. Slavery became the cornerstone of the continued prosperity of tobacco cultivation, as enslaved African Americans performed the demanding labor required to ensure profitable tobacco crops. Gadsden became one of the five "Black Belt" counties (along with Jackson, Leon, Jefferson, and Madison) in North Florida in which blacks accounted for half or more of the population.[20] The agricultural wealth produced a class of elite white planters and slave owners, but the prosperity was eventually interrupted by the outbreak of the Civil War.[21]

By 1865, the defeat of the South and the abolition of slavery meant the end of a way of life in Gadsden County, socially and economically, for both those who were formerly enslaved and defeated whites. A temporary changing of the guard occurred under Reconstruction as African Americans began to participate in government. The experiment was short-lived, however, because by the 1880s whites in Quincy and throughout the South began to reestablish white supremacy, establishing Jim Crow policies to curtail and control the social and political aspirations of African Americans. White landowners also desired to reestablish blacks as the cheap source of labor necessary to support economic recovery in the region. African Americans themselves needed a way to earn a living and provide for their families. These complementary dilemmas were solved by compromise with the advent of new labor structures—tenant farming, sharecropping, and wage labor.[22]

Agriculture in Gadsden County continued under these new systems. Farmers imported the shade technique of cultivating tobacco from Cuba around 1892 that allowed for the growth of a high-quality cigar wrapper leaf, which was previously exclusive to the island. The introduction and successful implementation of shade-grown tobacco resulted, once again, in an influx of people and capital into the region. Gadsden County was the center of it all, with 173 of 211 shade tobacco farms located in the Georgia-Florida District. Over the years, businessmen in the area established several small companies, which merged in 1910 to form the American Sumatra Tobacco Corporation, the "world's largest single producer and packer of cigar tobacco leaf."[23] Nestled between the Ochlockonee and Apalachicola Rivers, "aristocratic old Quincy" had become "the shade capital," the heart of the Georgia-Florida shade tobacco district.[24]

The good times, however, did not last, and by the 1920s an economic bust succeeded the boom. A crop disease known as black shank hit Gadsden County especially hard, affecting as much as 7 percent of the tobacco acreage under cultivation overall, and wiping out entire farms in some cases. Unfortunately, the 1930s held no more hope than the previous decade, as the country entered the grips of the Great Depression. In the ensuing economic reverberation, tobacco prices fell from a high of $1 per pound in 1918 to 30¢ per pound by 1934.[25] Recovery, however, was on the horizon. In the 1940s, tobacco prices stabilized and began to rise because of the economic stimulation caused by World War II. Driven by wartime demand, tobacco prices reached a high of $1 per pound in 1943, the first time in a quarter of a century.[26] Between 1939 and 1941, the per capita effective buying income for Gadsden County steadily increased, rising from $196 to $333. Still, these values were comparatively meager, representing 48 percent and 63 percent, respectively, of the statewide mean of effective buying income.[27]

Just as the main economic resource was the same, Gadsden County's racial composition, as well as its social and economic structure, remained relatively consistent between 1860 and 1940. In 1940, 56 percent of the county's 31,450 residents were people of African descent. Black workers comprised the majority of the area's agricultural labor force as well.[28] As long as Gadsden County farm owners relied on shade tobacco for the local economy, they depended on cheap black labor to produce it. As one observer noted, "the use of large numbers of Negro laborers is part of a regional cultural pattern. . . . Dependence upon Negro laborers is almost as striking a characteristic of that cigar-wrapper area as the use of shades and curing barns."[29] This dependence also created a need to control the labor force. Subjugation and control of blacks created a favorable balance of power for whites, which ensured continued economic and social stability; African Americans provided a "great, easily-exploitable, common-labor reservoir."[30] In Gadsden County, as throughout much of the South, racism sustained a paradigm of social and economic control based on fear and oppression. Any threat, real or imagined, to the white power structure required immediate attention and action.

The vast majority of black men living in Gadsden County worked either as wage laborers, tenant farmers, or sharecroppers. For many, tobacco farming was the only way of life they had known. One longtime Gadsden County resident who was born in 1912 recalled, "I was born on 'bacca. Married on a 'bacca farm. Four of my chillin' was born on a 'bacca farm." The work was tedious and the hours were long; workers recall "workin' from sun to sun, can to cain't."[31] Many still labored under the supervision of white farm managers, much like the white overseers who directed blacks during slavery. Also, blacks often resided on the farms at which they worked. One researcher noted this occurrence:

> The laborers (almost 100 percent Negro) are housed in shacks which are located conveniently near the barns and shades. A high dependence upon Negro laborers (which began on the early plantations) has evolved to the point where workers' houses are one of the most significant elements of the rural landscape.[32]

These arrangements ensured black workers' dependence upon white farm owners and managers, establishing living situations greatly reminiscent of slavery. As with other African Americans in the agricultural South, "the prospects for improving their position were not especially encouraging, as opportunities to escape the system contracted rather than expanded. . . . Rather than escaping the arbitrary power of whites, blacks found themselves firmly in their clutches."[33]

According to the design and the intended purpose of Jim Crow policies, combined with the exploitative nature of agricultural wage labor, a level of social and economic inequality thrived in Quincy.[34] Many African American families in Gadsden County earned just enough to live in the shadow of poverty. There were not many opportunities for blacks to accumulate wealth and land. Despite this trend, some African Americans in Quincy did manage to obtain higher education and acquire some material prosperity. Quincy did have a small black middle class consisting of a number of professionals, educators, and landowners. Some blacks took advantage of the forced social separation and started their own businesses. African American proprietors operated a string of businesses, including a dry cleaning shop, a pool hall, a juke joint with a piccolo (a jukebox), and a grocery store, in downtown Quincy on Adams Street, known to both blacks and whites as "Nigger Corner."[35] Dr. William Spencer Stevens, an African American physician, operated a hospital, drugstore, and soda shop on Adams Street. On the weekends, Adams Street became a "Mecca" where blacks made their weekly pilgrimages, congregating and socializing outside of these stores. People "would come in town on a Friday evening and they would congregate, walk backwards and forwards down the Adams Street," one resident recalled. "We'd sit on our cars down there. . . . It was just a place to be, place to go."[36] Additionally, there were black-owned barbershops, restaurants, insurance agencies, and various entertainment venues sprinkled throughout the town.[37]

Racial violence occasionally shattered the relatively peaceful atmosphere of Quincy. On November 9, 1929, a white mob killed forty-year-old Will "Bull" Larkins in Quincy. Local newspaper accounts reported that Larkins had been accused of attacking a thirteen-year-old white girl in the area of Midway, just east of Quincy on the way to Tallahassee. Given the fury that a crime of this nature was likely to inspire, Sheriff G. Scott Gregory moved Larkins to the jail in Leon County, and then Madison County. Unfortunately, his efforts were in vain. While transporting the prisoner to Duval County for even greater security, a mob ambushed law enforcement officers and took Larkins from them. The group then made their way back to Gadsden County, where they "trussed [Larkins] to the railroad crossing signal post with heavy galvanized wire, and shot [him] to death." Afterward, the mob tied Larkins's body to the back of a car and dragged it around the courthouse square.[38]

Generally whites in Quincy supported the lynching of Larkins. Sheriff Gregory took pleasure at "the prompt administering of justice" and in the fact that no innocent blacks had been killed.[39] The editor of the *Gadsden County Times* interpreted the occurrence as just another incident in the fight to maintain white supremacy, noting that "outraged girlhood or womanhood shall be avenged quickly. The brightest hope of our race depends on man's chivalrous attitude toward women. . . . Men spilling blood for worthy womanhood are a part of the scheme which will never permit the race to die."[40] The newspaper characterized Larkins as a "bad nigger," citing accusations that he harassed other white women prior to his alleged attack on the white girl. It also reported that Larkins had been accused of raping three young black girls. Accordingly, Sheriff Gregory claimed that the "better class of negroes" in Quincy supported the action of the mob. It seemed, however, that Larkins's supposed habit of sexual harassment and assault was not a problem until the victim was white; accusations that he committed the same crime against a white girl inspired swift and brutal action. The severity of his punishment served as a warning to other blacks: they could expect the same treatment if they challenged white authority. The threat succeeded. One resident recalled the feeling of Quincy's black residents: "They was frightened. It was pitiful during that time. [Violence] seems to have been a general practice."[41] The circumstances of the Larkins lynching and the community's reactions offer an important precedent to the later murder of Arthur Williams.[42]

*   *   *

The events leading to Williams's lynching began on Sunday, May 11, 1941, with his arrest. While patrolling the deserted Quincy streets in his car early that morning, the loud blast of gunshots startled Officer Dan Davis, deputy sheriff of Gadsden County. Anticipating trouble, he drove toward the sound. While en route, Davis saw a figure moving swiftly through the shadows. As he exited his car and continued to approach on foot through the darkness, Davis saw someone running from him. He pursued the man, who, in an attempt to elude him, ran behind a chicken coop and then entered the back door of a nearby residence occupied by an African American family. Officer Davis knocked on the front door, and once inside, found Williams there.[43]

After questioning Williams, he inspected the area behind the chicken coop where he saw Williams stop. Davis found several coins and a kitchen knife on the ground. When searching through Williams's clothes, he also discovered a pocket watch and a wristwatch. Davis confronted Williams with what he had found, asking Williams if the items belonged to him. After some hesitation, Williams confirmed that they were his and that he had won them in a gambling match. Suspicious of his elusive behavior and unconvinced by his claims, Officer Davis took Williams into custody.[44]

Meanwhile, the other officers on duty that evening searched for the source of the gunfire. They found William Bell, a white man, standing outside his home with a shotgun. He had fired his weapon, he informed the officers, to summon help because someone had broken into his house and attempted to rape his daughter. Upon learning of the alleged attack on the Bell family, Officer Davis arrested Williams. On Monday, May 12, 1941, authorities charged him with burglarizing the Bell home and attempting to rape twelve-year-old Thelma Bell. Davis placed Williams in the jail located at the Quincy courthouse, where he remained without guard throughout the night.[45] Sometime the next day Officer Davis spoke with the sheriff, Morgan P. Luten, and informed him of the incident. At that time, as they would later claim, neither one of the men thought that Williams's life would be threatened. Beneath the veneer of calm, however, news of the attempted assault quickly spread through the town.[46]

Later that night, Officer Davis conducted his rounds on foot in downtown Quincy. The sounds of an approaching car interrupted the still of the night. A vehicle pulled up beside Officer Davis, and four masked men exited. One of the men pointed a gun at the stunned Davis while the others forced him into the car. The driver took off into the darkness, in the direction of the county jail. As the kidnappers exited the vehicle, they informed Davis of their intent: "We just want that goddamn negro out of the jail and we don't want any fuss about it." Outnumbered and outgunned, Davis complied. As they entered the building, Davis attempted to turn on the lights. One of the men stopped him, saying, "We will furnish the light for this party." Davis pointed them in the direction of the cells. The masked men proceeded into the cell block and returned with Williams. Before leaving the building, the kidnappers locked Davis in a jail cell.[47]

Sheriff Luten, asleep in the cottage adjacent to the jail, awoke to the sound of Davis's yelling. Once in the jail, he found Davis locked in a cell.

As Luten released him, Davis divulged the morning's event: "they got my gun, my handcuffs, and that nigger."[48] After learning the details of the situation, Luten and his deputies scoured the town in search of Williams and his kidnappers.

Their efforts were too little, too late. During the course of their probe, the sheriff's search team discovered a severed rope hanging from a pecan tree with blood splattered beneath it near the Georgia, Florida, and Atlantic (G.F.&A.) Railroad station. From that spot, a bloody trail continued on the ground for fifty feet, leading underneath a nearby building. Luten and his men brought a bloodhound to the scene, and the dog followed a trail leading to the building but lost the scent. Other than the blood, there were no signs of Williams, living or dead.[49]

Since they could not locate Williams, Luten assumed he was alive. In a last-ditch effort, they proceeded to the Seaboard Quarters to visit Hattie Williams, Arthur's mother, to see if she knew of his whereabouts. Shocked to hear of her son's fate, she maintained that she had not seen him. Sheriff Luten and his party continued to search for Williams.[50]

Facing the specter of another lynching controversy that would stain Florida's reputation, state officials quickly sprang into action. On the afternoon of Monday, May 12, State Attorney Orion Parker began an investigation into Williams's abduction from the county jail. Several individuals testified during Parker's hearing: Officer Dan Davis; Sheriff Luten; William "Jabo" Pittman, a black man from Marianna who shared a cell with Williams; twelve-year-old Thelma Bell, the alleged victim of the attempted rape; her sister, Marie Bell, aged ten; and Annie Bell, their mother. Notably, William Bell was not questioned on record as to his whereabouts on the evening of the kidnapping.[51]

The testimony that afternoon described one version of what went on in the Bell home in the early morning hours of Sunday, May 11. On Saturday, the family had settled down for the evening. The two young girls, Maria and Thelma, slept in their bedroom. In the middle of the night Maria, the younger sister, awakened to Thelma's screams. As she opened her eyes, she claimed she saw a black man fleeing the room. Maria's screams woke the girls' parents, William and Annie Bell, who rushed into the room. After questioning the girls, William Bell dressed himself, retrieved his shotgun, and fired it into the air, signaling for assistance.[52]

In her testimony on May 12, Annie Bell revealed other important details about the discoveries made on the night of the alleged attack. She positively identified as hers the watches and the knife Officer Davis reported that he had taken from Williams. She also testified that on the night of the break-in, the officers found a crowbar on Thelma's bed and several burned matches on the floor. Bell concluded Williams intended to use them to harm her children, "Lord, have mercy!" she exclaimed. "He was going to kill my young girl." When testifying about her daughter's condition on that night, Annie Bell recalled that upon examining her daughter after the attack, Thelma was "as nasty there [genital area] as she could be," but she did not see lacerations in the area.[53] Subsequently, Annie Bell had difficulty explaining how Williams managed to maneuver through the house, first entering the parents' bedroom, burglarizing it, and then proceeding to the girls' room without being detected. In explaining the phenomenon, Annie Bell suspected that Williams used some sort of "black magic," either a spell or tranquilizing concoction, that deepened the family's slumber, thereby preventing his detection, suggesting that he "threw something over us to make us sleep."[54]

Thelma Bell took the stand next. When questioned by Parker, the girl only confided that there was a man in her bed who was "trying to do something nasty." When pressed further she declared, "I don't know what he was trying to do, only to rape me." However, only a few moments later in her testimony Thelma stated that the assailant had never been between her legs. Further, she testified that she was unsure of her attacker's race.[55]

Next the jury heard from Dr. Sterling E. Wilhoit, a local white physician, who examined Thelma Bell after the alleged attack. He testified that he saw bruises and scratches around her neck, and that the girl's vaginal area showed signs of trauma. He concluded that she had indeed been raped.[56] The doctor's professional analysis offered a sober finality to the proceedings, and a damning indictment of Arthur Williams.

At that point, State Attorney Orion Parker concluded his investigation. With the alleged perpetrator missing, there was nothing else he could do. That would change when, later that evening, Sheriff Luten learned Williams had returned to the Seaboard Quarters, severely wounded and in need of medical attention. In actuality, the Williams family and their neighbors had hidden him throughout the day. Although the family realized Williams needed medical care, they feared that his attackers would return to finish the job they started, or worse, that the lynchers would harm other family members.[57] In order to avoid suspicion, they denied knowing his whereabouts. They even went so far as to assist the sheriff earlier in the day to search for Williams. It was later suggested that another reason for the family's hesitance in contacting the authorities was that Williams asked his mother not to contact Luten because he had been involved with the first attempt on his life.[58]

With Williams located, Luten had to decide the proper course of action, an arduous task considering that one attempt on Williams's life had already occurred and that state officials from nearby Tallahassee were paying close attention to the case. If Williams was not protected or it was found that Luten failed to act properly, the sheriff could find himself in the middle of a national controversy, drawing negative attention to his hometown and the state. At the age of sixty-six, Luten had just been installed as sheriff five months earlier.[59] His reputation was on the line if he could not maintain good order or protect the inmates in his own jail. Given the gravity of the situation, Luten decided to consult with Edgar C. Love, the judge of the Second Judicial Circuit for the state of Florida and a Quincy resident. It was clear that Williams would need medical treatment; however, Jim Crow policies barred his admittance to the hospital in Quincy. The judge instead advised Luten to transport Williams to the Florida Agricultural and Mechanical College for Negroes (FAMC) hospital in Tallahassee, the only medical facility in the region that treated African Americans.[60]

After arriving at the Williams home, Sheriff Luten, Chief of Police Ed Wynn, and Dr. Sterling Wilhoit found Arthur Williams bloody and writhing in pain. Examining Williams, Dr. Wilhoit noted several gunshot wounds: two through the buttocks, two in the chest, one in the shoulder, and a grazed right wrist. Most of the gunshot wounds were on the right side of the body. He also observed that Williams had been beaten in the head. In the doctor's estimation, Williams was lucky to be alive. Despite his injuries, Dr. Wilhoit thought Williams to be in "damn good condition," still conscious and with a normal pulse; with adequate medical treatment, he had a good chance of surviving. Following Judge Love's advice, Wilhoit made arrangements with Dr. L. H. B. Foote, director of the FAMC hospital, for Williams to be transferred there. Meanwhile, Luten contacted Will Webb, a sixty-four-year-old African American funeral home director in Quincy, and asked him to take Williams to Tallahassee in his hearse.[61] Dr.

Wilhoit directed Webb to drive through what was known as St. Hebron, northwest of town, on his way to Tallahassee instead of taking the usual route through Havana. Perplexingly, neither the sheriff, the police chief, nor the judge thought it prudent to assign a guard or police escort to accompany the party.

In the early morning hours of May 13, the party of six black men set off for Tallahassee. Traveling with Webb were Rufus Williams, Arthur's brother; Sam Singleton; Jesse Lee Hill; and Horace Courtney. As they journeyed through the night toward Tallahassee, Webb noticed the glare of a pair of headlights in his rearview mirror. As the glow grew larger and the car drew closer, the men in the hearse became more apprehensive. In due course, the car overtook the hearse and sped ahead into the darkness. Webb continued and crossed over the railroad tracks about four miles outside of Quincy. Once across the tracks, the men inside the hearse noticed a light on the dark road ahead.[62]

As they approached, the men saw someone standing in the middle of the road, flashing a signal for them to stop. As Webb slowed the vehicle, he saw three masked men armed with shotguns emerge from the darkness and stand in the road. They demanded Williams. Reluctantly, Rufus Williams helped Sam Singleton remove his brother from the hearse and place him in the awaiting car. Rufus later testified that he knew his brother was alive at that point because he heard him exclaim "Oh Lord" as he was being placed in the vehicle.[63] The men stood by helplessly as the masked men drove off into the night with Arthur Williams. They were the last people, aside from his murderers, to see Williams alive. Later that morning, a passerby discovered Williams's body, riddled with buckshot and bullet wounds, lying face up on the bridge over the Withlacoochee River, five miles north of Quincy.[64]

After the discovery of Williams's body on the morning of Tuesday, May 13, State Attorney Orion Parker initiated a coroner's inquest. Called to give testimony were Chief of Police Ed Wynn; Sheriff Luten; Dan Davis; William Pittman, a black jail inmate; Dr. Sterling Wilhoit, the physician who examined Williams; Will Webb, the hearse driver; and Jessie Lee Hill, Horace Courtney, Sam Singleton, and Rufus Williams, all of whom were in the hearse when Williams was kidnapped for the second time.[65]

One by one, the witnesses spoke of the events the previous night and either denied involvement, vindicated themselves, or failed to identify any suspects. The most revealing portion of the session that morning, however, was not what was spoken but what remained unsaid. The African American witnesses, in particular, were nervous and evasive during questioning. The court transcripts reflect the state attorney's repeated attempts to extract information from these resistant witnesses. For instance, State Attorney Parker continuously coaxed Will Webb to remain calm while on the stand: "Now, Will, don't get excited. Just go on and tell us what happened." Later in the interrogation, Parker again urged Webb not to "get so scared that you can't tell this Jury what happened."[66] Early in Webb's testimony, he referred to the kidnappers as boys. However, when Parker pressed him about the reference, Webb quickly retreated: "I will tell this jury I was looking at that gun and my eyes got crossed and I wanted to get away from there." The next time Parker pushed him to estimate the ages of the kidnappers, Webb responded that he "would be afraid to say. You know a man just walked up and you see a thing like that and know a man wasn't joking, you would forget what you know."[67]

Will Webb occupied a precarious position. As a mortician serving a primarily black clientele, he enjoyed a certain level of economic independence. However, like many blacks living in the South, the attitude of the whites around him affected, directly and indirectly, his success. If Webb inspired the hatred of whites by cooperating with investigators, retribution could take a number of forms. Hostile bankers could contract his credit. Whites could "encourage" their black employees not to patronize his mortuary. A mob might run him out of town or do him physical harm. Having a gun aimed at him on the night of Williams's kidnapping certainly reminded Webb of his own mortality. Whatever the case, Webb had little recourse; he was an old man who could not afford the financial or physical consequences his testimony might bring.

At the conclusion of the inquest, none of the four black men who were in the hearse with Williams could positively identify the race or recognize the voices of the men who stopped them that night.[68] The results of the inquest were inconclusive. No suspects were identified, and, as Parker reported to the governor, "no evidence has been secured thus far showing any particular person to be involved in this lynching."[69]

This was not the end of the investigation, however. Governor Holland, upon learning of the incident, dispatched his own special investigator, Maurice Tripp, to Quincy to look into the situation. Within two weeks,

Tripp reported his findings. He informed Holland that "I have discussed this case with many people of prominence in Quincy and I find no mob sentiment. The largest number ever involved was only four persons. There has been no crowd or gathering of any great number of people. The sentiment of the general public is they feel that the officers did their duty."[70] Tripp suggested that the community supported their local law officers and did not want the sheriff to be the state's scapegoat. Williams was dead, and life in Quincy returned to normal; there was little support for further investigation.

Upon closer examination, however, Tripp's report contained information that contradicted some of the sworn testimony taken by State Attorney Parker after the murder. One point of contention involved Chief of Police Edward Wynn. Sheriff Luten, Dr. Wilhoit, and Will Webb stated that Wynn was at the Williams home when arrangements were being made to transport Arthur Williams to Tallahassee. Wynn testified that he received a call from Luten saying "that negro [Williams] is at his mammy's house and I want you to go out with me." Wynn said that he accompanied Luten to Williams's home and "was there all the time."[71] However, Tripp's report identified Luten and Wilhoit as "the only two white persons" present on that night.[72] This detail is important because few people knew of Williams's whereabouts and the plans for his transportation; it was likely that someone on the scene informed the individuals who kidnapped and killed him.

Unfortunately, Tripp's inconclusive report was about the extent of Governor Holland's activity, and he made no promises to take further action. When asked when the governor would announce his plan of action for dealing with the Quincy situation, a spokesperson claimed that Holland did not know when he "would be able to reach a decision on whether any action by him against Quincy law enforcement authorities was justified. The pressure of legislative business on the governor was heavy, and the inquest transcript is long."[73]

Details of the investigation of the murder of Arthur Williams were not turned over to the U.S. Department of Justice until July 1942, a full year later. After reviewing the evidence, U.S. Attorney Wendell Berge concluded that when the boy was placed in the ambulance for transportation to the hospital at Tallahassee, no armed guard or deputy sheriff was placed over him. The failure of the sheriff to take the necessary precaution to protect this negro from further violence merits criticism and any feeling on his part that the wrath of this small group of men had been spent, would hardly be an excuse. The situation was one that really justified and required an armed guard and protective custody in its best sense. The sheriff's failure to do this is perhaps directly responsible for the second episode in this unfortunate affair.[74]

Department officials admitted that Gadsden County officials were guilty of "ineptitude and negligence," but concluded that they did not "intentionally refuse" to protect the prisoner in their custody. Therefore, the department decided to close the case because of the amount of time that had passed since the incident occurred.[75] After a year, the inconclusive investigation uncovered no suspects, so there was no one to indict. The identity of Arthur Williams's murderers remained a mystery.

*   *   *

News of Arthur Williams's lynching stimulated considerable reaction both inside and outside the state of Florida. While far from a media frenzy, several newspapers across the nation reported the affair. By 1941, the overall frequency of lynchings in the United States appeared to be tapering off, in comparison to the numerous murders recorded in past years; during the previous decade, the number of reported lynchings decreased by half.[76] Because these types of extralegal murders occurred less frequently than they had in previous decades, the few reported instances of lynching seemed all the more appalling, and, as a consequence, many Americans became increasingly sensitive to them.

Many southerners, however, pointed to the decreasing number of lynchings as evidence that the problem would solve itself without the need for federal intervention and compulsory laws insisting upon justice for blacks.[77] They argued that white southerners would (eventually) experience enough compunction over the shameful legacy of extralegal murder and change their ways. However, as each year passed and more deaths were added to the lynching rolls, it became evident that whites in the South were having difficulty mustering the will to stop the extralegal murder of black citizens. Southern liberals like those in the ASWPL and the Committee for Interracial Cooperation (CIC), who wanted to see an end to lynching but without a federal antilynching law, it seemed, had placed too much hope in the saving graces of humanity and decency. The lynching of Arthur Williams confirmed what many African Americans already knew—that in the absence of legal restrictions, white southerners would continue to perpetrate these murders. Lynching was yet another violent example that old traditions died hard.

The response to the Williams lynching illustrated a slow but definite movement in public opinion away from silent acceptance of extralegal violence. The efforts of groups such as the NAACP, CIC, and ASWPL—as well as the African American press—and their work in investigating, reporting, and publishing information about lynching seemed to be reaping benefits. Detailed investigations into incidents combated the age-old justifications southerners used when arguing for the necessity of lynching; the image of the black bestial rapist was gradually being replaced by documentable instances of black men accused of nonsexual crimes who were then denied their right to due process. As more and more Americans became aware of the actions of Mussolini and Hitler in Europe, they also began to draw lines that separated that group of fascists from their own government and society. Adherence to the law and the equal application of the law were key elements of American democracy. Lynchings directly undermined the moral authority of the United States as Americans criticized the fascist regimes in Europe. Reports about lynchings made it more difficult for Americans to ignore extralegal murder, and harder for those in elected office to sweep such matters under the proverbial rug. At the same time, they fostered a new willingness on the part of many people, particularly white Americans, to speak out against the practice.

Because of the work of these groups and the media, the news of the kidnapping and murder of Arthur Williams rapidly spread across the country. The Associated Press picked up the story, and it was published by a number of newspapers throughout the state. The *Tampa Tribune* labeled the event a "double-barreled lynching." The *St. Petersburg Times* opined that "lynch law has reared its ugly head once more in Florida, and as a result of this latest mob violence, a new stigma is attached to the state's reputation." The editor pushed for an investigation into the matter and for the prosecution of the perpetrators. In a significant contrast to the other state newspapers, a *Tallahassee Daily Democrat* editorial claimed that the incident was not a lynching but an occasion of private vengeance, something the author seems to suggest was a normal and acceptable display of retribution.[78]

Nationally, news of Williams's lynching was carried in the *New York Times* and the *New York Herald Tribune*. Syndicated columnist Westbrook Pegler wrote what was by far the most critical commentary on the Williams lynching in his column "Fair Enough." Perhaps emboldened by recently receiving the Pulitzer Prize for his investigative reporting, he did not mince words in his condemnation of the city of Quincy and the state of Florida in general:

> The section of the country in which this horror occurred is in the social and intellectual slum which, according to the hearsay historians of Florida, was populated by low whites who fled from the other southern states, notably Georgia and Alabama, to escape service in the War Between the States, and the white population is distinguished from the Negroes only in the matter of complexion and other racial characteristics. . . .
>
> It is not to scold the people or the state that such observations are made, but rather to indicate how it can be that white men, claiming to be members of a superior breed, can so degrade themselves and embarrass the race in which they hold technical membership in an effort to impress their superiority on their Negro neighbors. Ignorance and brutality die hard and slowly in certain strains of Florida Caucasians and resist such refinements as electric signs, the radio, plumbing and paving, even on the luxury coast of the Atlantic. . . .
>
> Civilization can't be hurried in the Florida swamps and backwoods, on either the whites or Negroes. Each degrades the other, but the white man has moments when he can really show the Negro a very recognizable stump of the tail by which his not so remote ancestors swung from tangled vines amid the stunted trees.[79]

Pegler's stinging criticism (and the fact that his columns reached an estimated ten million households nationwide) deeply offended the people of

Quincy and individuals throughout the state, particularly his derogatory comments about the character and intelligence level of white Floridians. In response, Floridians picked up their pens and countered his attack. A *Tallahassee Daily Democrat* editorial, "Westbrook Pegler Lynches a Community," praised Quincy's "clean, shaded, paved streets, its well-kept homes and gardens, its air of culture and gentle living, its interest in the general welfare and in community progress, its ample income." Turning the tables on the attacking Pegler, the editors found him guilty "of the charges he hurls with abandon at the community, the section and the state."[80]

Others accused Pegler of abusing the power of his journalistic authority. Harold Colee, executive vice president of the Florida State Chamber of Commerce, believed "injustices, however small, should bring down the thunder of the strong muscled among journalists. This is not only their right, but their duty." However, Colee concluded that Pegler had "seized upon this Quincy incident . . . to display 'below the belt' shrapnel."[81] Many of the attacks against Pegler became personal barrages, characterizing the journalist as yet another northerner who had stuck his nose and pen where they did not belong. Others alleged that Pegler's article was "filled with inaccuracies as to fact and with what would be libel, if a community could sue for libel." Some dismissed Pegler's comments as "perverted intelligence," and that a "rational, sensible man would not raise an eyebrow." The residents of Marianna went so far as to organize the Society for the Dissolution of the Westbrook Pegler Column.[82]

Quincy's white citizens fumed over what they interpreted as underserved criticism of their community. T. R. Smith, president of the Quincy Junior Chamber of Commerce, wrote:

> First the decent people of Quincy and that includes all except a very few of your ilk with little respect for truth and order—condemn lynchings or murder, just as we do gang warfare, labor outrages, and love nest escapades so common to your urban provincial centers. . . . You speak of lack of due process of law, and yet you would lynch the citizenry of a small city. We give you the words of Daniel Webster "The law of the land hears before it condemns, proceeds upon inquiry and renders judgment only after trial." Good newspapermen adhere to this in their code of ethics. We suggest you try this in your future preachments.[83]

In addition to individual expressions of condemnation, the protest against Pegler's column on Quincy spread to the state legislature. Two state senators—Amos Lewis, of Marianna, and Pat Whitaker, of Tampa—denounced Pegler's writings, referring to him as an "alley-bat news sniper" and a "blasphemer" and cursing him to "drink the dregs of the shame that must be his inevitable reward for his earthly existence."[84]

While many spent their energy trying to defend the reputation of Gadsden County, others spoke in terms of moderation and a changing of the order. One enlightened response appeared in an editorial in the *River Junction Tribune*, the local paper for Chattahoochee, a small town in Gadsden County. The column maintained:

Without traditions, life would not be worth living. Without customs to meet the special needs of individual communities, life could not be lived. But tradition and customs must change in a changing world, and nations or communities that do not stay awake to this fact are in a tough spot indeed. . . . Gadsden County developed as a sort of island community with a tradition of lusty ability to take care of its own affairs and a strong feeling that what the rest of the world thought about it didn't matter. It was a tradition that developed from the necessities imposed by isolation and population balance. . . . Pegler's attack on the community was a vicious, libelous diatribe with no sound excuse in journalism. . . . Once—and not many years ago—it was possible to dismiss such comments by saying, "They're outsiders—they don't understand." But in this era of close integration between communities and nations, there are no outsiders in the sense of the possibility of isolationism. Anyone who thinks there is an "outside" world which we can ignore might ask the sheriff how many long distance telephone calls he received the first of last week, and where they came from. . . . [An elderly citizen remarked that] "a few years ago, we would have handled this differently; but that period is gone forever." We gather that he had no regrets for what had happened in the past, but was not sorry to see the change—a change that he fully understood, though some of his younger confreres, with far less excuse for traditionalism than he has, do not yet realize that community isolationism today is a hopeless myth. . . . There is increasing indication that Hitler's greatest help in conquering nations has not come from deliberate traitors; it has come from men who thought they were good citizens, but could not appreciate change. . . . Disciplined citizenship is the only way to meet the crisis of this decade. If that discipline is not self-imposed by us as individuals through obedience to law and to the principles of democracy, and through full respect for law enforcement agencies, it will be imposed upon us by dictatorship. Take your choice.[85]

The author of the editorial concluded that times were changing, and the stark realization that southern isolationism was a thing of the past. No longer could communities such as Quincy lynch their black citizens and expect the rest of the nation to turn a blind eye to the violence. There was the international context as well; the author made a specific reference to the specter of Adolf Hitler and the devastation he was wreaking in Europe. The editor pointed out that his rise had been facilitated by those who thought themselves "good citizens." He fell short, however, of comparing the brutality of Williams's lynchers to that of the Nazis against Jews in Europe; this was rhetoric that had been put to good use by the black press over the last few years. News of lynchings had the potential to besmirch America's international image as the "defender of democracy." Such activity also fed German propaganda mills, paralleling discrimination against blacks in the South with prejudice against Jews in Germany. In a strange twist on this international perspective, the Gadsden editor used the analogy to warn against an intrusive federal "dictatorship" that would rain down on the South if they did not prove themselves capable of abiding by the law.[86]

Another concern shared by citizens in Florida was that the lynching would encourage the federal government to take action to prosecute members of the lynch mobs and protect blacks against these types of crimes, since southern cities and states seemed unable or unwilling to do so. The threat of federal intervention was fresh on the minds of many southerners, especially since federal antilynching legislation had been brought before Congress in 1937 and 1940.[87] This latest occurrence of lynching could be used to bolster the argument for federal intervention. Bishop John D. Wing, of the Episcopal Church, publicly encouraged the governor to remedy the violence in Quincy, "otherwise, the outrage will furnish ammunition to those seeking enactment by congress of federal anti-lynching legislation."[88]

Many encouraged Governor Spessard Holland to initiate an inquiry into the Quincy lynching, not only because of the political implications but for moral reasons as well. A businessman from one of the more prominent Quincy families, Sanford May, wrote Governor Holland urging that the guilty parties be brought to justice, "whether they be among our county officials or not."[89] Also among those agitating for action by the state were members of the ASWPL. The organization's executive director, Jessie Daniel Ames, sent Governor Holland a brief letter encouraging investigation into the matter. Various state coordinators of the ASWPL from Mississippi, Alabama, and Virginia wrote to the governor as well.[90] Typical of their reserved approach, characterized by a combination of moral persuasion and feminine charm, their letters expressed regret that the state's reputation had been besmirched by the tragedy of lynching; this strategy was frequently employed by the women to tap into the southern sense of honor and reputation, thereby persuading officials to investigate these murders.[91]

Jane Havens, chairperson of the Florida council of the ASWPL, contacted Governor Holland, urging him to take action, arguing that "law and order as enforced by the state and counties can protect our whole society. When this process is taken away from the state and county by unscrupulous persons then an injustice is done to the people of the state and those who are responsible for law and order should be removed from office."[92] The regional heads of other Florida ASWPL chapters in Madison, Tampa, Miami, and Vero Beach each forwarded similar sentiments lamenting the fact that Florida was the first state to record a lynching that year.[93]

African Americans, individually and collectively, voiced their vexation over the failure of justice in Quincy. In nearby Tallahassee, a group of black citizens drafted a petition, warning that they were "seriously considering refusal to pay taxes without adequate protection of life, liberty and property" being ensured by the state. Among the petitioners was noted African American educator and community leader John Gilmore Riley.[94] The Miami Negro Youth Council took a different tack, denouncing the tragedy and pointing out that Williams was indeed "a prospective draftee" into the U.S. military. Among the voices of protest that rose from northern blacks were those of members of the Harlem Peoples Club of New

York, who pointed out Sheriff Luten's "criminal failure . . . to provide guard for the ambulance" and demanded his immediate suspension.[95]

The NAACP sought to exploit the tragedy of the Williams lynching to move its larger civil rights agenda forward. Instead of writing to Governor Holland, the group appealed directly to President Roosevelt, urging him to make a statement condemning the events in Quincy. Playing heavily upon the wartime ideologies of democracy being championed by the American government, Roy Wilkins stated that the NAACP was

> concerned with lynching as it relates to the aims in our national defense effort, to our aid to the democracies of the world, and to our declared opposition to the philosophy and practices of the dictator nations. . . . You have pictured this struggle as one to preserve the democratic freedoms against the assault of the forces of oppression, brutality, and death. In this immense effort our country is weakened morally and physically by the lynchers who kill at their whim, and by officers of the law who make no effort to protect their prisoners or to arrest lynchers.[96]

While pointing out the brutality of the murder, the group emphasized commonality between the struggle overseas and the plight of blacks in America, a strategic argument that they hoped would compel the country's leaders to take action to correct injustices. NAACP officials also used Williams's lynching to argue for federal antilynching legislation, which the agency continued to fight for in Congress.[97]

The black press used reports on the Williams lynching to draw parallels between racism in America and fascism in Europe, comparing the Nazis and the men who carried out the murder in Quincy. The *Baltimore Afro-American* proclaimed the Williams lynching "a story of bestiality and stupidity that rivals the crimes of Hitler."[98] The *Pittsburgh Courier*, in an article entitled "Warlike Florida," portrayed the state as a domestic war zone, in which blacks fought, however unsuccessfully, for democracy.[99] James Jackson, head of the Southern Negro Youth Congress, used rhetoric that tied Hitler's atrocities to the crimes of the Confederacy during the Civil War in an effort to mobilize black youth in the current struggle for black rights. "The slave-holding rebels march again," Jackson proclaimed.

> Behind Hitler, they march against our freedom and our right to live.
> A great union of Freedom forms to oppose them. Led by Roosevelt,

Churchill and Stalin, the peoples of the world rally to destroy the slave-masters. Take your place in the front ranks, Negro youth. Give your all in this war to drive Hitler slavery out of the world.[100]

Overall, the carelessness of legal authorities was the single most significant factor in Williams's lynching. The double kidnapping and eventual murder of Arthur Williams took place while he was under the general authority of Gadsden County law officials. Williams was accused of the attempted rape of a twelve-year-old girl, a crime certain to arouse Quincy whites, yet law officers did not think it necessary to guard the jail where Williams was being held. Once Williams was located, having survived the first attempt on his life, the officers of Gadsden County again failed to provide protection for him. Both Sheriff Luten and Chief of Police Ed Wynn were present when arrangements were made to transport Williams to Tallahassee, but neither thought it necessary to protect a man who had already been kidnapped from their custody once and almost killed. Later, Sheriff Luten claimed that after the first kidnapping, he was not aware of the seriousness of the charges against Williams. Following the second kidnapping and the eventual murder of Williams, Luten claimed that he did not think the murderers would be so bold as to make another attempt on Williams's life; he "wasn't dreaming of any such thing."[101]

According to authorities, in cases where people were abducted from jail, the facility was usually unguarded or significantly understaffed.[102] On this occasion, the performance of Luten and his staff walked the fine line between negligence of duty and human error. On the one hand, Luten could be viewed as the aging sheriff, overworked and understaffed, who was outwitted and outmaneuvered by the individuals who were determined to lynch Williams. Conversely, he could have been indifferent to the situation, doing enough to appear to be protecting Williams, thereby preventing the need for state intervention. Nonetheless, blacks in Quincy, like other African Americans throughout the region and nation, had enough previous experience with racist law enforcement officers to recognize that no sincere effort was made to protect the prisoner. One Quincy native recalled, "just look like to me, he could have actually protect that boy if he had got enough help. But he didn't. He just put him in the ambulance Sunday morning. Wasn't nothin' but the folks' duty to take him."[103] Just the same, many whites in Quincy believed that Williams got what was coming to him.

Similarly, because Williams was lynched without the benefit of a trial, the authorities failed to adequately investigate the charge of attempted rape made against him. The testimony from the Bell family was accepted without question, although their versions of events contained many troubling inconstancies. Thelma Bell, a scared and confused young girl, offered a puzzling description of what went on in her bedroom the night before. An especially glaring loophole centered on Thelma Bell's statement that her attacker was never on top of her. Furthermore, the Bell family claimed that Williams broke into their house, entered the main bedroom and stole valuables, then went into a room with two sleeping children and attempted to rape one of them without waking the other. Such a version of events represented an almost fantastic display of daring and stealth on the part of Arthur Williams, who decided to conclude his thieving expedition with the rape of a young girl while her sister slept in the same room a few feet away. At face value, this seems not only foolhardy on Williams's part but physically impossible given the relatively small size of the family's rented dwelling. It is hard to imagine that his presence would not have been detected as he maneuvered past unfamiliar furniture, stepped on creaking floorboards, or rummaged through the family's possessions as he looked for something to steal. Investigators failed to establish a timeline for these events to test the plausibility of these claims.

In the absence of a thorough investigation contemporary to the accusation made against Williams, modern observers can only tie together loose strands of facts in order to deduce other alternative theories and motives behind the crimes and claims. While seemingly circumstantial, the economic indicators of employment and housing, along with family size, imply that the Bell family belonged to a class of whites on the lower end of the socioeconomic scale in Quincy who lived near and possibly worked with blacks. According to reports and census information, William Bell worked as a laborer, specifically a woodcutter, to support his wife and their five children. The same census report suggests that the Williams and Bell families lived next to or in close proximity to each other in the county's Thirteenth Precinct. One newspaper reported that, at the time of the murder, one of the Bells' sons was serving time on the chain gang for auto theft.[104]

There seems to have been some familiarity between the families; some Quincy residents recall that Williams worked for the Bell family at some

FIGURE 1.1. Accused of robbery and the attempted rape of a twelve-year-old white girl, Arthur C. Williams was kidnapped from the jail in Quincy, Florida, by four armed white men who tried to kill him. Williams survived only to be kidnapped again and shot to death. Family members indicate that Williams was only visiting Quincy at the time of this death, after leaving Quincy for Illinois at a young age. This picture seems to confirm Williams's urban orientation. Source: *Pittsburgh Courier*, May 24, 1941.

point before his death.[105] Under the social structure of segregation and racism, such close contact could foster tension and resentment between the races. Evidence of such close proximity between the alleged victim and the alleged assailant, while not conclusive, provides another perspective on Williams's lynching, by introducing the plausibility of interpersonal conflict or an array of ulterior motives in the alleged encounter between Arthur Williams and the Bell family. Existing hostility between the two parties could have inspired a false rape accusation against Williams or, conversely, could have motivated an attack upon the Bells as retribution for a perceived insult or slight. This detail, if explored, had the potential to either substantiate or refute the allegation of robbery and attempted rape.

Despite questions raised by such prejudice, little information could be gathered about Williams, his personal life or his character. According to family members, he left his parents' home at an early age and went to live with relatives in East St. Louis, Illinois.[106] It is alleged that Williams was only visiting Quincy at the time of his death. If true, it opens the possibility of other factors in his murder. If Williams lived in the North for a significant amount of time, it is possible that he might have been killed because he breeched some convention of racial etiquette. A young black man like Williams, after growing accustomed to slightly more liberal race relations in Illinois or thinking himself above the omnipresent racial slights that he would have encountered in Quincy, may have exhibited an "uppity" attitude that would have made him a target for violence or retribution. Similar circumstances resulted in the death of Emmett Till, a fourteen-year-old native of Chicago who was killed in Money, Mississippi, for allegedly making inappropriate comments and gestures to a white woman.[107]

Within the black community, one detail that would be of great importance in establishing the guilt or complicity on the part of those charged to enforce the law was the route Will Webb traveled to Tallahassee. Before the construction of Highway 90, which has become the lifeline between Tallahassee and Quincy, travelers used a system of circuitous streets and back roads to reach the state's capital. The most common route went north from Quincy through Havana. The suspicious detour that Webb took became a revealing detail in the minds of Quincy's black residents. How did Williams's murderers know where to find him, given that there were only a few people who were aware that he was alive so late that evening? From the testimony, it was only a span of two-and-a-half hours between locating Williams and his departure for Tallahassee, roughly between 10:00 p.m. and 12:30 a.m. For some, it made sense that an "insider" with knowledge of Williams's whereabouts and the plans for his transportation to Tallahassee had to have leaked the information. Oral transmissions of the event maintain that it was Dr. Wilhoit who alerted the lynchers about the route Webb's party would be traveling.[108]

Both before and after Williams was lynched, bias concerning his culpability was so pervasive that records, court transcripts, letters, and newspaper articles assumed his guilt. Since Williams was murdered before he was officially charged or brought to trial, his version of the events that evening will never be known. In the absence of his testimony, legal defense, or a thorough investigation, the void was filled by biased assumptions that implicated Williams as a rapist, thereby reinforcing his criminal image. Williams's guilt was unquestioned, and, as a result, it seemed to be a foregone conclusion, in both the investigations and newspaper reports of the incident.

In the black press, the questionable accusations took another form. The *Baltimore Afro-American*'s headline for May 24 announced that "Florida Lynchers Forced Victim to Castrate Himself." In the article, reporter Denmark Vesey claimed that Williams's abductors had removed his handcuffs and forced him to castrate himself. Vesey learned this information after spending time in Quincy and talking to Williams's family members and people in the community. Vesey's is the only reference to castration that was made during the time, which is peculiar. Even more telling is that the claim of castration is not a part of the local lore surrounding the event. How did this claim appear and then seemingly disappear from the private discourse surrounding Williams's lynching? One possibility is that it was a useful fabrication. The accusation injected a level of sensationalism into the lynching incident, adding a familiar element of lynchcraft that readers had come to expect as a part of the brutality. The accusation of castration may have been added by the members of Quincy's black community, as they told, retold, and embellished their accounts of Williams's lynching to make them fit with their own expectations. Without this detail, many of the typical markers of a "traditional" lynching bee were not a part of the Williams lynching. There was no large and angry mob that broke into the jail and then filled the streets as they watched him hang or burn. In fact, the entire event had been carried out in a very quiet manner that bespoke a small, well-organized group of lynchers. Their only miscalculation was not ensuring their victim was dead before leaving the scene. Faced with this situation, Vesey and others may have borrowed from the details of the Claude Neal lynching in 1934, during which the victim was forced to eat his own mutilated genitals. Claiming that Williams had been forced to castrate himself added the familiar element of sexual torture that would be sure to enrage the *Afro-American*'s black readers. However, other evidence does not support the accusation that Williams had been castrated, either by himself or the mob. The detail was not mentioned in Dr. Wilhoit's report of Williams's injuries, and subsequently no other residents recounted the claim when interviewed, including the victim's sister.[109]

The lynching of Arthur Williams produced fear not only in the victim's family; the black community as a whole suffered repercussions as well. They were angry, but like other blacks in the South, they had learned to suppress their outrage as a matter of survival. Blacks in Quincy feared retaliation so much that they refrained from publicly discussing the lynching, dreading that doing so would invite the rage of Williams's attackers upon them and their families. As one resident remembered, "people was scared but you didn't hear them talk about it." And even though blacks were "absolutely afraid . . . [,] no one ever did anything about it," most likely because they acknowledged the futility of protest.[110]

Aside from the fear and anguish suffered by other blacks in Quincy, the Williams family bore the brunt of the tribulation. They would be forever changed. Within two weeks of her son's murder, a heartbroken Hattie Williams, unwilling to continue living at the site of her son's lynching, made arrangements for the family to move to East St. Louis, Illinois, with her sister. In addition to her grief, she feared the lynchers who killed her son "probably would have killed all of us."[111] According to her daughter, Hattie Williams continued to live with the pain of her son's lynching, grieving for him until her death in 1966. Ann Flipper, Arthur's sister, struggled for years with the hate she harbored for white people. In her mind, they had killed her favorite brother, caused the separation of her family, and were responsible for so much of the tragedy in her life.[112]

These testimonies offer deeper revelations about the echoes of lynching violence, a perspective that is often missing from histories. The lynching victims are not alone in their suffering; their families are forced to live with the fear, insecurity, shame, and anger that transpire after such blatant acts of injustice. African American women often found themselves particularly vulnerable. Unlike white women, who could rely on the code of southern justice to protect and defend them against aggressors, black women enjoyed no such assurances. Their menfolk were unable to ensure their own safety, much less the protection of them or their children. Thus Hattie Williams made the best decision she could at the time: to remove herself and her daughter from Quincy in order to achieve some level of protection for the two of them. The ghosts of Gadsden County, however, proved impossible to escape.

*   *   *

The lynching of Arthur C. Williams and the failed investigation into his death offer a glimpse of the difficult realities of race relations in Florida on the cusp of America's entry into World War II. For many whites in Quincy, Williams was no more than a would-be child rapist who received what he deserved. The stereotypes that abounded in the white southern mind during this era about black men defined them—sometimes alternately, sometimes simultaneously—as criminal, lascivious, and shiftless. Consequently, they failed to muster much sympathy or curiosity when black people generally, but especially black men, became victims of brutal, extralegal punishments.[113] Not all violations, however, were the same. The assault of a white female by an African American male, which Fitzhugh Brundage describes as an "elastic concept" broad enough to include rape, attempted rape, or even a nudge, was the ultimate crime in the minds of southern whites, rendering the perpetrator worthy of swift, painful, and deadly punishment within or without the scope of the law.[114] Accordingly, the mere accusation of rape could prove deadly to a black man. Blacks in Quincy clearly understood the danger such situations presented: "There was no use in denying it. They'd put you to a limb. You'd be lucky to make it to jail."[115] The outcome was so certain that in some instances accusers added false claims of rape to inflame passions and instigate the death of the accused. Such accusations were made directly or indirectly in every lynching examined in this work.

These perceptions predicated a grim reality for black southerners: the systematic devaluation of black life often translated into the systematic denial of due process and equal protection for black people in the southern legal system. In the case of Arthur Williams, the police failed to provide adequate protection for him under circumstances that clearly warranted special considerations. Similarly, the state attorney conducted what was billed as an investigation of William's abduction in the hours after his kidnapping in such a way that it served as a proxy for a rape trial, with the alleged victim and her family testifying about their encounters with Williams.

After Williams's murder, this established pattern of behavior continued. There was a rudimentary investigation into the kidnapping and murder that fell far short of a vigorous pursuit of justice. No law officers were held accountable for their failure to anticipate and act to protect Williams's life. Those who were charged with enforcing the law, didn't. Those responsible for initiating proceedings to prosecute the law did so in such a manner that reflected the racial biases of the day. Justice was not colorblind, and the machinery continued to operate in a way the reflected the racial bias of the population. In short, through the mechanics of the criminal justice system, the citizens of Quincy expressed tacit support for the actions of Williams's lynchers.

A DEGREE OF RESTRAINT

The Trials of Cellos Harrison, 1940–1943

When compared to the other extralegal murders that took place in Florida during the 1940s, the 1943 lynching of Cellos Harrison in Marianna is exceptional. Unlike the instances in which the victims were accused of rape or unacceptable contact with white women, Harrison's lynching was the result of the accusation that he, a black man, had murdered a white man. Moreover, the white community in Jackson County exhibited an unusual degree of restraint, initially allowing the court system to determine Harrison's fate. This fact may have owed less to the desire for due process on the part of Jackson County's white citizenry than to the painful memories of the national infamy the community suffered after the horrific public lynching of Claude Neal less than a decade earlier. Instead of immediately resorting to lynching violence, the community exercised forbearance in the expectation that the machinery of the southern criminal justice system—prosecutors, jurors, and judges—would quickly convict and execute Cellos Harrison.

The Florida Supreme Court disrupted those plans. Breaking with its previous history of indifference to the rights of African Americans, the court questioned the methods law enforcement officers used to extort a confession from Harrison. After two years of legal battles, members of the Jackson County community grew impatient and lost confidence that the legal system could deliver the punishment they desired. One quiet night in June 1943, a small group of lynchers kidnapped Harrison from the Jackson County jail and murdered him.

Although the lynchers acted in stealth, what was done in the darkness of Jackson County came to light in the national press. Civil rights activists and other citizens—black and white, northern and southern—rained letters and telegrams on Governor Spessard Holland and federal officials demanding that they take action. The NAACP and members of the black press waved the banner of "Double V," using Harrison's lynching along with the other outbreaks of racial violence that summer to point out America's hypocrisy in fighting fascism abroad while allowing black Americans to be terrorized, as well as to highlight the need for a federal antilynching law. Sensitive to the implications that Harrison's lynching would have as propaganda in the hands of the Axis powers, as well as the potential black eye to the nation's reputation as a bastion of democracy among its allies, President Franklin D. Roosevelt's administration, including the Department of Justice (DOJ) and the Federal Bureau of Investigation (FBI), made an uncharacteristically valiant effort to investigate the lynching. Despite this flurry of activity, the perpetrators of Cellos Harrison's lynching were never identified or brought to justice.

Jackson County is a quiet farming community situated in Florida's western panhandle. Bordered on the east by the Chattahoochee and Apalachicola Rivers and divided by the Chipola River, its terrain is interrupted by lakes, creeks, and caverns. Its alluvial and sandy soil had attracted planters from other southern states to the area in antebellum times. Along with them came their plantation society and commitment to racial hierarchy. The county, officially organized in 1822 by the territorial legislature of Florida, took its place as the westernmost of the five "Black Belt" counties in North Florida, known for their agricultural production and the extensive use of enslaved labor.[1] Blacks grew, picked, and ginned most of the cotton produced in the county, after which it was shipped on the Apalachicola River to Apalachicola and the rest of the world. The unpaid labor of enslaved blacks was key to the success of Jackson County's economy, as it was for much of the antebellum South.

The onset of the Civil War brought many challenges to the people of Jackson County. While Jackson County Confederates fought on faraway battlefields, the county's once bountiful agricultural production, and the plantation society it supported, suffered greatly under wartime pressures. The absence of white men truly put the county in a difficult position militarily. "So many men have left for service from [Jackson County]," one observer noted, "that the proportion of Negroes to white men is greater than twenty to one." This shortage of white males, coupled with the hope of freedom for African Americans that the Civil War represented, was a dangerous combination that Florida governor John Milton and other whites feared would destabilize the institution of slavery in Jackson County; such trouble could disrupt operations of his plantation, Sylvania, also located in the county.[2] Milton's fears proved prophetic, as Marianna itself became a battleground in September 1864. The Union army defeated Confederate forces at the Battle of Marianna and took control of the city. In addition to wrecking and pillaging the town, some 600 slaves left with the Union army when it departed.[3]

The conclusion of the Civil War in April 1865 marked the end of one struggle and the beginning of another. Black and white citizens in postbellum Jackson County had to deal with displacement, destruction, and poverty, in addition to the other, more significant consequences of emancipation. For whites, the most abhorrent changes were reflected in the social order; their former slaves were free and organizing to attain education and social equality. The fiercest struggles, however, would be waged over control of local politics. After the war, Republicans were successful in organizing black voters in Jackson County. As an indication of their success, several blacks were elected to local and state positions; between 1868 and 1872, two African Americans served as registrars, one as tax collector, one as treasurer, seven as county commissioners, seven as justices of the peace, two as constables, and five as city councilmen. During that same period, five black men were elected to the Florida House of Representatives, and one black man, Washington Pope, served in the Florida Senate.[4] Because of this success, whites turned to violence to counter the perceived threat of black political domination. As a result, Jackson County was the scene of violent fighting and murder during the Reconstruction period, primarily in an attempt by local whites to eliminate the leaders of the local Republican faction. Referred to as the "Second Battle of Marianna" by the historian Jerrell Shofner, violence claimed the lives of at least 170 people—black, white, men, women, and children—in Jackson County between 1869 and 1871.[5]

While Jackson County had been considerably altered politically and socially, the economy continued to thrive on cotton production, along with the introduction of some tobacco cultivation. When the boll weevil reached the Jackson County area in the mid-1910s, the local cotton economy was completely devastated.[6] Facing these new economic realities, local farmers turned to the production of peanuts, becoming one of largest producers of the legume in the United States. Complementary to the growth of peanut agriculture was the construction and operation of several peanut mills in the area. The Marianna Peanut Plant, established in 1923, would become the fourth largest such operation in the nation.[7]

Through the early 1900s, African Americans in Jackson County fared well economically. The rates of land ownership and occupational statistics for blacks in Jackson County were remarkable when compared to those of other blacks in the region. Of all black farmers in Jackson County, one-fourth owned their land, nearly twice the rate of land ownership for African Americans in other areas of the South. This high rate of land ownership was consistent with the trends reflected in the occupational indicators. Thirty-three percent of blacks made their living as farmers or managers, which were high-level occupations, as compared to 4 percent statewide, making it the largest job category for blacks in the county. Conversely, 32 percent of Jackson County's African Americans worked in the two largest areas of black employment, either in domestic service or as hired farm laborers, which were considered traditional lines of work for blacks.[8]

Despite the cruel reality of de facto and de jure segregation as the law of the land, blacks in Jackson County were creative in dealing with the reality of Jim Crow, as were other blacks in similar circumstances. During the late nineteenth and early twentieth centuries, the financial independence created by large numbers of black landowners supported the development of a number of black-owned businesses throughout the county, but primarily in Marianna. These businesses influenced the character of black life in Marianna, providing a self-sufficiency that helped blacks maintain their dignity. Charles Forrest, an African American, was part owner of the main local newspaper, the *Times Courier*, which was the predecessor to the

Jackson County Floridan, the major news organ for the area. Forrest also served as the paper's typesetter and printer. Another black man, former slave Armstrong Purdee, practiced law in Jackson County. In addition to his law practice, Purdee dealt in real estate and founded the *West Florida Bugle*, a black newspaper, in 1888. Lemuel Granberry operated his People's Funeral Home on the city's west side. Another member of that family, Henry Granberry, and his business partner, Ben Smith, manufactured cypress shingles. There were several skilled African American tradesmen, particularly in the area of brick masonry; these included Willie and Pete Harrison, and Alvin Swilley Sr. and his sons Lawrence, Alphonso, Alvin Jr., and Earnest. Other blacks operated businesses that catered exclusively to whites, such as Zannie Garrett's barbershop and Taylor's Restaurant.[9]

The Blue Front, as it was called, was a sizable black business district near downtown Marianna along Madison Street in which several black shop owners operated stores that were patronized by other blacks. During the early 1900s, Willie Horne and Jim Speights ran stores there, and William Holden operated a fish stand and a hotel. Dick Baker owned a pressing shop. Maggie Pinder Atwater operated a bakery on Madison Street, and Plessie Cook owned a popular restaurant called the Red Bird Café. The restaurant contained two separate dining areas, one for blacks and one for whites. Members of both races agreed on one thing: Cook served the best stewed beef around.[10]

During this time, other businesses were located in the black community west of town along St. Andrew's Street, known as Brookland to some. These establishments served the dining, shopping, and entertainment needs of many of Marianna's black citizens without the sting of racism. Cynthia Forrest, wife of printer Charles Forrest; R. T. Stinson; Aggie Bell Horne; and "Bunk" Wynn all operated food stores. Sam White ran the Cotton Club, where renowned entertainer Cab Calloway once visited. In the same area, E. E. and Edna DeVaughn operated the Holiday Inn Café, which later became home to W. C. and Curly White's beauty school.[11]

Despite their progress, blacks in Jackson County, like African Americans nationwide, lived with the constant threat of racial violence. There were seven lynchings recorded in Jackson County between 1890 and 1911; five black men, one black woman, and one unknown African American were murdered.[12] By far, the most notable instance of lynching to occur in Jackson County was that of Claude Neal in October 1934. Neal, a twenty-three-year-old black man, was accused of the rape and murder of Lola Cannady, a young white girl. Local law enforcement officers, under the leadership of W. F. "Flake" Chambliss, sheriff of Jackson County, arrested Neal on suspicion of murder. The sheriff made an effort to protect Neal from mob violence, shuttling him from Chipley to Panama City in the Florida panhandle, then on to Brewton, Alabama. While in Alabama, Neal allegedly confessed to raping and killing Cannady. Once news of the confession spread, a group of whites kidnapped Neal from the Brewton jail. They returned Neal to Marianna while making public their intention to lynch him.[13]

Most astonishing about the Neal lynching was the audacity and brutality of the lynch mob. Exhibiting no fear of interference by law enforcement officials, local radio and newspapers publicized news of the impending lynching. Eventually the information found its way to the wire for the Associated Press. Despite widespread knowledge of the ensuing events, the state and local governments did little to prevent the lynching. As a result, on October 27, 1934, Neal suffered terribly at the hands of his captors. In the last hours of his life, the mob stabbed, skinned, and castrated Neal, and then forced him to eat his own genitalia. Witnesses recalled a crowd of nearly 5,000 people, many of whom traveled from other states, including Georgia, Alabama, and Tennessee. The mob included small children who took part in the lynching spectacle, stabbing Neal's lifeless corpse with makeshift wooden daggers when it was brought to the Cannady farm.[14]

The lawlessness did not end with the execution of Claude Neal. Whites who traveled for miles but arrived late and missed their opportunity to participate in killing Neal were angry and disappointed. Over the next two days they vented their frustrations by assaulting some 200 African Americans. Fearing for their lives and desiring to defend their property, local blacks either avoided the downtown area or stayed home. The unrest was so great that the National Guard was summoned to quell the violence.[15]

With the lynching of Claude Neal, whites in Jackson County demonstrated their proclivity toward extralegal violence in seeking what they deemed justice against an alleged African American criminal. Nearly nine years later, with the lynching of Cellos Harrison, they would exercise a great deal more forbearance, but proved unable to eradicate their desire for vengeance.

*   *   *

The details of Cellos Harrison's life are few. Longtime residents recall that his mother, Mary Harrison, worked as a washerwoman. She lived with her three children—thirty-year-old Theresa, twenty-six-year-old Leverett, and twenty-year-old Cellos—in what was known as Russ Quarters, located near the corner of Borden and Clay Streets in west Marianna. Residents remember that, as a young man, Cellos helped his mother with the wash by picking up and delivering clothes to her customers. Physically, Harrison was of average height and slender, with a yellowish complexion. Some remember him as being particularly good-looking. In characterizing Harrison, residents remember him as "daring," and having "a mind of his own," meaning he more readily contested the status quo. Unlike his older brother, Leverett, who worked at a local lumberyard, the 1940 federal census marked the twenty-year-old Cellos as unable to work due to an unspecified physical disability. Still he managed to earn some money taking on odd jobs and working as a carpenter. At one time he was said to be employed at Daffin's dry goods store, directly across from the Jackson County courthouse in Marianna. Doc Grant, clerk of court for Jackson County, once hired him to assist with renovations to the attic in his home.[16]

Records of Marianna's Municipal Court indicate that Harrison had his share of encounters with the law. He was in court on August 7, 1939, and released with time served; a few months later, on November 27, 1939, the court gave Harrison the choice of paying a $10 fine or serving sixty days hard labor in the city jail, but ended up releasing him due to his physical condition, yet another reference to his disability. The following year, on November 19, 1940, Harrison's name appears in court records again when police arrested him for disorderly conduct and fined him $7.[17]

Cellos Harrison's fate intertwined with that of another Marianna resident, a local service station owner, a white man named Johnnie Mayo. In May 1939, Mayo and his wife, Nella, leased a service station from W. B. Sangaree for three years for the nominal fee of $1. The station was located on the road leading to the Florida Industrial School for Boys, a facility for delinquent youth three miles south of Marianna. Harrison frequented the service station for his supply of whiskey. Mayo and his brother-in-law, Frank Lee (the men married a pair of sisters), were part of a bootlegging ring in Marianna.[18]

The morning of February 5, 1940, marked the beginning of tragedy for both Mayo and Harrison. Harrison left his home on Clay Street carrying a jug. As a precaution, he also took along a hammer wrapped in a brown paper bag, which, learning from his previous arrests, he planned to use to destroy any evidence of his intent to purchase or consume an illegal beverage. Arriving at the store, Johnnie Mayo, who perhaps would have been expecting his regular customer, informed Harrison that he had nothing to sell him. Instead, he invited Harrison to leave his jug on the back porch and return for it after dark. He would have been resupplied by then, and they both could breathe a little easier under the cover of darkness. Meanwhile, Nella Mayo, on her way to a doctor's appointment, dressed herself in the makeshift bedroom she shared with her husband in the rear of the building.[19]

Nella left shortly after nine o'clock that morning. Soon thereafter Raymond Speights and William "Red" Hicks, two black men, passed in front of the store. They slowed their steps as they heard cries for help emanating from inside the filling station.[20] As they approached, the two saw Mayo lying on the floor in a pool of what appeared to be his own blood. Speights and Hicks faced a dilemma. Certainly Mayo needed help. The racial etiquette of the day, however, called for self-preservation on the part of these two black men. They knew what most black men and boys throughout the South were aware of: absence of a solid alibi meant that they could be accused of attacking Mayo. While the white man bleeding before them needed help to save his life, the two of them needed to save their own lives by getting a credible—white—witness on the scene as soon as possible. It was a matter of life and death for all involved. Their presence without white witnesses could lead to any number of tragic outcomes: accusation, pursuit, arrest, trial, imprisonment, kidnapping, beating, hanging, shooting, and, ultimately, death by either legal or extralegal means, all a result of being the wrong color at the wrong time and the wrong place.[21]

To avoid any possible suspicion that he or Hicks were involved, Speights later testified that he refrained from entering the building until there were "some white people there." To that end, the pair hurried down the road toward the boys school to look for help. Along the way, the two men waved down the next vehicle they saw, a truck being driven by Charlie Reiff, a white man.[22] They told him about Mayo and his need for help.

They hopped on his truck and rode with him to the school, where Reiff contacted Walter Watford, sheriff of Jackson County, and a local white physician, Dr. C. D. Whitaker.[23]

Within the hour a crowd descended on the filling station now turned crime scene: Sheriff Watford and his deputies; Reiff, Speights, and Hicks; Dr. Whitaker; and a driver from a local undertaker, whose hearse doubled as an ambulance. They found Johnnie Mayo, lying on the floor, bleeding from his head, groaning as he faded in and out of consciousness. As Watford and Whitaker examined him, it appeared he had been struck twice, once over his right temple and once on the top of the head, fracturing his skull, leaving a hole in the hat he was wearing. Brain matter had begun to seep from his skull in places.[24] As the doctor inspected Mayo's wounds and his condition, the sheriff and his deputies inspected the rest of the building. In the back room of the station—the bedroom—they found an overturned muffin pan resting on the bed, and money scattered on the covers and on the floor. It had been the Mayo's makeshift cash register, where he deposited proceeds from the sale of both gasoline and illegal liquor. Whoever attacked Johnnie Mayo also took the money.

Whitaker directed the men on the scene to move Mayo into the hearse and transport him to his office in town. Mayo, jolted by the movement, briefly regained consciousness. He spoke to the doctor, babbling somewhat incoherently, as brain matter continued to leak from his head. As Whitaker listened, he heard what he would later testify to as Mayo's dying declaration: that a "yellow negro" had "shot" him. Nella Mayo, also at her husband's bedside as he lingered near death, asked her husband about this attack. When she asked him if his attacker was a "negro," Johnnie nodded his head. When Nella asked him if he knew the person, however, Johnnie shook his head no. Dr. Whitaker did what he could to stabilize his patient's injuries. Before long, Mayo slipped into unconsciousness. Shortly afterward, Johnnie Mayo died from his traumatic injuries, just sixteen days short of his thirty-fifth birthday.[25]

Almost immediately, local law enforcement officers instituted a dragnet to identify the perpetrators of the murder and robbery of Johnnie Mayo. Despite their precaution and their willingness to assist at the crime scene, both Speights and Hicks were arrested and jailed, a realization of their fears. Three other black men, including Cellos Harrison, then age twenty, were also taken into custody. They all had the misfortune of being black men seen in the vicinity of Mayo's store the morning of February 5. Sheriff Watford and his staff questioned all of them, but finding no strong evidence, released the men. With no concrete evidence other than the decedent's incoherent last utterance, Mayo's tragic murder would remain an open case for the time being.[26]

*   *   *

While Johnnie Mayo's murder went unsolved for the moment, the desire for answers and justice resurfaced during the heated electoral campaign for sheriff of Jackson County during the fall of 1941. Barkley Gause, a local white man, had thrown his hat into the contest for sheriff. The Gause family resided in the Magnolia community, just southeast of Marianna, and were no strangers to public office in Jackson County. J. P. Gause, Barkley's father, had served on the Jackson County Board of Commissioners, representing the county's Third District between 1933 and 1937.[27] A minor scandal marked his term, however, when local residents reported Gause's flagrant nepotism to Governor Fred Cone. In all, Gause had six members of his family on the county payroll: his sons, J.P. Jr. and Addis; his wife's nephew and her niece's husband; his stepmother's husband; and a second

FIGURE 2.1. W. Barkley Gause ran a successful campaign for sheriff of Jackson County in 1940, in part because of his promises to bring Johnnie Mayo's murderer to justice. His record would be marred not only by the events surround Cellos Harrison's lynching but also by the accusation that he took kickbacks from bootlegging and gambling interests in the county. Courtesy of the State Archives of Florida.

cousin. Governor Cone wrote J. P. Gause directly in January 1937 demanding the dismissal of all but one of his relatives, as prescribed by law.[28]

In order to win office, Barkley Gause recognized he needed to distance himself from his father's tarnished reputation. Johnnie Mayo's unsolved murder offered an opportunity to win the community to his side. As part of his campaign, Gause publicly promised Nella Mayo that he would find her husband's killer. His proclamations represented more than soothing words to comfort a grieving widow; they were part of a savvy campaign strategy. Gause knew that the unsolved Mayo murder weighed heavily on the minds of many of Marianna's white residents, including Johnnie Mayo's numerous relatives. Additionally, because law enforcement officers were on the front lines of maintaining white supremacy during the age of Jim Crow, southern communities typically desired officers who would be tough on crime, specifically, on crimes committed by African Americans against whites. By promising to find Mayo's killer, Gause sought to earn the good graces of a significant segment of Jackson County's white voters. Gause's strategy worked, and he won the election.[29]

Despite Gause's promises, no new leads in the Mayo case appeared until May 1941, nearly sixteen months after the killing. Deputy Sheriff J. C. Hornsby received a tip that if he wanted to crack the case, he needed to talk to Jabo. That was the nickname of a black man, William Pittman, a member of the Pittman clan of Jacob City, a small majority-black community just northwest of the county seat, Marianna. Interestingly, in the months after Mayo's murder, Pittman relocated to St. Petersburg, leaving behind his pregnant wife. Based on the new tip, Sheriff Gause's office issued a warrant for his arrest and had him returned to Jackson County for interrogation.[30]

During questioning, Pittman revealed details about his activities around the time of Johnnie Mayo's murder. He confessed that shortly after Mayo's murder, he and Cellos Harrison had been in DeFuniak Springs attending a basketball game in which the boys and girls from the Jackson County Training School (JCTS), the local black secondary school, were competing. Pittman recalled that Harrison was exhibiting what he believed to be unusual behavior. Harrison, he claimed, spent money very loosely and gambled heavily that night. He did not usually have that kind of money to burn. Pittman also remembered that most of the money that Harrison used for his extravagance that evening was silver coins.[31]

These crucial details gave new life to the investigation. Based on this new information, Marianna police rearrested Harrison on May 19, 1941. This must have come as a surprise to Harrison, since he had previously been cleared of any suspicion. In the months after his arrest and release in connection with Mayo's murder, Harrison had moved on with his life. Unlike his earlier days of gallivanting and drinking, Harrison seemed to be settling down into family life. He had married his sweetheart, Bessie McClinton, a local schoolteacher, in February 1941 and had taken a job working in a hardware store downtown, across from the courthouse.[32]

In the meantime, Sheriff Gause, determined to capitalize on this break and solve Mayo's murder as he had promised, requested assistance in attempting to obtain the truth from Harrison and Pittman. To this end, Governor Holland sent William "Buddy" Gasque, an experienced investigator for the state of Florida who had served under four governors, to assist in the case. Over his eight years as an investigator, he had earned a reputation as an astute investigator, winning him the respect of law enforcement officers around the state. This case in particular fit Gasque's talents: murder investigations were his specialty.

After arriving in Jackson County and being brought up to speed on the case, Gasque first needed to have someone identify who, between Harrison and Pittman, had been near the Mayo store closest to the time of the attack. That role fell to Earl Daniels, who, fifteen months earlier on the morning of the murder, had been riding in a car headed for the Florida Industrial School for Boys and remembered seeing a black man in a blue jumpsuit. Daniels now lived in Quincy, nearly fifty miles east of Marianna in Gadsden County. It is unclear why Daniels had not been able to identify Harrison back in February, but Gasque decided to transport both Pittman and Harrison to Quincy to have Daniels identify them.[33]

On May 21, Gasque transported Harrison to Quincy. Apparently, Pittman had already been transported to the Quincy jail, where he had the misfortune of witnessing the kidnapping of Arthur Williams from that facility on May 13. Williams was eventually lynched by an unknown group of white men.[34] Unbeknownst to them, Earl Daniels was about to change the course of one of their lives. Gasque found Daniels waiting surreptitiously atop his tractor at a prearranged meeting point. Gasque told both his prisoners to go get a drink of water under a nearby tree, giving Daniels a chance to look at both of them. Which of these two men, Gasque wanted

FIGURE 2.2. William "Buddy" Gasque served as special investigator for the state of Florida during the 1930s and 1940s, specializing in solving murders. Controversy and suspicion over his methods, however, clouded the confession he obtained from Cellos Harrison in May 1941. Photograph by Jack Spottswood. Courtesy of the State Archives of Florida.

to know, had he seen that morning near the Mayo filling station? Daniels identified Cellos Harrison.[35]

When Gasque returned to the car, he drove into Quincy and headed to the Gadsden County jail. He ordered Harrison out of the car and took him inside. Pittman remained behind. He explained to Harrison that he was now being charged with the murder of Johnnie Mayo and was being left in the Quincy jail for his own safety. Once the news broke that Harrison was the suspect, it would be too risky to take him back to Marianna. This certainly provided little comfort for Harrison, given what had happened to Arthur Williams just weeks earlier. The Gadsden County jail was certainly not a fortress, but no southern jail was when it held a black man accused of murdering a white person.[36]

A frustrated, confused, and scared Harrison remained in the Gadsden County jail for the next several days. Gasque left strict instructions with the sheriff and his deputies that Harrison was to have no visitors, but despite this specific order, a stream of Jackson county law officers visited Harrison. Among them were Deputy Hershel Malloy and Deputy

Charles Standland.[37] Harrison later stated that Sheriff Gause visited him also, showing him fingerprints that Gause claimed would be used to convict him. Using a combination of threats and enticements to confuse and frighten Harrison, the law officers pressured him to confess to murdering Johnnie Mayo; they knew that, given the limited physical evidence in the case, a confession would be necessary for his conviction. Harrison adamantly defended his innocence and refused to confess to a crime that he had not committed. Fine, the deputies told him, but they threatened him that "some dark night he would be taken out and then he would talk."[38] These threats, coupled with his knowledge of Arthur Williams's recent kidnapping and lynching a few weeks earlier, no doubt clouded Harrison's mind with fear.

Meanwhile, back in Jackson County, authorities moved swiftly in an attempt to win a conviction against Harrison. If they could achieve a guilty verdict and legal execution of the alleged killer, members of the community would be unable to take matters into their own hands as they had in the case of Claude Neal. Harrison's ordeal in the Gadsden County jail came to an end on May 30, 1941. That day Sheriff Gause, Deputy Jack McMullian, and W. B. Gasque, the state's investigator, retrieved Harrison and transported him to Tallahassee. Gasque sat in the back with Harrison, while Gause drove with McMullian in the passenger seat. During the ride, Gasque made attempts to befriend Harrison. When Harrison asked for a cigarette, Gasque gave him the remainder of his pack and lit one for him. Their conversation soon turned to more serious matters. Gasque chided Harrison for attempting to blame Pittman for Mayo's murder; it was wrong and cowardly to frame an innocent man, Gasque told him. Harrison smoked and listened. The topic then turned to a black man named Slim Williams, a mutual acquaintance of both men. Gasque shared with Harrison that he had once read a death warrant for Slim, but had recently seen him walking the streets of Cottondale as a free man. Apparently, serious charges were not always hopeless. Harrison, however, was not the only one in the backseat blowing smoke.[39]

In the front seat, Sheriff Gause sped down the road toward Tallahassee as if he were rushing to avoid something. At one point, he decided to stop for gas, and Harrison overheard Gause and another officer mention that they were being pursued by people who wanted to kidnap Harrison. Is that why he was being moved again, even farther from Marianna? Was there a mob planning to kill him like they had killed Arthur Williams and Claude Neal? It didn't have to be that way, Gause implied. Harrison could avoid the death penalty, or receive a reduced sentence, if he admitted to the crime.[40] If he handled the situation correctly, Harrison could survive the charges he faced.

After eleven days in custody between two jails, traveling hundreds of miles, and with an increasing sense of danger, Harrison began to show signs of worry. Perhaps Gause and Gasque were right: the only way to stop a lynching, to ease the wrath of the mob, was to confess. Better to have a day in court than to be tortured at the hands of hundreds, mutilated, burned, or hanged. What hope did he have? Once the party reached the Tallahassee jail, without the benefit of legal counsel and under the impression that this was the only way to save his life, Harrison confessed to Mayo's murder.[41]

The *Jackson County Floridan* printed the full content of Harrison's written confession, taken in the presence of Investigator Gasque; Sheriff Gause; Cecil Gatlin, deputy sheriff for Leon County; and Deputies Porter Holland and Jack McMullian in its next edition. According to the document, at 7:00 a.m. on February 5, 1940, Harrison visited Mayo's service station, with a carpenter's hammer and a jug to buy liquor. Mayo told Harrison that he did not have any liquor to sell him, and suggested that Harrison leave his jug and return for it and the liquor later that afternoon. Harrison reputedly returned a few hours later and found Mayo alone behind the counter. He asked Mayo for some cigarettes, and when Mayo turned around to get them off the shelf, Harrison hit him in the back of the head with the hammer. After Mayo fell to the ground, the confession claimed, Harrison hit him again. He then proceeded to the room in the back of the station and took money from a muffin pan he found there. He put some money, about $30, most of it in silver coins, in his pockets, and left some on the bed. Harrison then crossed the highway and escaped into the woods.[42]

With Harrison's confession in hand, Jackson County officials were eager to begin the trial process and expected "a speedy conviction."[43] The state attorney for the Fourteenth District, seventy-one-year-old native of Wakulla County LeRoy Devilla McRae, prosecuted the case against Harrison. A grand jury in Jackson County heard the charges against Harrison on Monday, June 9, 1941, and agreed to the indictment, and the trial was set to begin the following day. The task of defending Harrison fell to Benjamin Franklin Barnes Jr. A native of Jackson County, Barnes had grown up in Chattahoochee, where his father worked as a physician. Tall and dark-haired, he was just two years out of law school and had recently relocated to Marianna with his new bride. The case would help him make a name for himself in the local legal community. Barnes, however, faced an uphill battle in preparing a defense for his client in such a short amount of time.[44]

The grand jury indicted Cellos Harrison for first-degree murder, just ten days after his confession, to which he pleaded guilty. Things, however, did not go as smoothly as court officials wished. Judge Ernest C. Welch, finding error with the first indictment, quashed it. The attention to detail exercised by the judge reflected the eagerness of the Marianna authorities to deliver an airtight case without grounds for any challenges on appeal. A matter of this importance required at least the appearance of judicial prudence. Reconvening on Friday, June 13, the grand jury once again reached the same conclusion and indicted Harrison for a second time on the charge of first-degree murder.[45] Unlike the first occasion, however, Harrison, with guidance from his legal counsel, replied to the charge with a plea of not guilty, denying premeditation.[46]

The trial began ten days later, on Monday, June 23, 1941, with Judge Welch presiding. During the trial, the jury heard testimony from twenty-five witnesses, including Nella Mayo and Harrison, Dr. C. D. Whitaker, Raymond Speights, Red Hicks, Charlie Reiff, T. C. Carr, and John White. All testified about the circumstance of Mayo's death on February 5, 1940. The most evidentiary statement came from Dr. Whitaker, who told the jury that in his dying breath, Mayo claimed a "yellow negro" had attacked him. This statement, while circumstantial, worked against Harrison, who was a light-skinned black man. Several other witnesses who lived in the area near Mayo's filling station acknowledged seeing Harrison either heading to or returning from that direction on the morning of February 5. Some noted that they had seen him carrying two packages, a jug and another "long" package, presumably the hammer discovered at the crime scene, that was used to bash in Mayo's skull.[47]

Other witnesses took the stand and gave critical, albeit suspicious, glimpses of Harrison's behavior in the hours after Mayo's murder. Jabo Pittman, who had originally implicated Harrison in the murder, testified that he was with Harrison the night of February 5. He traveled with Luke Coleman, another African American, and Harrison to watch the boys' and girls' basketball teams from the JCTS play against the Tivoli School in De-Funiak Springs, two counties and sixty miles west of Marianna. Pittman claimed that Harrison gambled heavily that night using "silver money." This provided a crucial link to Mayo's murder because of the theft of nearly $30, mostly in change. The next witness was Luke Coleman, who was a known bootlegger in the community with a history of arrests for possession and consumption of alcohol. Just that past January Coleman had been convicted of unlawful possession of intoxicating liquor. On the stand, Coleman corroborated Pittman's statements, noting Harrison's relatively lavish spending. Harrison, he said, purchased eight gallons of gasoline for the car they were driving over to DeFuniak Springs. It was noticeably unusual generosity from a man who rarely had that type of money.[48]

Two other witnesses, Lawrence Swilley (son of one of the leading African American families in Marianna) and Abraham Robinson, twenty and twenty-one years old, respectively, played for the JCTS basketball team back in February 1940. After the JCTS Panthers' victory over Tivoli the night of February 5, they testified Cellos Harrison bought the members of the winning teams, boys and girls, Coca-Colas to celebrate. The witnesses painted a damning image of Harrison on the night of February 5, detailing his abnormally extravagant spending on gasoline, gambling, and drinks that evening. Their collective testimony depicted him as a remorseless murderer, lavishly spending his ill-gotten gains.[49]

Next, a series of law enforcement officers took the stand to testify about their experiences with the defendant. Deputies Standland, Joe Sims, Joe B. Dykes, McMullian, and Gatlin, one by one, told the jury of their interactions with Harrison. They reported that he had admitted that the hammer they found at the crime scene belonged to him. Harrison claimed he had loaned it to Pittman to work on some jukeboxes. The most contentious part of the testimony, however, came when law enforcement officers began to explain the circumstances of Harrison's confession, marked by rigorous interrogation by the counsel for the defendant, Ben Barnes. Before beginning his interrogation, Barnes asked that the jury be removed. It quickly became clear that Barnes suspected that his client had been unduly pressured to make a statement of his guilt. He asked Investigator

FIGURE 2.3. Benjamin F.
Barnes represented Cellos
Harrison during his first
murder trial in 1941, a successful appeal before the
Florida Supreme Court in
1942, and his second murder
trial in 1942. A native of
Jackson County and a graduate of Vanderbilt University's
law school, Barnes vigor-
ously defended Harrison, an
African American, against
charges that he murdered
Johnnie Mayo, a white man,
in February 1940. Courtesy
of Ruth Barnes Kinsolving.

Gasque to go over the details of his involvement in the case—from his interaction with Harrison during the trip to Quincy to their subsequent time together on the trip from Quincy to Tallahassee. Had he, Barnes asked Gasque, insinuated to Cellos Harrison that he might receive better treatment if he confessed? Gasque denied making such statements. How did the subject of Slim Williams and the death warrant come up? Barnes asked. Gasque could not remember if he or Harrison brought it up, but insisted that it came up in the natural course of the conversation, not as an attempt on his part to influence Harrison. Similarly, in question-ing Sheriff Gause and Jack McMullian, attorney Barnes challenged their actions and conversations with his client during the trip on May 30. As Deputy McMullian left the stand, Barnes moved that Harrison's confes-sion be deemed inadmissible because of the "inducement of hope" these law officers gave his client. Judge Welch summarily denied the motion.[50]

After Barnes's unsuccessful challenge of the admission of Harrison's confession, Judge Welch readmitted the jury into the courtroom, and Wil-liam Gasque returned to the stand. Now he and the prosecution were fully aware that the defense counsel planned to challenge the confession on the grounds that it had been coerced. It was at this point that Gasque made some subtle but significant changes in his testimony. When questioned by State Attorney McRae this second time, in describing what he initially learned during Harrison's trip to the Mayo filling station, Gasque mentioned that when Harrison went to place his jug on the back porch of the building, he saw Nella Mayo dressing in the couple's bedroom. It had been well established that Nella was preparing for her trip to the doctor that morning, but why now, all of a sudden, had Gasque decided to mention that relatively insignificant detail in his testimony, not once but twice? The inflammatory nature of this detail—an alleged criminal black man like Harrison leering lustfully through a window while an unsuspecting white woman, Nella Mayo, walked around in a state of undress—was sure to incense the white men on the jury. Likewise, while he admitted to talking about reading a death warrant for a man who was later freed, Gasque, in contrast to his previous statements in which he was uncertain who had brought up Williams's name, now stated unequivocally that Harrison had brought up his name. He emphatically denied that it was an attempt to give Harrison hope that he too could beat his charges, and testified that Harrison's confession had been made freely and voluntarily.[51] After Gasque, Sheriff Gause returned to the stand, and added little other than to confirm Gasque's interpretation of the events and that Harrison had not been pressured to make his confession.[52]

When he took the stand, Cellos Harrison painted a very different picture of the circumstances surrounding his confession. It was a brave move that placed his word against that of three sworn officers of the law. Harrison's action demonstrated his determination to stand up for himself and not be railroaded by a criminal justice system eager to rectify the death of Johnnie Mayo. On the stand, he testified that Gasque told him that he would "burn" if his case went to trial and the jury returned a guilty verdict. Harrison also claimed that Gause told him a confession would soften the jury's condemnation, making it possible for him to receive a life sentence instead of a death sentence. It was for these reasons, Harrison claimed, he confessed to the murder.[53] Based on his client's testimony, attorney Barnes requested again that the confession not be admitted as evidence "on the ground that the inducement of hope was given to this defendant."

Judge Welch, unmoved by Harrison's version of the events, denied the motion, and the jury was allowed to hear the confession.[54]

After testimony concluded, the case was turned over to an all-white, all-male jury for deliberation. Within forty minutes, they returned a guilty verdict. Because the jury did not recommend leniency, it was certain that Harrison would be sentenced to death.[55] Ben Barnes, steadfast in his belief that Harrison's confession was inadmissible, requested a new trial for his client, a motion Judge Welch rejected.[56] A few days later, on June 27, Harrison was sentenced to die in the electric chair. For Cellos Harrison, this was a whirlwind of events. Within the course of a month he had gone from a working newlywed to a convicted killer facing a death sentence.[57]

THE FAILURE OF FORBEARANCE

The Lynching of Cellos Harrison, Jackson County, 1943

With Cellos Harrison's conviction and sentencing, Jackson County's white community breathed a sigh of relief, especially the members of Johnnie Mayo's family. The successful conclusion of a case more than a year old, with so few leads, stood as a tribute to the work of Sheriff Gause's office. Even more significant, they maintained law and order and avoided a lynching, which, given Claude Neal's murder seven years earlier, was a significant accomplishment. Sheriff Gause and his officers would have surely been in a self-congratulatory mood, as accolades flowed into his office from the community. On July 18, the *Jackson County Floridan* published a letter of thanks written by Nella Mayo, Johnnie Mayo's widow, expressing her "deep and sincere appreciation to all the persons who contributed in any way to the apprehension and conviction of the Negro who so brutally killed my late husband." She gave special regard to Sheriff Gause, his deputies, and William Gasque.[1]

Despite the conviction, Harrison's attorney took issue with the fairness of the trial, particularly with the charge given to the jury. On September 18, 1941, Ben Barnes appealed Harrison's conviction to the Florida Supreme Court. He argued that Judge Welch did not properly instruct the jury to cautiously weigh the contents of the confession, in consideration of the circumstances under which it was given. There was sufficient indication, Barnes argued, that Harrison had been pressured into the confession, believing that it would save his life. The confession could be considered as evidence only if it was "freely and voluntarily made by the defendant" and if "the mind of the accused [was] uninfluenced by fear, hope, promise of reward or other inducements."[2] Barnes, perhaps strategically, touched on a very sensitive subject with the court, as the court had recently been admonished in the U.S. Supreme Court's reversal in the case of *Chambers v. Florida*. Isiah Chambers, Charlie Davis, Jack Williams, and Walter Woodward were four black men who confessed guilt in the murder of a white man in Broward County in 1933, after being held and questioned over the course of five days without the benefit of counsel. On the birthday of the "Great Emancipator," President Abraham Lincoln, in 1940, Justice Hugo Black, writing for the majority, delivered a scathing decision that criticized the state of Florida for failing to protect the Fourteenth Amendment rights of the defendants, noting:

> Today, as in ages past, we are not without tragic proof that the exalted power of some governments to punish manufactured crime dictatorially is the handmaid of tyranny. Under our constitutional system, courts stand against any winds that blow as havens of refuge for those who might otherwise suffer because they are helpless, weak, outnumbered, or because they are non-conforming victims of prejudice and public excitement. Due process of law, preserved for all by our Constitution, commands that no such practice as that disclosed by this record shall send any accused to his death. No higher duty, no more solemn responsibility, rests upon this Court, than that of translating into living law and maintaining this constitutional shield deliberately planned and inscribed for the benefit of every human being subject to our Constitution—of whatever race, creed or persuasion.[3]

The U.S. Supreme Court's reversal in the Chambers case was a significant precedent of the 1966 *Miranda v. Arizona* case and was widely praised in the civil rights community. Justice Black's words also represented the chilling winds of change that were blowing down on sunny Florida. No longer could the nation allow its African American citizens to suffer such blatant abuses under the American justice system, especially as the nation watched the specter of fascism and Nazism rage in Europe. Instances of lynching and other forms of racial injustice were being used as propaganda by both the Germans and Japanese to discourage African American troops in the field and to discredit American democracy abroad. They also had the added effect of demoralizing African American support for the war effort and advancing demands by civil rights groups for more action to protect the rights of blacks in the United States. Perhaps with this recent defeat in mind, the Florida Supreme Court concurred with Barnes's assessment and on January 20, 1942, by a vote of six to one, with only Justice Rivers Buford dissenting, ordered a new trial for Cellos Harrison.[4] Tellingly, Justice Roy Chapman, writing for the majority, quoted generously from the U.S. Supreme Court's verdict in the *Chambers* case.

* * *

News of the Florida Supreme Court's decision most certainly came as a shock to the residents of Marianna. The local community perhaps believed they had been vindicated in the eyes of the press and the nation because they had been able to maintain law and order by giving a black man accused of the murder of a white person a "fair" trial. Despite the ugly occurrences of the Neal lynching in 1934, Jackson County had proved itself capable of reining in "Judge Lynch," only to have the Florida Supreme Court question their effort. On the other hand, although the successful appeal of the first conviction represented a significant victory for Harrison, the decision did not guarantee his freedom. He would face another hostile all-white jury whose members would have read his confession. Despite the circumstances of the confession or the admonition of the Florida Supreme Court, public knowledge of it suggested Harrison's guilt to any potential jurors.[5]

For the second summer in a row, Cellos Harrison awaited trial for the murder of Johnnie Mayo. One testament to the tension surrounding the case was Judge Welch's order on May 13 to have Harrison held in Tallahassee "either to prevent his escape or to safe guard him from mob viloence [sic] and upon request of . . . Barkley Gause, Sheriff of Jackson County."[6] When a new trial began on Tuesday, June 2, 1942, the jury heard testimony for most of two days from the same witnesses who were called in the previous trial. One significant change came with Judge Welch's instructions to the jury, which addressed how the jurors should weigh the confession, based on the Florida Supreme Court's vacating of the first trial. The jury began deliberations on Wednesday at 5:00 p.m. and returned with a verdict in twenty-two hours. This was considerably longer than the forty minutes the first jury took, and may have been calculated to avoid any future accusations of partiality that the defense counsel could make on appeal. On June 4, 1942, for the second time, a jury in Jackson County convicted Harrison, and a second death sentence was handed down.[7]

Defeated again, but not outdone, Barnes began to consider his next steps. His commitment was remarkable and offered a rare example of a white attorney from and in the South providing a thorough and vigorous defense of a black defendant in a capital murder case. This contrasted greatly with the usual court-appointed lawyers who represented black defendants in capital cases. On the occasions when black men managed to escape a lynch mob and stand trial, they frequently suffered through inadequate legal defense. Southern courtrooms were notoriously hostile to black lawyers, while many white lawyers who were secured by the family or appointed by the court displayed bad behavior or complete malfeasance—from failing to call witnesses or adequately cross-examine witnesses to being asleep, drunk, or both, during the trials. This happened in the famous case of the "Scottsboro Boys," nine black youths falsely accused of raping two white women in 1931, when the attorney for the young black men was alternately drunk and asleep during their trials. So appalling was the behavior that the U.S. Supreme Court moved to right the situation in its 1932 decision in *Powell v. Alabama*. The court also intervened nine years previously in 1923 in *Moore v. Dempsey*, when twelve African Americans had been placed on trial without adequate access to legal counsel for the death of five whites during a 1919 race riot in Elaine, Arkansas.[8]

Barnes was clearly cut from different cloth. But what was in it for him? There is no clear explanation why Barnes was committed to putting up such a vigorous defense. There was no financial benefit, as there was no civil rights organization footing the tab for Harrison's defense. If not for external reward, perhaps Barnes was motivated by a sense of duty, a deeply held commitment to his profession, and, perhaps, a sincere belief that Harrison was being framed or had not been dealt with fairly by the authorities. The two men, while not very far apart in age—Barnes was six years Harrison's senior—and both recently married, had a wide gulf of social, racial, and educational experiences that separated them. Whatever his motivation, his persistence did not come without a personal cost; Barnes and his wife would experience some alienation from Marianna's white community as a result of his work in this case.[9]

After Harrison's second death sentence, Barnes once again appealed his client's conviction to the Florida Supreme Court. In contrast to his previous argument that the jury had not been properly instructed on how to consider the alleged confession, this time Barnes argued that Harrison's confession should be thrown out altogether because it was coerced. Unfortunately for Harrison, it seemed that Barnes's good fortune with the high court of Florida had run out; on December 18, 1942, unconvinced by Barnes's appeal, the justices upheld the verdict of the Jackson County court.[10]

The attorney's work would be sidetracked for another reason: Barnes was going to be leaving to train with the U.S. Navy reserves in a few months, officially ending his connection with the case in October 1942. To carry forward with the defense effort, Barnes and Bessie Harrison, Cellos's wife, brought in Clyde "Gus" Atkinson to work on the case. Atkinson's first action was to submit a motion requesting that the Florida Supreme Court rehear the case. Technically, the deadline for filing the appeal had passed, but Atkinson beseeched the court to approve the request and the appeal. He argued that his client, in the midst of securing new counsel, was unaware that he could appeal for a rehearing.[11]

Surprisingly, the court granted Atkinson's petition for a rehearing, which took place on January 28, 1943. Even more surprising, the court, sharply divided over the case, handed down its decision on February 19, in which the majority of the justices now agreed that the confession, due to the conditions under which it was obtained, was inadmissible. Justices James B. Whitfield, Rivers Buford, and Alto Adams had sided with Justice Elwyn Thomas, who had written the previous majority opinion rejecting the appeal in December 1942. Justice Roy Chapman, along with Justice William Terrell and Chief Justice Armstead Brown, had voted in favor of the rehearing. The scales tipped in Harrison's favor this time, however, when Justice Adams changed sides, making the dissenting opinion the majority.[12] Writing for the new majority, Justice Chapman argued that "the attending circumstances shortly preceding the signing of the alleged written confession by the appellant [created in his mind] an abiding conviction that it was obtained by influences calculated to delude the mind of an immature and ignorant colored boy."[13] Chapman also pointed to the conditions surrounding Harrison's arrest in May 1941. He cited the fact that Jackson County law enforcement officers took Harrison to the Quincy jail, knowing that Arthur Williams had been kidnapped from that same jail and lynched just a few weeks earlier. Knowledge of those events undermined Harrison's sense of security. Chapman also criticized the fact that although Sheriff Gause had ordered that Harrison not be allowed to receive visitors, he was visited in jail and threatened by Sheriff Gause's own deputies. Furthermore, he noted that while being transferred from the jail in Quincy to Tallahassee, Harrison was given the impression that a mob was pursing the party. Officers led him to believe the only way to escape death was to admit to the murder. They convinced Harrison that with his confession, he might even reduce the amount of time he spent in jail. Chapman surmised that

> poverty, like a huge stone hung about the neck, deterred the development of beneficial facts of the controversy from the moment of appellant's arrest until the death penalty was imposed. . . . It is established that in order to render a confession voluntary or admissible, the mind of the accused should at the time it is obtained or made be free to act uninfluenced by fear or hope.[14]

Just as he had when writing the 1942 decision granting Harrison a new trial, Chapman cited the *Chambers* decision as the judicial basis of his objection to the admission of Harrison's confession. These conditions were enough to convince a majority of the court that justice had not been served, and the Florida Supreme Court ordered that Harrison be given a new trial.

As a result of Justice Adams changing sides, Justices Thomas and Harold L. Sebring, who replaced Whitfield on the bench on January 5, 1943, joined Chief Justice Buford in dissenting. Chief Justice Buford, who had remained steadfast in his opposition to Harrison's repeated appeals, wrote for the dissenting justices. He argued that the same confession had been introduced in the first appeal and that the court had not then been compelled to withdraw it. Moreover, he thought that the other justices acted as usurpers in overturning the verdicts of the juries in Jackson County. "Two fair and impartial juries," Buford argued, "have considered all the evidence and returned like verdicts. . . . [The majority opinion] is the invasion of the province of the jury by substituting the court's finding as to the probative force and effect of the evidence for that of the jury and thereby allowing a [self]-confessed twice-convicted murderer to go free."[15]

Why in the course of a month did the Florida Supreme Court pendulate from refusing to hear an appeal, to not only agreeing to hear it but concurring with the appellant? Some significant personnel changes took place in the weeks between December 18 and January 28. Justice James B. Whitfield, the longest-serving justice in the court's history at the time, retired and was replaced by Sebring. When it came to the vote in Harrison's 1943 appeal, Justice Sebring, perhaps owing to his newness on the bench or out of deference to Justice Whitfield's previous negative vote, stood with Buford and Thomas as Whitfield had done. Meanwhile, Rivers Buford succeeded Armstead Brown to the position of chief justice. In the spectrum of the court opinions, Chapman, Terrell, and Brown voted on Harrison's behalf in all of his appeal decisions. Conversely Rivers Buford demonstrated a consistent opposition to Harrison's plight, as demonstrated by his sole dissenting vote in the first appeal in 1942 that resulted in a new trial. Since then, both Buford and Thomas sided against Harrison on his appeals. The swing vote on the decision, however, came from Justice Alto Adams. A veteran of World War I and a graduate of the University of Florida's law school, he had been elected to the Florida Supreme Court in 1940, and had developed a close friendship with Justice Buford.[16]

Aside from these basic facts, several intangible factors—political, legal, and social—surely influenced most of the justices on the Florida Supreme Court as they pondered their decision. They stood on the precipice between the state's past and future, especially when it came to the issue of civil rights. The real signs of transition were inescapable, with the tidal wave of soldiers and sailors flooding into military training camps in the state. All of this bustle also signaled wider changes that would manifest in American society. The U.S. Supreme Court's decision in *Chambers* was clearly another shot across the bow, warning Florida and other southern states that the Court was reconsidering its tacit support of Jim Crow policies. Racial issues in the South could either empower or disempower the rhetorical battle over the value of American democracy in a global context. The nation's leaders in the Roosevelt and Truman administrations were increasingly sensitive to the issue of racial injustice and its international implications. Surely the Florida justices were aware of the consequences that their actions had on the struggle against the Axis powers. Their dictates from the bench in Tallahassee would echo in faraway Berlin and Tokyo as examples of American values in action. In a speech in 1941, Justice Sebring reflected on the crisis of the time:

> The Axis leaders would like nothing better than to see the American principles of free speech, free press, freedom of assemblage and worship, and all the other freedoms embodied in the Constitution, overthrown as a "war measure." . . . Such a surrender of our freedom would be the first step in the giving up of all we are fighting for. . . . A sane people need not fear that the complete exercise of their freedom will weaken them or disrupt their war effort. We must be intelligent enough to realize that only by utilizing all of our freedoms and hampering none of them can we build a war machine greater than that developed by the enslaved peoples of our enemies, and win this war which is dedicated to the simple purpose of proving that freedom is better than slavery.[17]

Despite these implications, some of the justices, led by Chief Justice Buford, reflected the more conservative and traditional values, which rejected federal meddling and refused to bow to outside pressure.

*   *   *

Despite the setback of the appeal verdict, State Attorney J. Tom Watson, lead prosecutor in the Harrison case, was determined to place Harrison on trial for murder. On March 2, 1943, he applied to the Florida Supreme Court for clarification of the verdict: was the confession altogether inadmissible or was it simply insufficient in itself to warrant a conviction? In their response on March 16, the court stated plainly that, because of the circumstances surrounding Harrison's confession, it was inadmissible as evidence. This decision dealt a blow to the prosecutors in the case. Harrison's confession had been the cornerstone of their case. Attorney Watson had no choice but to abandon the prosecution, and, subsequently, the Florida State Prison at Raiford released Harrison from custody.[18] After two years of legal battles, Cellos Harrison became a free man again in March 1943.

Stunned, but unprepared to cede defeat, Jackson County officials refused to let go of their desire to see Cellos Harrison convicted for the
crime they were certain he had committed. The Florida Supreme Court, in
throwing out Harrison's confession, left the state attorney with no concrete evidence in the case. That fact, however, seemed insignificant. The
court in Jackson County instituted a new measure to prevent any further
hindrances to Harrison's conviction. One major change came just four
days after news of Harrison's successful appeal. After learning that a black
lawyer in Pensacola had been able to win reprieves for many of his black
clients after citing that blacks were routinely omitted from jury duty, the
Jackson County Board of Commissioners submitted a petition to the local
court to change this process. In response to the petition, on May 20, 1943,
Judge Welch ordered that the jury box be refilled and include blacks in the
jury pool. While at first glance this seemed a rather progressive move on
the part of white leaders in Marianna, in actuality their motives were less
than altruistic. "It would be a travesty of justice," Judge Welch explained,
"to say that a Negro could commit a heinous crime—murder or rape—and
go free of punishment, while a white man would have to pay the penalty." The Board of Commissioners and Judge Welch successfully closed a
significant legal loophole that could have been used by the defense during the inevitable next round of prosecution in the Harrison case. This
justification, however, illustrated a conveniently historical myopia that
failed to consider incidents when whites were either rarely or unsuccessfully brought to justice for horrendous crimes committed against black
victims.[19]

Jackson County officials wasted no time in pursuing their next effort
to convict Harrison. Just two months after he had been released from Raiford, on Friday, May 28, 1943, a specially impaneled grand jury in Jackson
County indicted Harrison for first-degree murder for the third time. The
Jackson County Floridan took special note that one black person had been
included on the jury and that "the new indictment was speedily brought."[20]
That token black grand juryman was Essex Davis, a self-employed shoe-
shine man who was well respected in the white community. More than
likely Davis was hand-selected by the city's ruling fathers for the task,
not only for having an amenable character but also because his livelihood
depended on the patronage of the city's white business professionals. The
court wasted no time scheduling a new trial for June 21. A warrant was

issued for Harrison's arrest. Law enforcement officials located Harrison in Orlando and returned him to Jackson County to stand trial.[21]

In response to the latest indictment, Harrison's attorneys moved to prevent further prosecution. Encouraged by the success of the previous appeals, on June 4, a week after the third indictment was handed down, Atkinson and Weldon G. Starry, another white attorney who was now assisting on the case, applied to the Florida Supreme Court for a writ of habeas corpus and a writ of prohibition. They argued that Harrison was being subjected to malicious prosecution and that another trial would constitute double jeopardy.[22] Given the court's previous favorable decisions, chances were high that the body would once again vote in Harrison's favor.

With this latest move, the patience of Jackson County's white community began to wear thin. It had been three years since Mayo's murder and two years since Harrison was first convicted. Somehow, Harrison had survived four indictments and two death sentences and won two reprieves from the Florida Supreme Court. For a black man repeatedly convicted of the murder of a white man in a small southern community, Harrison had beaten considerable odds. His luck, unfortunately, was about to run out.

*   *   *

For the third consecutive summer Harrison's fate was set to play out in the Jackson County courthouse. In late May 1943, Harrison was in jail in Marianna, conferring with his lawyers and anxiously awaiting the outcome of Atkinson's latest legal challenge. Meanwhile, news of the application for the writs was reported in the *Jackson County Floridan* on June 11. Those awaiting Harrison's prosecution had to be apprehensive. His lawyers had been successful in every appeal to the Florida Supreme Court either on the first or second attempt. If they were successful this time, all legal avenues would have been exhausted, and Harrison would be beyond the reach of the law. For those who believed him guilty and wanted to see him executed, this conclusion was unacceptable. Some decided to take measures into their own hands.[23]

The events that led to Harrison's demise began to unfold in the middle of June 1943. Sheriff Barkley Gause, out of town the week of June 13 attending a sheriffs' convention in Ocala, left Chief Deputy Jack McMullian in charge. On the evening of June 15, three officers from the sheriff's office supervised the jail. Tom Belcher, a sixty-five-year-old former deputy sheriff in Calhoun and Jackson Counties, had been hired a few weeks earlier to work as the night jailer after complaints about long hours from the regular deputies. Deputy Sheriffs Joe Sims and Lewis Rogers, both of whom lived at the jail, were also on duty that night.[24] Around six o'clock that evening Deputy Rogers and Patrolman E. B. Jordan, of the Florida Highway Patrol, began their watch. After they were finished, Jordan dropped Rogers off at the jail at ten o'clock. Exhausted after a long day, Rogers went to bed. The other deputy, Joe Sims, was on patrol with Sergeant D. W. "Red" Wells of the Marianna city police, pursuing illegally towed cars in the western part of the county. While they were in the area, they stopped by the Kokomo Club, a troublesome juke joint in that section.[25]

Back at the jail, as the midnight hour approached, Belcher sat on the porch, reading the newspaper. Suddenly a car pulled up in front of the building. The street was dark because the Board of Commissioners had recently instituted a policy of shutting off all streetlights in Marianna during "moonlit" nights as a cost-saving measure. Belcher, standing under the porch light, could not identify the men as they exited the car. When he asked their business, the men yelled to Belcher that they had a drunk for him to put in jail. In the darkness, Belcher could make out two figures, one man standing behind another man with his head wrapped in what appeared to be bandages.[26] As he proceeded to open the gate, Belcher noticed that the second man was wearing a paper bag over his head. Startled, he looked at the car just as two other masked men exited the vehicle.

"We want Cellos Harrison," the men told Belcher. They surrounded Belcher, forcing him back toward the front door of the jail. The men commanded Belcher to turn the lights off. Annoyed by the elderly Belcher's slow pace, one of the men turned them off himself. Next, one of the men demanded from Belcher the keys to the jail. He lied and told them that one of the other deputies had them. The men laughed, amused by his attempt to deceive them, and repeated their demand. Belcher relented and pointed out the keys, which hung behind the door down the hall. One of the intruders stumbled down the hallway in the darkness, bumping into the door and jingling the keys. Belcher then called out to Deputy Sims, whom he believed to be asleep in his room at the jail. Two of the men pulled guns on Belcher, pointing one at his side and one at his back. "Keep going. We don't want to hurt anybody, but we come after Cellos Harrison."[27]

Belcher and the four kidnappers ascended the stairs to the second floor, where the holding cells and "bull ring," the outer chamber before the cells, were located. After unlocking the door, one of the men called for Harrison.

"What do you want with me this time of night?" asked Harrison.

"Come on," one of the men replied, "we want to take you to a better jail. You're liable to get hurt here."

"Mr. Joe, is that you?" asked Harrison.[28] As the men entered his cell Harrison, suspicious of these late-night visitors, resisted their grip. The kidnappers then grabbed him and began pulling Harrison from his cell. In the tussle, Harrison pulled the bag off one of the kidnappers' heads.[29] With Harrison in tow, the kidnappers left the jail.

Rogers, who had slept through the kidnapping, awakened at the sound of the gate slamming as the kidnappers exited. As he followed the sounds of the commotion, he caught a glimpse of the "bullet back" car as it drove off. He found Belcher, who informed him of what had just transpired. Cellos Harrison had been kidnapped. Rogers then called McMullian, who in turn called Patrolman Jordan. Jordan called to notify his boss, Lieutenant Reid Clifton, who was stationed in Chipley, of the kidnapping. Clifton left Chipley en route to Marianna with Patrolmen Henry Mills and W. E. Butler. Meanwhile in Marianna, McMullian reached out to Chief of Police Turner and asked him to have the streetlights turned on.[30]

Word spread through the community about the jailbreak and kidnapping, and other agencies offered to assist local law enforcement officials. Bunny Sims, who sat on the town council and was also in charge of the local American Legion, wanted to take action and call up his members, fearing that widespread violence might occur as it had in the aftermath of the Neal lynching years earlier. Sims and his men could help prevent another embarrassing episode in the city's history if they could locate the kidnappers and Harrison. Regrettably, his superior commander, located in faraway Jacksonville, remained unconvinced. Failing to see an immediate threat, he told Sims not to take action unless the governor called for it.[31]

If the commander could have heard from Marianna's black residents, however, he might have reconsidered. In the wee hours of the morning, many of them were awakened by frantic screams echoing through the night. It was Cellos Harrison pleading for his life, as he was being driven by his kidnappers through the black neighborhood on the southwest side of town, down the main thoroughfare of Orange Street. He called for someone, anyone, to come and save his life. His pleading was more than likely encouraged, or demanded, by his captors. They had no intent of letting him go, but the memory of the doomed man's cries sent a clear message to those who heard Harrison that night, or who would be spooked by the tale of horror in the days, months, and years to come: step out of line and what happened to Cellos Harrison could happen to you.[32]

Within a few hours, law enforcement officers from different agencies arrived on the scene. Lieutenant Clifton and his men, after hurriedly driving the twenty miles from Chipley to assist in the manhunt, were surprised to find the members of the sheriff's department at the jail, busily engaged in a game of dominoes. Appalled by their lack of interest in pursuing the criminals, Lieutenant Clifton refused to stay in the company of "that bunch," and he and his men began their own search for the kidnappers and Harrison. After Clifton and his men left, the remaining officers, including Chief of Police Guy Turner, Joe Sims, Red Wells, Leo Kirkland, and Tink Reddick, went to Tee's Restaurant for coffee at half past two in the morning.[33]

Hoping to locate Harrison and his kidnappers before any violence occurred, Lieutenant Clifton and his patrolmen traveled Highway 84, heading south. While they drove along the road at twenty minutes after four that morning, one of the men spotted a mass on the ground a few feet from the road. As they approached they could make out a body clothed only in shorts. It was Cellos Harrison's lifeless body. He had been severely beaten in the face; there was a hole in his jaw, and he had been hit along his temples. The most damaging blows were made to the top of his forehead, presumably with a hatchet; with two blows, a piece of his skull had been removed, and his brains spouted from the wound. His injuries were consistent with the manner in which Johnnie Mayo had been killed and inflicted with an instrument similar to that used to kill Mayo.[34]

With the lynching a fait accompli, the officers on the scene transitioned from searching for a kidnapping victim to processing a murder scene and began looking for evidence that would identify the perpetrators. The condition of Harrison's body told part of the story. While there was blood on his head and on the ground immediately beneath it, there was no blood anywhere else on Harrison's body. The officers concluded that Harrison must have been lying unconscious on the ground when the deathblows were dealt. The officers failed to locate any clearly identifiable footprints on the ground surrounding the body. The only piece of useful evidence that the officers found at the scene was a paper bag similar to the ones Belcher said the kidnappers were wearing. It was collected and taken to the sheriff's office. After officers were finished with the crime scene, someone called for local black funeral director Lemuel Granberry to pick up Harrison's body. The only other action taken by law enforcement officials that evening was to institute a ban on the sale of beer.[35]

With the discovery of a murder victim, standard procedure called for State Attorney LeRoy McRae to convene a coroner's inquest to investigate the circumstances of Harrison's kidnapping and murder. On the morning of June 16, several witnesses gave testimony at the inquest, but none of the testimony proved to be particularly revealing. Tom Belcher had been too surprised and overwhelmed during the kidnapping to stop the men or to remember any identifying features. Deputy Rogers, while at the jail, slept through the kidnapping. Deputy Sims claimed to be in another part of the county on patrol.[36] Another set of possible witnesses turned out to be of no use to the case. During the coroner's inquest, several black inmates who had been incarcerated with Harrison came to court to testify to what they saw the night he was kidnapped. At the same time, about fifty white men positioned themselves around the perimeter of the courtroom. As each man took the stand, he was asked if he knew anything relating to the kidnapping of Harrison. Each answered negatively, after which the whites in the courtroom smiled and nodded encouragingly. Their strategy worked; none of the inmates were able to give any significant information about the kidnapping, even though at least one of the four kidnappers had his mask removed.[37] As the inquest concluded, no one was able to identify any distinguishing traits or provide clues that would have indicated who was responsible for the kidnapping and lynching. In the absence of any physical evidence or corroborating testimony, the jury concluded that Cellos Harrison met his death "at the hands of a person or persons unknown."[38]

*   *   *

With Harrison dead, whites in Jackson County eagerly moved to put the incident behind them. Their experiment in providing the rudiments of due process for an African American accused of a capital crime failed, and some people had taken it upon themselves to do what they believed the court system could not accomplish: dispense retribution. In many ways, Harrison's guilt or innocence was inconsequential. A black person had taken a white life, presumably, and "balance" had to be restored. An example needed to be made. Guilty or not, Harrison was a suitable ram in the bush, sacrificed on the altar of white supremacy.

William Gasque, the lead investigator in the case who was credited with obtaining Harrison's confession, immediately wrote Governor Holland's assistant Ralph Davis when he received news of the murder. He expressed his regret at the situation and placed the blame at the feet of Justice Roy Chapman and his opinion disavowing the verdict of Harrison's second murder trial. "My every action during the two trials," Gasque wrote, "was to keep them from getting him which was the plan on both occasion[s]." Clearly, Gasque was connected enough to the community to be aware of not one but two secret plots to kidnap and lynch Harrison. What remains unclear is why he waited to report this knowledge until after Harrison had been killed.[39] Gasque may have felt relieved by the lynching, as his methods of obtaining the confession from Cellos Harrison became a central matter in Harrison's appeals to the Florida Supreme Court. With his kidnapping and murder, the focus would now be placed on capturing Harrison's lynchers, as opposed to blaming Gasque for muddling the confession.

The vengeance achieved by Harrison's murder, however, came at a price that included media headlines. News of the incident spread rapidly around the state and nation. The *Tallahassee Daily Democrat* published a brief report of the lynching on the same day that Harrison's body was discovered. The *Tampa Morning Tribune* and the *Atlanta Daily World* covered the story the following day with short summaries of the events. The Associated Press distributed the news to other newspapers throughout the nation.[40]

In the African American newspapers, news of Harrison's lynching took second billing under the headlines reporting and condemning the race riots in Beaumont, Texas; Los Angeles; and Detroit, where racial resentment and competition for jobs and other scarce resources bubbled over into the streets. Just two weeks before the Harrison lynching, fighting broke out between soldiers and sailors stationed in Los Angeles and members of the Mexican American community, resulting in the arrest of about 600 Latinos.[41] Similar racial tensions brought about rioting in Beaumont, Texas, on June 15 and 16, 1943, where violence erupted after a white

woman claimed a black man had raped her. When the victim failed to identify her attacker, the angry crowd unleashed their wrath on the local black
community, burning and plundering black homes and businesses. Three
people died in the fighting.[42] On June 20, Detroit exploded after rumors
spread through the city that whites had killed a black woman and her baby
and threw them into the river, and conversely, that blacks had raped a
white woman and killed her boyfriend. Police arrested some 2,000 people,
and thirty-four people lost their lives in the violence, including twenty-
five blacks and nine whites. The aftermath of the riot left $2 million in
property damage and a loss of one million hours of labor, negatively affecting the area's defense industry.[43] Altogether, there were 242 recorded
instances of interracial violence in forty-seven U.S. cities recorded for the
year.[44]

Black journalists like Marjorie McKenzie, of the *Pittsburgh Courier*, used
the painful episodes of Harrison's lynching and other violent outbreaks
across the nation as leverage in the argument for the need of a federal antilynching bill, as the Dyer Anti-Lynching Bill was then being considered
in the U.S. House of Representatives. McKenzie fumed: "The real remedy
for lynchings still lies about as quiescent as a hand grenade in the clutches
of Congress. The war of telegrams ought to be waged unceasingly in the
direction of federal anti-lynching legislation. . . . The imperative need for
federal intervention and for the implementation of democratic principles
grows apace. As never before there is no time nor place for blundering,
uninformed or wasteful leadership."[45] The *Atlanta Daily World* reported
on the NAACP's interpretation of the event as evidence of the need for
passage of federal antilynching legislation, noting:

> "The NAACP warned that the tragic growth of mob violence which
> threatens to become nationwide will inevitably seriously hamper
> successful prosecution of the war. The rioting in connection with
> the Packard upgrading of qualified Negroes, the outbursts against
> zoot suiters which has been shown to be directed almost exclusively
> against persons of dark skin, and the clashes in the Mobile ship-
> yards are tragic examples of a dangerous situation which can be
> checked only by the strong arm of the Federal Government," the
> NAACP contended. " . . . Opponents of federal anti-lynching legisla-
> tion," the NAACP continued, "have for years asserted that the states

themselves would do the job of preventing lynching and punishing lynchers. The record demonstrates that these promises have not been kept. In view, therefore, of the immediacy of the situation it is imperative that the Congress act without fail to add the strong arm of the federal government to those of the several states to stop this tide of mob violence at once before it causes us either to lose the war or to prolong it at the cost of the lives of Americans.[46]

In closing, McKenzie reminded readers that Marianna had been the scene of the gruesome lynching of Claude Neal in 1934, tying together the atrocities of the past and present. Nine years later, African Americans were still being victimized by lynching violence. Marianna's example provided a very strong argument in favor of a federal antilynching bill.

John McCray, writing for the *Atlanta Daily World*, captured the frustration of many black Americans when it came to the continued terrorism they faced at home. "The riots at Detroit, Beaumont, Mobile and several other centers during the past month, and the lynching of Cellos Harrison at Marianna, Fla.," he fumed,

> aside from the shock, disgust and shame they have brought America, have combined to emphasize the Atlantic Charter signed by President Roosevelt and Mr. Churchill, in the summer of 1941. The Atlantic Charter, as creed for democracy's purpose in this war, sets forth four Freedoms: Freedom of Speech, Freedom of Worship, Freedom from Want and Freedom from Fear. . . . The chief weapon used against Negroes from their settling in America to the present day has been one of the goals announced in this Charter—Fear. . . . Were we Negroes to have this day "Freedom from Fear," our many problems and worries would crumble like a sand castle, struck by a bomb.[47]

In reporting Harrison's lynching and the other violent outbreaks, members of the black press captured the sentiments of black Americans, particularly black soldiers, by articulating their frustrations at American hypocrisy on the issues of race and democracy. The United States could not ask blacks to fight for democracy in foreign lands and deny them the benefits of democracy in their own country. Blacks would be unwilling to accept second-class citizenship after returning home from the war, and whites, the black press asserted, knew this. The rash of racial violence that occurred during this period was evidence in their eyes that whites were aware of the desire for change among blacks, but were willing to fight to preserve the status quo. Journalist Cliff Mackay, in speaking of the wartime violence, confirmed this tendency:

> It is this fear that motivates the growing attacks in Mississippi, Georgia, South Carolina and Arkansas on brown boys wearing the brown uniform of the United States Army. The fear is real among these elements in America that these brown boys taught to kill and sacrifice their lives if need be for freedom, will no longer be willing to accept the sub-standard status of second class citizenship upon their return. . . . The same fear lies behind the sudden outbreak of attacks against Negro workmen, not only in the South, but in Northern Industrial centers as well.[48]

Despite the sense of righteous obligation the United States claimed it felt for its European allies, the lynching of Cellos Harrison proved that not all of America's white citizens were as obligated to the welfare of their African American neighbors. "The most horrible Nazi atrocity stories coming from occupied Europe are no worse than these home front outrages," the *New York Age* reminded its readers. "The desire for liberation from such oppression can be no greater in the minds of Nazi-dominated Europeans than in the hearts of prejudice-flayed Negroes in America."[49]

Several interested parties, including civil rights organizations and civil rights advocates, wrote directly to state and federal officials encouraging an investigation of the Harrison lynching. Pearl S. Buck, winner of both the Nobel and Pulitzer Prizes for literature, dashed off a telegram to Governor Holland:

> MAY WE HAVE YOUR ASSURANCE BY WIRE COLLECT THAT PROMPT ACTION WILL BE TAKEN TO BRING TO JUSTICE THOSE RESPONSIBLE FOR THE LYNCHING OF COLES [SIC] HARRISON AT MARIANNA SUCH MOB INTERFERENCE WITH THE ORDERLY PROCESSES OF THE COURTS MUST BE SPEEDILY DEALT WITH IF WE ARE TO PRESERVE NATIONAL UNITY AND SUCCESSFULLY PURSUE THE AIMS OF THE DEMOCRATIC CAUSE[50]

Buck's interest in matters of civil and human rights was well documented, and her unique perspective as a Sinophile foresaw the import of American race relations writ large in a global context. In 1942, Buck had pushed for the creation of the Committee Against Race Discrimination within the American Civil Liberties Union (ACLU). As chair of the group, she worked on behalf of a number of causes that benefited African Americans, including fair employment opportunities and support of an antilynching bill in Congress. Buck earned her stripes as an unflinching supporter of black rights in a speech given during a luncheon sponsored by the American Booksellers Association. She had been invited to speak about China but focused instead on the meaning of the Second World War for the "colored people"—the Japanese, black Americans, and all dark-skinned people around the globe. "Every lynching, every race riot," Buck entreated her audience, "gives joy to Japan."

> The discriminations of the American Army and Navy and air forces against colored soldiers and sailors, the exclusion of colored labor in our defense industries and trade unions, all our social discriminations, are of the greatest aid today to our enemy in Asia, Japan. "Look at the Americans," Japan is saying to millions of listening ears, "will white Americans give you equality?" . . . If we intend to persist blindly in our racial prejudices, then we are fighting on the wrong side in this war. We belong with Hitler.[51]

Harry T. Moore, president of the Florida State Conference of the NAACP, also wrote to Governor Spessard Holland on July 12, 1943. As he characteristically did after lynching incidents in the state, Moore provided the governor with details surrounding Harrison's murder and urged Holland to investigate. Strategically, Moore based his protest of Harrison's lynching in the wartime language of patriotism and democracy, reminding the governor that

> it is hardly necessary to say that such incidents only tend to create a spirit of doubt and fear among Negro citizens. While our country is engaged in a gigantic struggle against the forces of hate and evil abroad, it is even more important that a stronger spirit of unity and hope should exist among all American citizens, regardless of race or color. Nothing could do more to lift the sagging morale of colored Americans than to see justice done in a case like this. If the morale

of American Negroes is to be lifted to a higher level in this fight for democracy abroad, it must be done through a more practical application of the fundamental principles of democracy at home.[52]

Other activists focused their efforts on prodding the federal government to take action and investigate Harrison's lynching. George Haynes and James Myers, of the Federal Council of the Churches of Christ in America, sent a telegram to U.S. attorney general Francis Biddle on the day after the murder urging federal investigation. Speaking of the lynching in Marianna and racial violence in Beaumont, Texas, in the context of the international implications, Haynes and Myers argued that such incidents

> jeopardize not only the lives and liberty of many innocent law-abiding citizens but the very power of our nation as it struggles for its life. It doubtless also gives aid and comfort to axis enemies. Such outrages within our own land will greatly reduce our influence with our many colored allies who will judge what we say over there by what is done over here. . . . We urge therefore that the federal department of Justice exhaust the possibilities of federal action to assure that those responsible for these outrages be apprehended and prosecuted as criminals impairing the national order.[53]

The collective voices of the civil rights community and the subsequent media attention forced the federal government to respond to the events in Marianna. Once apprised of the situation in Marianna, Attorney General Biddle requested that Assistant U.S. Attorney General Wendell Berge take action. President Franklin Roosevelt had ordered the Department of Justice (DOJ) to investigate all instances of lynching and do everything in its power to bring the lynchers to justice, especially in light of the lynching of Cleo Wright in Sikeston, Missouri, in 1942. In January of that year, Wright, an African American man, was accused of attempting to rob two white women and stabbing a marshal in the mouth. He was captured and taken to a Sikeston jail, sustaining eight gunshot wounds during the process. A few hours later, a mob kidnapped Wright from the jail, beat him, and dragged him behind a car through the street, followed by a crowd of more than 300 people. The mob then doused Wright with gasoline and set him on fire in front of a church. Despite the large number of spectators, a grand jury failed to indict the perpetrators of Wright's lynching.[54] The event became a national and international scandal, and Roosevelt wanted to avoid another calamity.

At the urging of Attorney General Biddle, Berge wrote to George Earl Hoffman, U.S. Attorney for the Northern District of Florida in Pensacola, on June 17, 1943, requesting a report on recent events in Marianna. Hoffman replied on June 25, sharing with Berge what information he discovered surrounding the Harrison lynching.[55] More than simply informational, however, Hoffman's correspondence downplayed the need for federal intervention or investigation. He characterized the violence as isolated, maybe even justifiable, and that in the aftermath, all things were under control. In Hoffman's view, the lynching was a case of retribution for the murder of Johnnie Mayo, of which Hoffman claimed Harrison was guilty, despite two successful appeals to the Florida Supreme Court. "While the case is one that presents a violation of the Federal law with reference to guarantee of civil liberties," Hoffman admitted, "it may be noted that this lynch-murder was committed without any public clamor, rioting or racial clash." Sounding very much like a southern apologist advocating "home rule," Hoffman emphasized that the situation was under control; federal authorities need not worry that Marianna would be another Detroit. As further evidence of the local sentiment against the lynching, Hoffman included a clipping of an editorial condemning the lynching from the *Pensacola Journal*.[56] In his estimation, it was a minor event that did not warrant federal attention.

Despite Hoffman's attempts to characterize Harrison's lynching as an isolated but regrettable episode, representatives of the federal government were not convinced. Given the recent rash of racial violence throughout the nation, members of the Roosevelt administration did not want to appear to be sitting on their hands. On the same day that Berge wrote to Hoffman, he forwarded a memorandum to J. Edgar Hoover, director of the FBI, referencing President Roosevelt's request that the DOJ thoroughly investigate instances of lynching and seek to bring the perpetrators to justice. Hoover complied, despite his general hostility toward African Americans and a disinclination to use his office to investigate lynchings.[57]

As a result of this request, the FBI became involved in the attempt to identify Harrison's lynchers. Beginning in July 1943, six FBI agents from the Miami office worked the case for nine months, interviewing nearly sixty people.[58] While the FBI agents failed to uncover any tangible evidence to substantiate prosecution, the information they gathered pointed to several possible culprits and suspicious characters.

One name that rose to the top of the list of likely suspects was that of Frank Lee. Lee was Johnnie Mayo's brother-in-law (his wife and Nella Mayo were sisters) and operated a campsite, filling station, and hotel on the west side of Marianna. He had a checkered background and a reputation as an illiterate but ambitious man who was involved in a number of legal and illegal pursuits—bootlegging and prostitution. He was also allegedly involved in *bolita*, Spanish for "little ball," the Cuban gambling racket based in Tampa that dominated the underground economy in Florida during these decades. In most communities, blacks and Hispanics played the game, which could earn them 70-to-1 or 90-to-1 odds, while white community leaders, primarily law enforcement officers, were paid to turn a blind eye to the illegal activity. Lee would become one of the city's biggest vice traders over the next two decades.[59]

Besides his illicit enterprises, Frank Lee also had a history of violence against African Americans. In May 1940, Governor Fred Cone received a complaint from prisoners in the Jackson County jail alleging that several inmates had been severely beaten in their cells. The victims—James Green, James Meeks, and Jess Meeks—were held on charges of stealing gas and money from Lee's service station. Upon learning of the robbery, Lee visited the jail with two other men and, apparently with the permission of the jailers, viciously beat the three men in attempts to extract confessions. The victims and witnesses later claimed that they were beaten at intervals ranging from twenty minutes to an hour. James Meeks had a bottle broken over his nose.[60] Deputy Dykes admonished the attackers to "leave life in them." Cries from the victims could be heard outside the jail, causing a small crowd to gather. As a result of the abuse, the three confessed to the crime. This incident occurred just three months after Johnnie Mayo's murder. Frank Lee's rage may have been sparked by that memory, and the fact that trouble had found its way to his doorstep. He responded viciously. Complaints from the prisoners and members of the community forced Governor Cone's hand, and he called for L. F. Cawthon, state prison supervisor, to investigate the matter.[61]

During the course of their investigation into the Harrion lynching, FBI agents learned that members in the community initially suspected Frank

Lee as Mayo's murderer, although they failed to note any specific motive. After Mayo's murder, Lee was rumored to have become close friends with Mayo's father. It was known that the two were involved in the sale of bootleg liquor. In an interesting turn of events, Lee was subpoenaed as a witness in both the 1941 and 1942 trials against Cellos Harrison, although he was not called to testify either time. Why would the prosecutor trouble himself and the sheriff's office to require his presence in court both times, and then fail to call him to the stand? There are no other mentions of Lee's activities on the day of the murder, excluding him as a witness. Perhaps any information he might have provided about the case would be colored by his illegal activities, his disreputable character, or both. Frank Lee's name came up frequently in the FBI's interrogations, with several Jackson County residents mentioning that Lee publicly suggested that Harrison be lynched. Former officer W. R. Davis, who worked for the police department when Mayo was killed, remembered that Lee made the statement in the weeks before Harrison's death, "He ought to be lynched," referring to Harrison.[62] While some people told the FBI they had heard Lee suggesting that Harrison be killed, others doubted that Lee was capable of carrying out the lynching. Some described Lee as "an illiterate person and that he was somewhat given to exaggeration," and they "did not believe Lee had sufficient courage or initiative to execute the type of lynching involved here."[63] When questioned by FBI agents, however, Lee and his wife insisted that he had been at home at the tourist camp they operated on the night in question.

Another white man who drew strong suspicion was Lonnie Walls. A former police officer from Savannah, Georgia, Walls had lost part of his left arm to a gunshot injury and wore a steel claw in its stead. During the time he lived in Jackson County, Walls had a shadowy reputation in the community. He once operated a juke joint in Marianna, where he had beaten some young men with a blackjack. Afterward Walls was arrested for carrying a concealed weapon.[64] In the months after Harrison's murder, Walls frequented Taylor's Pool Room and bragged about killing a black man while he was in law enforcement. Other times he talked about breaking a black man's arm with his claw. Moreover, town gossip insinuated that Walls and Nella Mayo, the murdered man's wife, were romantically involved, some even suggesting that he lived with her.[65] Walls came under suspicion primarily because of his activities after Harrison's murder.

Witnesses remembered seeing him downtown with a visible bloodstain on his shirt. More interestingly, on the morning that Harrison's body was found, Walls used a telephone in Nifty's Cleaning Shop to call Nella Mayo and tell her that Harrison was dead. Additionally, the day after the lynching, Walls was overheard at Taylor's Pool Room talking loudly about being the one to inform Nella Mayo that Harrison had been executed. He even bragged that he took her to the spot where the murder took place and "showed her the nigger."[66]

The tone of his conversation, his disdain for blacks, his alleged relationship with Nella Mayo, and the bloody stain on his shirt made some people wonder if Walls had been involved in Harrison's lynching. One FBI agent questioned Walls about what he had learned. While he admitted his acquaintance with Nella Mayo, Walls insisted that the extent of their relationship was an occasional ride to town, as he did not have a car. As far as the telephone call he made to Nella Mayo the day Harrison was killed, it was simply a courtesy call to a friend whom he knew would be interested in the news. Walls claimed the blood on his shirt came from a sore on the back of his hand, which Agent Carter claimed looked like an "infected mosquito bite." Because of his disability, Walls claimed, he had to use the back of his hand to fasten his shirt buttons, thus the sore was the origin of the blood on his shirt. Despite his comments at the bar and his association with Nella Mayo, there was no physical evidence to link Walls to Harrison's lynching.[67]

What about Johnnie Mayo's relatives? Might they have been so disappointed in the outcome of the case that they would have resorted to lynching? In its truest form, the practice of lynching sought to right a perceived wrong and satisfy a desire for justice. It was still true that in many areas in the South, a community sanctioned extralegal violence when the wheels of justice did not move fast enough or effectively enough. Mayo's relatives, three years after his murder, might have been the only people in Jackson County who harbored enough anger to be motivated to kill Harrison. FBI investigators followed this lead as well and began to trace the activities of Johnnie Mayo's immediate family around the time of Harrison's murder. Since Mayo's murder in February 1940, the Mayo family had relocated to Tallahassee. His parents and three brothers—Roy, Wilbur, and Frank—resided there, and a fourth brother, Milton, was serving in the U.S. Navy. FBI agents interviewed the neighbors of the Mayo family

in Tallahassee. The investigation revealed nothing that led the FBI to suspect their involvement. Coworkers and neighbors characterized Mayo's
family members as hard-working and peaceful. No one had heard any
member of the family talk of taking vengeance against Harrison. Further,
they verified that the Mayos were in Tallahassee on the day that Cellos
Harrison was lynched. Ultimately, the FBI's investigation failed to reveal
the complicity of Johnnie Mayo's father, mother, and brothers.[68] While
Mayo's immediate relatives lived in Tallahassee, the family was large, and
many of his cousins still lived in Jackson County. Many people suspected
that Mayo's local relatives had played a role in Harrison's death. Sergeant
Wells, of the Marianna police force, commented on the night of Harrison's
kidnapping that he would have looked for Harrison's body along Highway
84, because that road led to the community where many of Mayo's relatives lived. Notably, this was where the body was eventually found.[69]

Of all the suspects in the Harrison lynching, law enforcement officers,
individually and collectively, aroused the most suspicion. Sheriff Barkley
Gause's activities during his campaign for office in 1941 showed that he
was not above opportunism to gain political office. During the FBI's investigation, several people spoke negatively of Sheriff Gause's character.
Gause's predecessor, Sheriff Watford, had a reputation for aggressively
pursuing lawbreakers, especially violators of the county's gambling and
liquor laws. Gause, however, was not cut from the same cloth. At least two
individuals told the FBI that Gause took money under the table from the
gambling and liquor interests in the county. The accusation gained trac-
tion when Charles Guyton, an attorney in Marianna and deputy commissioner of the Florida Industrial Commission, wrote Governor Holland to
notify him that he had learned from reliable sources that Gause regularly
took kickbacks from local bootleggers. Based on these reports, Governor
Holland instituted an investigation into the allegations; the findings,
however, provided insufficient grounds for his dismissal.[70]

In addition to comments against Sheriff Gause's supposedly scurrilous
character, residents apprised the FBI agents of his feelings in regards to
Cellos Harrison. One individual recalled that Gause had been less than
pleased with the outcome of Harrison's first appeal. While in the car returning from Tallahassee to Marianna after Harrison was granted a new
trial, Gause angrily blamed bribery for the Florida Supreme Court's decision. The subject said that Gause believed "the whole layout [meaning the

court justices] divided the money between them and turned the nigger loose." The same individual saw Gause at a local fish fry after the lynching. He heard Gause stating that Harrison's lynching "had all blowed over pretty smooth."[71] This was a strange assessment considering that Gause and his men had failed to solve the case, which might have caused other officers of the law great consternation. Gause's comments suggest he may have shared the sentiment of the lynching party: in order for justice to be served in the Mayo case, Harrison had to die.[72]

One of the individuals who spoke against Sheriff Gause was Joe Sims, a former deputy of Gause's. He left Gause's administration after coming into conflict with him after arresting Sheriff Gause's brother, Addis, on a liquor violation. Even when pressured by Gause to drop the charges, Sims refused, resulting in the increased tension between the two.[73] Interestingly, subsequent investigation revealed that Sims, the former deputy sheriff who spoke so negatively about Sheriff Gause, may himself have been involved in Harrison's kidnapping and lynching. Interviewed in 1944 by FBI agents, Tom Moore, a black man who had been in the Marianna jail the night Harrison was kidnapped, shared some critical information about that night. Moore told the agents about the conversation he overheard between Harrison and the men who kidnapped him, something he could not share when testifying before the jury during the coroner's inquest when he and other blacks had been threatened into silence. His recollections confirmed statements by Robert Hadley, another inmate, given to the agents about the incidents at the jail on the night of Harrison's kidnapping. Moore, however, recalled that Harrison called one of his kidnappers by name. Moore told agents that when the kidnappers first called Harrison, he replied by asking, "Mr. Joe, is that you?" Could he have been referring to Joe Sims? This explanation makes sense because Harrison would have concluded that Sims, as an officer of the law, had the authority to remove him from jail. If Harrison had been unable to identify the person coming for him in the middle of the night as an officer of the law, would he not have resisted more forcefully? Until that point, the agents had been unable to identify any of the kidnappers. Moore's statement was the most specific in that direction, and is as revealing as it was speculatory. Still, because none of the men in the jail—neither the inmates nor the officers—saw the faces of the men, Moore's recollections were circumstantial. Deputy Sims claimed that on the evening of June 15, he had been out towing cars; Red Wells, a police officer for the city of Marianna, confirmed his alibi. There is no way of knowing if Harrison's statement was factual and based on his recognition and positive identification of the source, or if it was simply a guess on his part. According to Moore, however, the person addressed as "Mr. Joe" responded to Harrison's question.[74]

One of the most damning critics of the performance of Jackson County law enforcement officers was Lieutenant Clifton, of the Florida Highway Patrol. He was interviewed by agents in DeLand, Florida, in March 1944, nearly a year after the lynching. Although several months had passed, Lieutenant Clifton readily articulated what had gone wrong during the Harrison lynching. He squarely blamed the kidnapping and murder on the inactivity and disinterest of local law enforcement officers. From what he observed, the officers from Marianna made no attempt to investigate the lynching and were generally unconcerned with trying to find Harrison and his kidnappers, or to prevent his possible lynching. The statements given by Jackson County law officers about their activities on the night that Harrison was killed confirmed Lieutenant Clifton's observations. After Harrison had been kidnapped, instead of patrolling the county in search of the lynching party, they drank coffee and played dominoes. As Clifton plainly stated, they engaged in recreational activities while a man was being killed.[75] Attorney Starry, a member of Harrison's legal team, also relayed a story that spoke to the disinterest of law enforcement officials in preventing his murder, pursuing his kidnappers, or solving Harrison's murder. When Starry inquired about the state of the investigation, specifically asking if the officers tried to lift fingerprints from the paper bag found at the crime scene where Harrison's body was discovered, he said the officers looked amused and laughed at him.[76]

Ultimately, there are no clear answers about the role of law enforcement officers in Cellos Harrison's lynching. In the worst-case scenario, the lynchers coordinated their plans with law enforcement officers. Perhaps they were surprised and outmaneuvered, but that tied into another important issue: the protection of Cellos Harrison. The most obvious problem was the failure of Sheriff Gause and his staff to adequately protect the prisoner. After Harrison's first arrest, Gause had been prudent enough to move him to Quincy and then to a jail in Tallahassee. Why, after two murder convictions were set aside, did Gause not take the precaution of moving Harrison? Sheriff Gause defended his actions by pointing to Harrison's successful appeals. Part of the reason Harrison's second appeal was successful, and his confession was thrown out, was because of Harrison being transported to a safe location by law enforcement officers. Harrison claimed, and his lawyers argued, that instead of seeking to protect him, Gause and his men used the process of transportation from Marianna to Quincy as an opportunity to intimidate Harrison. The sheriff and his men heightened the perception of a possible lynching by encouraging the belief that the group was being pursued by a mob. By giving Harrison the impression that he was about to be lynched, law enforcement officers coerced his confession, leading him to believe it would save him from a violent death at the hands of a white mob. These circumstances gave Harrison's attorneys the grounds for successful appeals before the Florida Supreme Court. Gause later claimed that because of the criticism of the Florida Supreme Court of his actions in the previous incident, he did not attempt to remove Harrison from Jackson County again.[77]

While Sheriff Gause's reasons for not removing Harrison from Jackson County seemed understandable, his failure to provide adequate protection for him was not. Tom Belcher's role in the events of June 16 become even more suspicious because of the conflicting reasons Sheriff Gause gave for hiring him. Tom Belcher was an experienced, but aged, lawman who had served sixteen years in law enforcement at the time he was hired. A few weeks before Harrison was kidnapped and lynched, Sheriff Gause hired Belcher to work at the jail. When asked by FBI agents, Gause claimed that Belcher had been hired at the request of his officers for relief on their overnight shift. However, in a letter to Governor Spessard Holland reporting on the Harrison lynching, Gause claimed that Belcher had been hired for the specific purpose of protecting Harrison.[78] This claim raises several red flags. Why would Gause hire a sixty-five-year-old man, who admittedly weighed only 110 pounds, to defend a prisoner in jail? Furthermore, if this were true, why would he change his story? The claim that Belcher was only hired to "protect" Harrison was confirmed when a few days following Harrison's lynching, Belcher was no longer working at the jail.[79]

Given his extensive background in law enforcement, Belcher's behavior on the night of Harrison's kidnapping was inconsistent with his reputation as a stern, veteran lawman. In his testimony before the coroner's jury, he claimed that he was surprised and tricked by the men at the gate who told him they had a drunk for him to lock up. Belcher also claimed in his testimony that he could not resist the kidnappers because he was afraid and overpowered. For those who knew Belcher, this claim did not have the ring of truth. Amos Lewis, a longtime Jackson County resident and former state senator, spoke candidly with FBI investigators about Belcher. He claimed that in his years of being acquainted with Belcher, he had never known him to fear anyone. If he claimed any different, Lewis insisted, Belcher was lying. Another man, local attorney Thomas Walker, thought that Belcher was central to the success of the kidnapping. He insisted that Belcher knew more than he was telling. Walker, corroborating Lewis, described Belcher as "fearless" and rejected the claim that he did not know more about the lynching.[80]

Aside from the suspicion surrounding Belcher, FBI interviews revealed misgivings held by other members of the Marianna community concerning Deputy Lewis Rogers. Rogers was on patrol with E. B. Jordan, who dropped him off at the jail at ten o'clock that night. Later, Deputy Rogers claimed that he went directly to sleep and awoke to the sound of the front gate of the jail slamming, after which he only saw the tail end of the car that carried Harrison and his kidnappers. This meant that Rogers slept through the kidnappers' entry into the jail as well as Belcher's alleged calls for assistance before the kidnappers silenced him. Not everyone believed Rogers's account of events. Officer Jordan told the FBI that he was "certain" that Rogers heard the activities and knew the participants. He based his claims on his prior experiences with Rogers. Jordan claimed "that he has recently attempted to enter the jail during the night time without awakening Rogers and that as careful and quiet as he may be Rogers always opens the door just as he gets there and asks him what he has."[81]

Despite the diligent work of the FBI and the clues, rumors, and innuendos gathered during the course of its investigation, there was simply not enough evidence to identify the persons responsible for the kidnapping and lynching of Cellos Harrison. After months on the case, the DOJ was satisfied that all possible leads had been investigated with inconclusive results. Even if the agents had discovered the identities of Harrison's murderers, the odds of justice being served were slim. The federal government had only recently achieved its first indictment in a lynching case in the 1942 murder of Howard Wash, only to have a Mississippi jury find the five defendants not guilty.[82] Southern ideas of justice remained firmly

anchored despite the changing national currents. On July 19, 1944, thir-
teen months after Harrison's murder and a year since the federal investigation into the incident began, Assistant Attorney General Tom Clark
wrote to J. Edgar Hoover, calling off any further investigation and closing
the case.[83]

*   *   *

In the aftermath of Harrison's lynching, blacks in Jackson County tried
to go on with their lives. Many stayed home in the days following the
lynching, fearing a violent outbreak similar to the one that followed the
Neal lynching in 1934. The immediate members of Cellos Harrison's family
left the area. His wife, Bessie, left for New York in May 1943, just before
Harrison was killed. His sister, Theresa, had already moved to Newark,
New Jersey. After Harrison's lynching, Theresa came and took her mother,
Mary, to live with her.[84] Ben Barnes, Harrison's first defense attorney,
returned to Marianna after his naval training and opened a successful
general law practice.

It is probable that most whites in Jackson County believed that justice had been served. Prior to the lynching, remarkable restraint had been
exercised in giving the wheels of justice an opportunity to operate. To
avoid the appearance of impropriety, Judge Welch took the precaution of
throwing out the first indictment due to complications. After the Florida
Supreme Court ordered Harrison's retrial, officials in Jackson County followed the order. The city fathers of Marianna took the unusual step of
allowing blacks to serve on the jury, again to project the façade of fairness.
It was only when the wheels of justice slowed, and it looked as though the
confessed murderer of Johnnie Mayo would go free, that whites began to
take matters into their own hands.

After all these years, the question still remains: was Cellos Harrison
actually guilty of killing Johnnie Mayo? Aside from the flawed confession, there was no concrete evidence that he committed the crime. Because Harrison was killed before his case reached its legal terminus, and
no other statement about his guilt or innocence has been found, we are
left to wonder. Might Jabo Pittman have committed the murder, as Harrison initially claimed? Pittman's behavior in the months after Mayo's
death looked like the behavior of a man eager to leave the location of a
crime, especially when he was leaving his new wife and his unborn child

behind. What about Frank Lee, Mayo's brother-in-law, who had been initially suspected by some as the culprit? He was clearly a man with a history of violence and a lengthy career in illegal activity. Was Lee involved
in the lynching of Cellos Harrison? Despite the rumor and finger pointing,
there was not enough evidence gathered by the FBI to bring him or anyone
else to trial for Harrison's murder.

Many white observers blamed the Florida Supreme Court for the
lynching. Some believed that northern influence had been injected into
the case, hinting that the NAACP or some similar organization was attempting to use the Harrison incident for political gain. Others believed it
was the legal maneuvering of Harrison's lawyers that raised the ire of the
lynchers; it was the application for the writs of habeas corpus and prohibition that made people angry. Others believed that Harrison simply got
what he deserved. In the end, it was the fear that Harrison would evade a
suitable legal punishment, death being the only appropriate answer, that
spurred vigilantes to take action.[85]

While the evidence is inconclusive, it could be argued that whites in
Jackson County were just as calculating when they finally decided to take
matters into their own hands. There were an inordinate number of coincidences leading up to Harrison's kidnapping and eventual lynching, making it difficult to believe that they all occurred without the knowledge or
support of local law enforcement officials: an absent sheriff; the age and
feebleness of the jailer hired to "protect" Harrison; the failure to remove
Harrison to a safer jail; a normally alert jailer who slept through the kidnapping; the other deputy sheriff on pursuit and patrol in the far end
of the county; the sheriff's men who played dominoes and drank coffee
instead of going to look for Harrison.

More than anything, the lynching of Cellos Harrison in Jackson County,
a community already smeared by the legacy of a large spectacle lynching,
during a time when the United States was taking a critical step forward
as the world's leading democracy, offers an intriguing perspective into the
factors that ultimately led to the decline of lynching in Florida, and the
transition to "legal lynchings" as a way to resolve the community's desire
for retribution. The would-be lynchers seemed to have yielded to the court
system, which suggests that members of the Jackson County community
learned a painful lesson about the power of the national media after the
lynching of Claude Neal just seven years prior to Harrison's arrest. For

years afterward, the notoriety of that incident hung like a dark cloud over the town's collective consciousness. The citizens of Jackson County certainly realized that allowing another instance of extralegal murder to take place in their community, especially with the nation in the midst of fighting a war for democracy in Europe, would invite a flood of negative attention and possibly outside interference in the form of a federal investigation. Moreover, the ripple effects of allowing Harrison to be killed once he was arrested would embarrass not only the local community but also the state before the nation, and, perhaps more important, the United States before the world.

Motivated by concerns over negative publicity, the members of Marianna's white community who desired an old-fashioned response to Harrison's indictment waited (or were restrained by others, as the case may have been) to allow the legal process to run its course, instead of quickly resorting to murder. The desired outcome was a "legal lynching" that would give them the satisfaction of Cellos Harrison's death without the chaos, spectacle, and negative uproar that would have accompanied a traditional lynching.[86] The community could claim to have upheld the banner of "law and order" while still offering Harrison as a sacrifice on the altar of white supremacy. This struggle against the lynching impulse ultimately failed. Once it appeared that Harrison would possibly escape punishment, lynchers sprang into action to restore balance to the racial order.

Harrison's lynching, however, would not be carried out in the same manner as the Neal lynching; it was, by contrast, secretive and summary. The efficiency seems to have been specifically calculated to avoid the worse aspects of a spectacle lynching. From a purely technical aspect, Harrison's lynching was not as "bad" as others; there were no large crowds, no lengthy and public torture of the victim, no mutilation of the body in search of souvenirs, and no open display of a lifeless body in the town square. Was this a deliberate attempt to communicate "progress" by stripping away the worst aspects of ritualized bloodletting that typically characterized an extralegal execution, to somehow make it less newsworthy? Whatever its origins, the change represents a significant juncture along the path of declining lynching violence in America, and mirrors the trajectory described by Fitzhugh Brundage in his research on patterns of lynching in Georgia and Virginia, as well as a finding by Walter Howard in his research on lynchings in Florida.[87]

While avoiding negative publicity served as a powerful external deterrent to carrying out a lynching, there may have also been considerations closer to home that motivated the subdued format that followed Cellos Harrison's murder. The change could indicate a lack of support, either real or perceived, from the key members of the community for extralegal violence. One determinant that fueled lynching violence for decades was the wall of silence the white community erected around members of the mob and their ringleaders. Even if participants were identified and charged, they could count on a lily-white court for vindication. Now, in the midst of World War II–era rhetoric, could these lynchers rely on a significant majority of the white community to protect them or to at least turn a blind eye to their actions? Even if the local white community protected the lynchers, would they have to face state and federal investigations? Would they be able to hide their identities and avoid prosecution by those agencies? While Jackson County officials faced less political pressure, the governor and the president could be forced to act by individual activists and pressure groups like the Association of Southern Women for the Prevention of Lynching (ASWPL), the NAACP, and the ACLU.

In the end, observers can only make inferences from the behavior of silent actors responsible for the lynching of Cellos Harrison in order to illustrate patterns of change among lynchers in the Florida, and their horrendous and terrifying practices. Fear of publicity and prosecution may have modified their behavior, but that fear was not powerful enough to override the abiding impulse for vengeance among those whites in Jackson County who were willing to lynch in order to uphold white supremacy. Cellos Harrison's lifeless body was proof of that fact.

"A VERY CHEAP ARTICLE"

The Lynching of Willie James Howard,
Suwannee County, 1944

> Way down upon de Swanee Ribber,
> Far, far away,
> Dere's wha my heart is turning ebber,
> Dere's wha de old folks stay.
> All up and down de whole creation
> Sadly I roam,
> Still longing for de old plantation,
> And for de old folks at home.
>
> **Stephen C. Foster, "The Swanee River
> (Old Folks at Home)" (ca. 1851)**

While thousands of people lost their lives to lynching violence during the late nineteenth and early twentieth centuries, some of the most egregious instances of extralegal violence involved youthful victims. In October 1942, two black teens, Ernest Green and Charles Lang, were kidnapped from a jail in Quitman, Mississippi, castrated, and lynched, for the "crime" of playing tag with a white girl. Similarly, one of the most tragic and well-known examples of the senselessness and indiscriminant violence characteristic of lynching was the brutal murder of Emmett Till in Money, Mississippi, in 1955. Aside from the fact that he was kidnapped and later killed for allegedly making inappropriate comments and gestures to a white woman, it was Till's age, a tender fourteen years, that made the tragedy seem much more callous.[1]

While Till may be the best-known young victim of southern violence in the twentieth century, another African American teenager was killed for similar reasons nearly ten years earlier in Florida. One Sunday morning in January 1944, eleven years before Till's tragic death, three white men forced fifteen-year-old Willie James Howard to jump at gunpoint into the frigid waters of the Suwannee River to his death, all while his father help-lessly watched. His crime: overstepping the bounds and taboos of south-ern culture by passing a note to a white girl with whom he was acquainted. This simple action cost him his life.

Even though Cellos Harrison had been killed just six months earlier, the threat of negative press or potential federal involvement did not deter Howard's killers. Events proved that their confidence was warranted; un-like the prior lynchings of Arthur Williams and Cellos Harrison, Howard's lynching did not garner national media attention, nor did it inspire inves-tigations by the state or federal government. Despite these facts, his mur-der was perhaps more tragic than the others because of Howard's young age and the trivial nature of his offense. In the larger scheme, Howard's lynching illustrates the continuing pattern of small groups of secretive actors who relied on the tradition of white communal solidarity to escape punishment for extralegal murder. Aside from the historical patterns and what they reveal about the forms of antiblack violence in Florida in the twentieth century, the aftermath of Willie James Howard's lynching re-veals how members of a marginalized community craft their own private discourse to construct their own separate interpretation of these events. Oral history from community members who lived on opposite sides of the racial divide allows modern observers to understand the role of collective memory in forming and re-forming communal views of lynching.

*   *   *

For many, their only association with the Suwannee River comes from its mention in Stephen Foster's famous minstrel song "The Swanee River (Old Folks at Home)," adopted as Florida's official state song in 1935. Sandy soil, pine trees, sinkholes, and springs dominate the landscape of the land that the placid river circumvents on three sides as it meanders to the Gulf of

Mexico. After Florida was ceded to the United States in 1821, the present area of Suwannee County was included within the boundaries of Duval County, which was chartered in 1822.[2] It would be another twenty-three years before Florida became the twenty-seventh state in the Union. By 1860, Suwannee County's 687 square miles were home to 1,467 whites, 835 enslaved blacks, and one free black man. Live Oak, which would eventually become the county seat, was officially recognized in 1863. While slavery existed in antebellum Suwannee County, it would be inaccurate to describe the county as having a plantation economy, which was more associated with the five more notable "Black Belt" counties in North Florida—Jackson, Gadsden, Leon, Jefferson, and Madison.[3]

Suwannee County's small size and relative youth did not exempt it from the disruption and turmoil caused by the Civil War. For whites, the coming of the war brought a combination of exhilaration, uncertainty, and fears, which later turned into the misery of defeat in April 1865. For enslaved African Americans in Florida, as with other people in bondage throughout the South, the most anticipated change to occur came with emancipation. With the close of the war and the end of slavery, former bondspeople began exploring their freedom. To that end, a select number of African American men pursued and held elected offices. Between 1870 and 1877, nine African Americans served on the Suwannee County Commission, one on the city council, and two as justices of the peace. A decade later, a black man, Thomas Harris, served as Live Oak's postmaster from 1889 to 1905.[4]

As the disruptions caused by the Civil War subsided and the nation refocused on its economic pursuits, Suwannee County experienced a relative boom in growth and expansion. Its central location, approximately halfway between Tallahassee and Jacksonville, and the proximity of the Suwannee River made it a convenient regional crossroads for both transportation by rail and communication by telegraph. Additionally, steamboats on the Suwannee River moved goods and supplies from the interior of North Florida to the Gulf of Mexico, as well as providing recreational cruises for those who could afford it; however, water travel would be surpassed by rail in the coming years.[5] Trains supported the burgeoning economy built around lumber, turpentine, and resin, all derived from the long-leaf yellow pine trees that were abundant in the area. Several rail systems emerged in Live Oak and the surrounding areas during the early

1900s—the Live Oak-Rowland Bluff Railroad; the Live Oak, Charlotte-Harbor Railway; the Live Oak, Perry and Gulf Railroad; and the Savannah Western Railroad. Many would dissolve or merge before being taken over by the Atlantic Coast Line Railway.[6]

Inevitably, the aggressive harvesting of pine trees for timber outpaced nature's ability to replace them. The reduction in the availability of pine and pine products simultaneously diminished the importance of the local railway system, which was already being surpassed in importance by the automobile. By the 1930s, the economy of Suwannee County began to depend on other, more diverse agricultural products, tobacco key among them. Despite the transition from timber to tobacco, one fact remained the same: a successful local economy depended upon black labor. The main crops growing in Suwannee County in the 1940s were corn, peanuts, tobacco, cotton, and watermelon. Fifty-six percent of the working population engaged in some type of farming, compared with a statewide average of 16 percent. Race, however, influenced where blacks and whites fit into the strata of farm labor. Most African Americans were employed as farm workers, or earned wages as hired laborers.[7]

As in other southern towns, life in Live Oak was dictated by the rules of segregation and a rigid code of racial etiquette. As a result, African Americans in Live Oak created and maintained their own society, including their own neighborhoods, schools, churches, and businesses. The main school for African Americans, established in 1868, had roots in the Reconstruction era and was named after the famous abolitionist and lecturer Frederick Douglass. Located on Houston Street, along the invisible border between the black and white communities, the Douglass School stood just a few hundred yards away from the town's all-white high school.[8] Blacks lived among each other in mostly all-black sections of town like the West End and Sugar Hill, or in the numerous other rural communities such as Houston, Rocky Sink, Falmouth, and Fort Union. In Live Oak, a few blacks owned their own businesses. Several of these businesses were grouped at the Hopps Building in downtown Live Oak on Howard Street. Called "The Hill" by local blacks, the building housed several African American–owned businesses, such as Eddie Holmes's laundry, a bar operated by Ike Smith, Mary Bell's restaurant, and Gertrude Solomon's restaurant. Besides this concentration of businesses, other black entrepreneurs and professionals lived and worked in the community.[9]

to legitimize his right to make such a claim, Howard turns to the heavens, claiming that God caused him to love her. He acknowledges the fact that she does not like black people, but it is not clear how he came to that conclusion. Does he know this from observation, or did the issue come up in a previous conversation between them? The next few lines in the letter are simultaneously bold and foolhardy. The author brashly declares that he wishes that he and Goff were in a northern state, believing a change in geographic location and social atmosphere would open the possibility of Goff warming up to him. Seeming to recognize the dangerous forwardness of his words, Howard requested that Cynthia not show the note to anyone. His hesitation was fleeting, as he concludes the letter with a clear statement of his feelings for her: although Willie James knew that Cynthia may judge him as forward or "fresh," he concluded the note by declaring that he had a crush on her and wanted to know if she reciprocated. Given the letter's contents, its author, and its intended recipient, as well as the era in which it was written, it was as baffling as it is brazen.

It is important to note here different and conflicting claims about the nature of the communication between Howard and Goff. Central to the controversy is the content of the original handwritten note. The Howards' later statements confirm that a letter or note was the cause of the conflict. However, interviews conducted with members of the Live Oak community who remember the incident offer a different interpretation of the events. When asked, several residents who recalled the rumors circulating in the days and years after the lynching claim that the words Howard had written to Goff were not his own but the words of a song. Supposedly, she overheard him singing the song and asked him to write down the lyrics for her. One of his classmates recalled: "First they say it was a note, next thing I read, they say it was a song he wrote and gave it to her."[27] Another interviewee claimed the song was "If This Ain't Love, It Will Have to Do until Then." Both insisted that the note Howard gave to Goff contained words to a love song.[28] Parts of this interpretation make sense, especially given the fact that Howard, by all accounts, always had a tune on s. Interestingly, famed jazz singer Billie Holiday recorded a song that featured a similar sentiment, entitled "Until the Real Thing long." The song included the refrain: "If that isn't love, it will have until the real thing comes along."[29] One Suwannee County resietta Haynes, remembers shopping at Van Priest's store in the days before Howard's death. While purchasing cloth to make dresses, Haynes recalled seeing both Goff and Howard in the store that day and overhearing a conversation between the two of them. She recalled that Goff repeatedly asked Howard to write down the lyrics. He did not respond to her, but continued to collect the trash and boxes around the store, as were his duties.[30] Haynes completed her purchase and left the store, thinking nothing of the exchange. It was only after Howard's lynching that she understood the significance of what she had witnessed. Haynes's recollections represent the closest substantiation of the "written lyrics" version of the incident, undergirding a plausible counternarrative to what has been accepted as truth in this matter.

The full truth about the circumstances and contents of the note Willie James Howard passed to Cynthia Goff may never be known. Nevertheless, the essence of his perceived violation is clear. The controversy crossed a critical threshold when Goff's father discovered what had transpired. He was outraged. Who was this black boy writing notes to his daughter? Despite what was written on the note, the simple act of conveyance of a message that was private, intimate, and clandestine represented a transgression that could not be ignored. This was a serious violation of the southern social code. Of all of the rules of racial etiquette governing the separation of the races, the need to separate, and keep separate, black men and white women was loaded with sociosexual connotations. Control of interracial sexuality—specifically, preventing black males from gaining access to white females—was key to maintaining white (male) supremacy.[31]

Southern psychosis surrounding rape meant that even trivial contact between black males and white females could become a deadly matter. Seemingly insignificant contact—a nudge, a direct look, and in the case of Willie James Howard, the transmission of a note on a piece of paper— fit into a grossly exaggerated social definition of "rape," as it applied to the safety of white, and not black, women. As W. Fitzhugh Brundage acknowledges, "in the popular usage of white southerners, rape, at least when white women were involved, was an elastic concept that extended far beyond the contemporary legal definition of the crime to include attempted rape, aggravated assault, and even acts as apparently innocent as a nudge."[32] This meant that any slight to a white woman, whether real or perceived, could be met with, in the eyes of white southern men, deadly and justifiable violence. Making eye contact, brushing against, or otherwise intimidating or threatening a white woman was punishable by death. Howard's seemingly innocent and insignificant act crossed a perilous racial boundary, beyond which awaited brutality and death.[33]

The other component of this southern sexual myth was that it was the duty of white men to protect their women by any means necessary. As such, it was Phil Goff's duty as the protector of his daughter's honor to deal with the matter firmly and directly. His standing in the community was at stake. A former elected official and leading man in his community, rumors of his daughter's indiscretions across the color line would cause irreparable harm to both of them. In defense of his manhood, and to defend his daughter's honor, Goff moved to address the perceived threat that Howard represented. After gathering his resolve, Goff sought help for what he had in mind. He called on his neighbor, Seldon "Mack" McCullers, a forty-two-year-old local white salesman, and McCullers's brother-in-law, Reginald H. Scott Sr., a forty-year-old local white farmer.[34] Goff told them about the letter, and that a black boy had been getting "fresh" with his daughter. They no doubt shared Goff's outrage. It was their duty as southern white men to put this boy in his place.

Goff, McCullers, and Scott embarked on their mission the morning of January 2 with a stop at the home of Edward McPherson, the principal of the school Howard attended. They asked McPherson for directions to the Howard home, and he pointed them to the east side of town, and described the Howard homestead near the railroad tracks. According to family members, Willie James had been at work that morning and learned that he was being pursued. He ran home as fast as he could from Van Priest's and explained to his mother that he was being chased by white men who wanted to kill him. A few moments later, a car pulled up at the Howard home, and three white men identified as Goff, Scott, and McCullers exited the vehicle. Goff spoke, inquiring of Lula Howard the whereabouts of her son. She replied that he was at home. Just then, Willie James walked out on the porch. Goff reached out, grabbed him, and attempted to drag him off the porch. Lula Howard grabbed Willie James and pulled him back toward the house. At that point Goff reached into his pants and pulled out a gun that he aimed squarely at Howard. Facing the barrel of Goff's pistol, she stopped resisting and allowed her son to slip from her grasp. It would be the last time she would see him alive.[35]

The three white men forced Willie James Howard into the vehicle, and the party sped off. Frightened and not knowing what to do next, Lula Howard rushed to her sister's home, where her niece, Corrine Dunbar, recalled seeing her walking nervously back and forth across the porch. "What was wrong?" she asked. "Where was Giddy-Boy?" Howard, despondent and terrified, continued to pace the length of the porch, wringing her hands. Three white men took him, she explained, but they promised to bring him back. She then decided that if she could find her husband, James, he would know what to do. She hurried to the Bond-Howell Lumber Company, where her husband worked, only to be informed by Mrs. Howell, the mill owner's wife, that the same party of men had picked up the elder Howard as well.[36]

Just as in the case of the contents of the note Willie James Howard passed to Cynthia Goff, the sequence of events that occurred the morning of January 2 is disputed. The end, however, is conclusive: Willie James Howard drowned in the Suwannee River on Sunday, January 2, 1944. Phil Goff, Reginald Scott, and S. B. McCullers, along with James Howard, signed an affidavit in the presence of Sheriff Tom Henry, of Suwannee County, that same day claiming that their only purpose that morning was to have James Howard punish his son for giving a letter to Cynthia Goff. In their view, Willie James had committed a serious transgression, and they wanted to ensure that his father properly disciplined him. The men admitted that they assisted James Howard by binding Willie James's hands and legs to prevent him from running. Then, according to Goff, McCullers, and Scott, as the elder Howard prepared to discipline his son, Willie James became hysterical. Not wanting to be humiliated, he declared that he would rather die than to be beaten by his father or the white men. They said that he began moving away from the four of them and closer to the edge of the riverbank. The men then claimed that Willie James jumped into the Suwannee River of his own volition, despite their attempts to prevent his fall. James Howard, they insisted, "stood by and viewed the son without attempting to prevent this happening." Willie James Howard, they claimed, had committed suicide. After taking the statements from the other men, Sheriff Henry compelled, through intimidation, James Howard to sign the affidavit as well, effectively cosigning their version of the events. Further, the officer had James Howard sign a document stating that he did not want a coroner's inquest performed to determine his son's cause of death. Armed with these statements, Sheriff Henry reported the incident to Acting State Attorney David Lanier at about eight o'clock that same evening.[37]

That Sunday morning the town's black and white residents worshipped in their segregated sanctuaries, but by that afternoon news of the tragic events spread through town, shattering the fragile peace. The task of retrieving Howard's body fell to Ansel Brown, the local African American undertaker, who quietly and quickly embalmed the body himself in preparation for a speedy funeral. Brown did not openly discuss the condition of Willie James's body at that time. Years later, however, one of Brown's former apprentices claimed that Brown later told him that Willie James had been beaten and castrated. The rumor, while unsubstantiated, reflected the eerily familiar ritual surrounding lynchings of black males accused of sexual transgressions.

That Monday, the day after Willie James Howard was lynched, the students from Douglass School were allowed to view the body of their classmate before it was hastily buried without the benefit of a ceremony, or even the presence of his parents.[38] James and Lula Howard quickly sold their home and property and moved to Orlando within days.[39] Their speedy departure from Live Oak was a clear indication of the fear they felt and the realization that there was no prospect for justice on behalf of their son, especially when it was evident that Sheriff Henry conspired to cover up their son's lynching.

In the wake of Willie James Howard's murder, the secrecy surrounding the handling of his body and the speed at which it was interred raised suspicion within Live Oak's black community. The reactions ranged from enraged shock to fearful silence, all characteristic of a people held captive by racist institutions in the South that provided no real avenue to justice for African Americans. The leaders in the black community weighed their desire for justice against the potential for retribution—ranging from economic to physical—from the local white community if their efforts to seek an investigation into the lynching was discovered. Despite the desire to have the lynching publicized and investigated, there were clearly forces conspiring to cover up any evidence of the murder and to silence any discussion. The absence of Howard's parents left a void in the leadership in the call for justice. Who would risk stirring the pot and advocating an investigation and the arrest of Howard's murderers? Written communication was risky because one of the alleged murderers, Phil Goff, ran the post office. Many of Live Oak's elected officials—the sheriff, the tax collector, and the chief of police—had been purportedly involved in the cover-up of the murder. Consequently, the initial protests over the matter would come from outside of Suwannee County, led mainly by the NAACP, at both the state and national levels.[40]

One of the first letters that Walter White, executive director of the NAACP, received was from Elbert C. Robinson, an African American attorney in Washington, D.C. Robinson spent the Christmas holidays in Florida and had heard of Howard's murder. In his correspondence to the NAACP, he spoke of the fear on the part of blacks in Live Oak: "It appears that the conditions here are so tense, and the colored people (high and low) are so freightened [sic] that they are afraid to have their names identified with cases of this type. . . . The hush, hush, fear and secrecy surrounding this whole miserable thing is beyond comprehension and description."[41] Robinson's letter confirmed a sad reality: blacks in Suwannee County desperately needed outside assistance to attain any justice in this case.

Another concerned observer, Robert Jackson, wrote to Walter White on January 7, 1944, but listed no return address. Other letters reached the national office of the NAACP in the following weeks, one from A. L. King, of St. Augustine, and another from Edward Davis. Davis served as the president of the Marion County branch of the NAACP, and his letter conveyed the contents of a note he received from an anonymous minister from Live Oak. The secrecy surrounding the transmission of the letter testified to the fear that blacks in Live Oak felt. "The colored citizens are much disturbed," the letter read, "but are afraid." Edward R. Dudley, assistant special counsel for the national NAACP office, responded to both letters, warning of the difficulty presented by lynching cases in the South due to the reluctance of local law enforcement officials to investigate. Instead, Dudley thought that the best course of action would be to write to the governor of Florida, Spessard Holland, as well as the state attorney general, requesting that they take action.[42]

In line with this approach, Thurgood Marshall, special counsel for the NAACP's Legal Defense and Education Fund, contacted Governor Spessard Holland, requesting an investigation into the matter. The pressure from the NAACP and others paid off, as Governor Holland in turn requested that Acting State Attorney David Lanier hold a grand jury hearing investigating Howard's death. The governor assured Marshall that proper protection would be provided for James Howard, the victim's father, when he came to testify; it was understood, as the governor's comment acknowledged, that James Howard's willingness to confront the power structure in Suwannee County would endanger his life. However, Holland did issue a warning to Marshall not to expect too much. "I am sure you realize the particular difficulties involved where there will be testimony of three white men and probably the girl against the testimony of one negro man."[43] After receiving word from the governor's office, Lanier issued a subpoena for James Howard to appear at the Suwannee County courthouse on May 8, 1944.[44]

In addition to writing Governor Holland, Thurgood Marshall also corresponded with Florida's best-known U.S. senator, Claude Pepper. Consistent with the African American war mantra of the "Double V" strategy—winning victories for democracy both at home and abroad—Marshall sought to draw parallels between injustice and terror instituted in Europe by the Nazis and atrocities committed by American whites against black citizens in the United States. "Yesterday," Marshall began,

> the War Department released stories of Japanese torture and inhumane treatment of American boys in prison camps after the fall of Corregidor. At the same time, numerous letters reached our office concerning a vicious crime committed in Live Oaks [sic], Florida. . . . This is the type of material that radio Tokio is constantly on the alert for and will use effectively in attempting to offset our very legitimate protest in respect to the handling of American citizens who unfortunately are prisoners of war.[45]

Senator Pepper, a staunch supporter of Franklin Roosevelt and the New Deal, proved to be no easy audience; he had joined the rank-and-file southerners in a filibuster against antilynching legislation just a few years earlier, in 1937. In his response to an inquiry about the lynching of Willie James Howard, the senator seem unconcerned. In a terse response to Milton Konvitz, assistant special counsel for the NAACP's Legal Defense and Education Fund, Pepper wrote, "I have heard nothing of the report of the lynching of a fourteen-year-old-boy in Florida and know nothing of the facts in the case. Consequently, I am unprepared to make any statement concerning it."[46] Apparently, he was equally as unwilling to use the weight of his office to call for an investigation into what might have happened in Suwannee County.

This pattern of disinterest would be repeated. Compared to other lynchings that occurred in the 1940s, Willie James Howard's murder barely generated any publicity. There was no report of his death in the local newspaper, the *Suwannee Democrat*. During the same week there were, however, reports on the deaths of two white Suwannee County residents published in the *Florida Times Union*.[47] The omission of reports on Willie James's death, and others like it, confirmed the marginalization of black people in Florida society. Whites controlled most media outlets and were in a position to control both the content and tenor of the information the public received, thereby manipulating both the validity and visibility of people and events. Howard's lynching did receive some attention in the African American press. Dated January 22, 1944, the report (most likely from Jacksonville's black newspaper, the *Florida Tattler*) claimed that a seventeen-year-old black male had been arrested and released as a part of the plot to murder him. Although the article does not name Howard specifically, despite other inaccuracies, it verified that the victim was killed on January 2, 1944, and that he had been accused of writing a love note to a white girl.[48]

As they settled into the relative safety of their new home, James and Lula Howard, along with local NAACP leaders, strove to make the public aware of their son's murder. After they moved to Orlando, Rev. R. H. Johnson, vice president of the Orange County branch of the NAACP, befriended the couple and invited them to live with him and his family. While the Howards were in Johnson's care on February 6, State Attorney David Lanier came to interview the two of them about the events surrounding their son's death. The events the elder Howard outlined were at odds with the previous version he offered back in Suwannee County and full of heart-wrenching details of the last moments of his son's life. James Howard told Lanier that on the morning in question, he had gone to work to assist his employer, R. L. Howell, with inventory. Later that morning,

Phil Goff arrived at the lumberyard and told Howell he needed Howard to come with him on "business." As Howard approached Goff's car, he saw his son sitting in the backseat. He also saw Mack McCullers sitting next to him. Then he saw the gun in McCullers's hand.[49]

Once in the car, the men drove the Howards down Suwannee Springs Road. Goff then turned the car onto a red clay road that led through the woods toward the Suwannee River. During the trip, James Howard attempted to speak to his son, but Goff told him to shut up. Once they reached the river, Goff parked the car. Then, Goff and McCullers retrieved rope from the trunk and tied Willie James's hands and feet. Afterward, Goff told James Howard to guide his son to a spot just a few feet from the embankment. Acting as jury and judge, Goff asked Willie James, who was crying, if he understood the penalty of his crime. "Yes, sir," he answered, weeping. Goff then asked James Howard if he had anything to say to his son. Powerless to intercede in his son's fate, James Howard offered his son some words of comfort in what he now knew were his son's last moments of life: "Willie, I cannot do anything for you now. I'm glad I have belonged to the Church and prayed for you." Willie James's final request of his father was that he take his wallet, which Howard did.[50] At that point, Goff gave Willie James a choice of how he would die: "You can either jump into the river, or take what is in this gun." Willie James chose the former, backing off the edge of the bank and falling into the water below. Howard stood by and watched, helpless to intervene.[51]

Upon returning to the car, the men threatened James Howard with the gun, warning that if he contradicted their version of events, he would receive the same treatment his son had, "with pleasure." After returning to town, the men took Howard back to work. He met his wife, who was anxious to know what was going on. Howard ignored her questions, took her home, and then returned to work. When he arrived at the lumberyard, Chief of Police William Hunter and Wylie Byrd, a former police officer with a sinister reputation when it came to dealing with blacks, met him.[52] They asked him to go with them to the courthouse, where they were joined by Sheriff Tom Henry and Phil Goff. The three white men made their statements before Sheriff Henry. Once they transmitted their account of the events, they forced James Howard to sign the affidavit, agreeing to their version. There was little else he could do; he had just watched them murder his son, and if he did not cooperate, it was likely that James Howard would lose his life as well.[53]

The ordeal, however, did not end there. Later that same night, the sheriff came to the Howards' home and asked James Howard to accompany him again. This time, Sheriff Henry took him to the courthouse. Goff and H. H. Hair Jr., the tax collector for Suwannee County, were there when they arrived. They had prepared a document stating that Howard did not want a coroner's inquest into his son's death. The statement was read aloud to Howard, but the presence of Goff filled him with fear. He signed that document, just as he had the false statement, because he was frightened and intimidated.[54]

The revelations James and Lula Howard shared with David Lanier were just one part of their continuing effort to draw attention to the lynching of their son. NAACP officers embraced the couple, assisting them as they transitioned to their new home in Orlando, and coordinating efforts to seek an investigation. The Howards were invited to speak before the statewide NAACP board of directors at their Orlando meeting on March 12, 1944. There they retold the story of their son's writing to a white girl, the kidnapping, and the murder. By that time, Harry T. Moore, president of the Florida State Conference of the NAACP, had begun to use his eloquent pen to press for justice in the Howard murder. Moore wrote to Roy Wilkins at the national NAACP office in New York to bring him up to date on the situation.[55]

This case struck a chord with Moore, who was a native of Suwannee County, having grown up in Houston, a small province just outside of Live Oak. Moore had also grown up with Lula, the victim's mother. As a native of the area, Moore was familiar with the local power structure and, more important, the activities of the Ku Klux Klan (KKK). "The Ku Klux Klan has been active around [Suwannee County] during recent years," Moore wrote to Wilkins. "Negroes have suffered much brutality at the hands of white people [and] are so cowered that there is never any talk of voting or exercising any of the fundamental rights of citizenship by Negroes." Moore urged Wilkins and the national office to intercede in the Howard case and help the family seek justice. Based on his prior experiences with Governor Holland, Moore expressed doubt that the state government would take positive action in the situation. Cellos Harrison had been lynched the previous summer, and, despite pleas from the state NAACP, the governor's office had not responded to them. Moore maintained that if anything were to come of the Howard case, they needed to seek assistance from a higher level.[56]

When the grand jury met in the Suwannee County courthouse on May 8, 1944, it was scheduled to hear a manslaughter case that, strangely, listed no defendants. James Howard was, however, listed as a witness. As the day proceeded, nearly all the cases listed were called except the one Howard had come for. The bailiff simply ignored him. Apparently, court officials did not intend to call the case. James Howard, however, would not be ignored any longer. He had lived for five months with the tortured memories and stewing anger and had spent time bolstered by the support of the NAACP and Orlando's black community. He was not the same man who had cowered before Sheriff Henry months earlier and signed his name to a falsified statement. Howard may have been powerless to save his son's life that January day at the river, as he faced armed and determined men, but he wanted justice. He was there to tell the full truth to whomever would listen and to hold Goff, McCullers, and Scott responsible for his son's lynching.[57]

The next time the bailiff emerged from the courtroom, Howard stood, walked over to him, and presented him with his subpoena to testify. The bailiff then gave the document to Sheriff Henry. Henry approached Howard and asked where he had received the document. Howard replied that the sheriff of Orange County had delivered it to him. Sheriff Henry approached State Attorney Lanier and asked him if he had any knowledge of the case, to which he replied that he had. This seemed to catch Henry off guard. According to Howard, who described him as visibly upset, Henry "looked surprised and started pacing up and down the floor from the back door to the front door and then to his office." He came back to Howard, asking him to stay around and saying that he would call him soon.[58]

Eventually, Lanier called James Howard to testify. Once on the stand, Howard recounted his version of events, how Goff, McCullers, and Scott forced Willie James to jump into the river at gunpoint. However, the only questions the grand jury asked Howard were his son's age at the time of his death and if Willie James had passed the note to Cynthia himself. After hearing from him, the jury dismissed Howard and did not call anyone else to testify, even though his wife, Lula, and his former employer and his wife had come in order to give statements. In his closing argument, State Attorney David Lanier encouraged the jury to return a true bill against Goff, McCullers, and Scott, stating to the jury that, if anything, the three were guilty of murder. As Governor Holland predicted, no indictment was returned against the three white men.[59]

After the grand jury failed to indict anyone for the murder of Willie James Howard, Moore continued to ask for advice and intervention from the NAACP's national office. Moore acknowledged that he was not surprised by the verdict but detailed the suspicious behavior of Sheriff Henry. He was disturbed at Sheriff Henry's reaction to Howard's presence in court that day. Henry's visible frustration and hesitance to allow Howard and others to testify indicated something more than surprise to Moore. "We are forced to wonder," he wrote to Marshall, "if the sheriff himself is not involved in this crime. It is very probable that he at least has tried to help cover up the facts in this case."[60]

As the months went on, Thurgood Marshall did what he could to prompt the federal government to investigate the Howard murder by writing the U.S. Department of Justice (DOJ). Tom Clark, assistant attorney general for the DOJ, responded to Marshall and informed him that the Civil Rights Section of the Justice Department had already begun a preliminary investigation into the matter. To help with the investigation, Clark requested contact information for James Howard from Marshall so that the FBI could interview him.[61] Moore replied to Clark's request, sending him Howard's new address, along with contact information for T. R. Reid and Rev. Johnson, who could assist the effort. In his correspondence, Moore expressed his gratitude to Clark that the federal government had taken an interest in the case.[62]

Moore's gratitude, however, may have been premature. After a year of silence, with neither the attorney general nor any other representative from the DOJ contacting the NAACP about the case, Moore again wrote to the attorney general in September 1945 seeking information about the status of the investigation. Moore was barely able to hide his disenchantment with the situation. He was keenly aware of the inability of the state of Florida to protect the lives of its black citizens. Federal intervention seemed to be the only solution. The tone of the letter shows Moore's frustration at the lack of action. Because of these circumstances, "The life of a Negro in Suwannee County," Moore grimly surmised, "is a very cheap article." "We need positive action by the Federal authorities," he reminded the attorney general, "to curb such horrible crimes against Negroes in Suwannee County, and in other counties of that section in Florida."[63] Without federal intervention, all hope for justice in the murder of Willie James Howard, or any other case of racial violence, faded. Since local whites controlled the avenues to justice, African Americans in Suwannee County, or anywhere else in Florida, lived without the assurance of equal protection of the law or due process. During the previous four years, North Florida had been a hotbed of lynching activity, and there seemed to be no end to the violence. A few weeks after Moore wrote to the DOJ to inquire about the status of the investigation into the Howard murder, Sam McFadden, a sixty-three-year-old African American World War I veteran, was forced by a Suwannee County constable to jump to his death in the Suwannee River. The following month, on October 16, 1945, Jesse James Payne, an African American sharecropper in neighboring Madison County, was kidnapped from the county jail and lynched.[64]

By the time of Moore's last letter to the DOJ in 1945, it was apparent that justice would not be rendered in the murder of Willie James Howard. The local, state, and federal powers proved unwilling or unable to prosecute the guilty parties. African Americans were angry, but fear suppressed their rage, and a general feeling of helplessness was in the air.[65] According to one resident, blacks "had to pretend that it didn't bother them . . . but it really tore us up. . . . It was just terrible and we had to, we had to keep it under [our] breath and talk to each other, how terrible it was and how we hated [it] but wasn't nothing that could be done, that they could do, 'cause the law here was for the white man."[66] Another resident recalled that "it wasn't nothing at that time for them to go get two or three of 'em and go to a house and get 'em out right in front of you and take 'em on out there and give 'em a good beating or killing and throw them in the river."[67]

These fears were justified. The Ku Klux Klan was active and highly visible in Suwannee County, and throughout the state of Florida, during these years. KKK members frequently paraded through the main streets of Live Oak. Growing up in the 1940s, Dorothy DePass, a former schoolmate of Willie James Howard, recalled being warned of the Klan's presence in town: "When we were younger, I remember us coming to town on

Saturdays. . . . They would say 'Oh, ya'll better get out of town 'cause the Klu Klux coming.'"[68] The local newspaper, the *Suwannee Democrat*, printed a resolution from the Suwannee Klan No. 114, Knights of the Ku Klux Klan, adopted on January 6, 1944, just a few days after Howard's murder. The declaration paid tribute to one of their recently deceased members, W. J. Warner, for his "noble and Klanlike life."[69] For the Klan to publish the names of its members implies a high degree of community support or sanctioning, at least enough not to risk social ostracism that may have accompanied public knowledge of such an affiliation. However, despite their fears and the odds against them, and as evidence of the strength gained in the aftermath of Howard's lynching, blacks in Suwannee County mustered the courage to organize a local chapter of the NAACP in 1944.[70]

The lives of blacks involved in this incident were forever disrupted. The tragedy of Willie James Howard's murder haunted family members for years. While visiting Daytona Beach several years after Willie James's death, Dorothy DePass, a native of Suwannee County, encountered Lula Howard. During the course of their conversation, Lula Howard became hysterical and began to cry, lamenting, "They killed my child in Live Oak."[71] While there was an eyewitness to the continued manifestation of Lula Howard's pain, what of her husband, James Howard? He was forced to live with the compounded tragedies of witnessing the murder of his son and having to internalize the humiliation that death represented. Goff, McCullers, and Scott could have carried out their intention without the presence of the father—they had kidnapped Willie James from his home before they picked up James Howard from his job. However, the lynchers made the decision to intentionally emasculate him, forcing him to stand by and witness the murder of his only child. While James Howard was not physically harmed, he was socially castrated by being forced to witness the symbols of his manhood being destroyed: his ability to protect his child and the loss of his progeny—his male heir who would have borne the standard of his family's name and lineage—that was represented in his son's death. He was forced to relive his son's lynching, to wallow in his social impotence, when he had to face Lula and explain what had happened to their son. In the end, Howard was forced to flee his home, compounding the humiliation that he had already experienced. When told of the accusation made by Goff, McCullers, and Scott—that Howard stood by and watched his son drown—his sister-in-law, Mamie Perry, responded: "What was James gone say? They'd a killed him [snaps fingers] on the spot. . . . What could he do with a bunch of men standing 'round and they got they guns and he ain't got nothing?! Nothing. . . . That's that slavery mess they had going on. They'll kill you if you look at them straight."[72]

The tragedy of Willie James Howard, as with all lynchings, represents a unique set of occurrences that reflect the disastrous intersection of gender, race, and power in southern society. Scholar William F. Pinar has described this as "homosocial rape"—a forced racial and social dominance between men of different races. "Lynchings," according to Pinar,

> represent the final stage of an emasculation process that white men conducted every day by word and deed, a culmination of a psychosexual war on black men. Black men were not allowed to forget that they were commodities, bodies not citizens, objects not men. . . . If black men dared to claim any privileges of (white) manhood, whether sexual, economic, or political, they risked lynching. Lynching was then, primarily, an "affair" between men.[73]

Pinar's interpretations of black manhood follow those of Trudier Harris, whose writing on the subject combines the historical and literary representations of lynching violence by black writers. Both life and art reinforced the fact that if a black man "could be emasculated politically in the symbolic counterpart of the physical emasculation, then he was made to feel in several arenas that he was expendable. How could he assume the role of man when he could not protect his own bed?"[74] In the case of James Howard, and many other black men, this extended to his inability to protect his home or his family.

Extending this line of thinking, Robyn Wiegman points out the role of racial violence, specifically lynching, in reshaping the boundaries of political control in the post-Reconstruction South, describing it as "the means for (re)articulating white masculine supremacy within the social and economic specificities of slavery's abolition" and, through the violence of lynching, "reclaiming . . . [white male] masculine potentiality for citizenship."[75] These hard realities reinforced for James Howard, and many other disempowered black men living in the South, the limits of southern black masculinity. In the bitterest of ironies, white southerners claimed the need to lynch black men because of their hypersexuality, which was also interpreted as "uncivilized manliness," but in turn they created a society that almost completely stripped black men of nearly every privilege of manhood.[76]

For the white men involved in this incident, their lives continued as usual. The society page of the local newspaper, the *Suwannee Democrat*, noted that Mack McCullers and Sheriff Henry went out of town on business within a week of Howard's murder.[77] Later that same month, Sheriff Henry began his reelection campaign. He argued that he had "in all my dealing with different classes of people, tried to be fair to them all, trying to serve the people with one thought at all time—to do unto them as I would have them do unto me."[78] Life went on as usual for the Goff family as well. That June they held a swimming party at the Suwannee Springs— the very place six months earlier where Phil Goff forced Willie James Howard to jump to his death—to celebrate the thirteenth birthday of Phil Goff Jr. Later, in September, Cynthia Goff was elected junior class treasurer at Suwannee County High School.[79] Four summers later, she married Homer Blankenship and began building a family of her own.

And what of Cynthia Goff's role in these events? She is at the center of this entire tragedy, but nothing is known about her exact actions, thoughts, and reactions to this affair. Nevertheless, her role in this drama is critical to the deconstruction of its meaning. Was she as much an innocent victim of the irrational sexual paranoia of the day, or did she intentionally breech the invisible boundary that she had been taught to observe between herself and African American males like Willie James Howard? At the turn of the century, Ida B. Wells, in her international campaign to shine light on the scourge of lynching that pervaded the American South, used her statistical research to blast the idea of the black male rapist, while at the same time drawing attention to the role that white females played in this continuing tragedy. Wells described black men as "poor blind Afro-American Sampsons who suffer themselves to be betrayed by white Delilahs." While southerners continued to perpetuate the image of southern white women as innocent victims of black male lust, in Wells's analysis it was white women who enticed black men to cross the deadly sexual color line, or who falsely accused them of doing so.[80]

In the situation with Willie James Howard, did Cynthia Goff play the role of temptress? She, just as much as Howard, would have been well versed in the racial etiquette of southern society. Lillian Smith, who spent much of her girlhood in neighboring Hamilton County and is author of the controversial 1944 novel *Strange Fruit*, which took up the subject of interracial relationships, described the "soul-splitting" lessons on race and gender handed down to her by her parents: "The mother who taught me what I know of tenderness and love and compassion taught me also the bleak rituals of keeping Negroes in their 'place.' The father who re-buked me for an air of superiority toward schoolmates from the mill and rounded out his rebuke by gravely reminding me that 'all men are broth-ers,' trained me in the steel-rigid decorums I must demand of every col-ored male."[81] Similarly, Virginia Durr, a white civil rights activist, testified to the messages she absorbed about her value as a young white woman growing up in Alabama: "the politicians would make speeches about pure white womanhood—and I believed it. I was pure white Southern woman-hood and Southern men had died for me and the Confederate flag was flying just to save me. I got to thinking I was pretty hot stuff, to have the war fought for me."[82]

Did Cynthia Goff maliciously flout the rules of her station and encour-age Willie James Howard's affections? Did she innocently, harmlessly, seek to interact with Howard by asking him about the lyrics of the song he sang? Was she devious enough to intentionally allow whatever was written on those sheets of paper to be discovered by her father? Did she take satisfaction in his death, or did she grieve for him? Did Goff detest her father's actions, taken on her behalf, or did she revel in the potent power of her pedestal, recognizing that she possessed something for which men would kill? The answers to these questions and others about Cynthia Goff's involvement and feelings may never be known, but there are numerous examples of incidents of this sort. In 1931, the false rape accusations of Victoria Price and Ruby Bates ruined—after nearly cost-ing—the lives of nine black youths, the "Scottsboro Boys," the youngest of whom were two thirteen-year-olds. In 1923, Fannie Taylor's lie about being beaten and raped by a black man resulted in the murder of dozens of blacks and the destruction of the entire black township of Rosewood, Florida. In 1955, the brutal lynching of fourteen-year-old Emmett Till for simply making what was deemed an inappropriate comment to a white woman became a national and international outrage and provided one of the many sparks that led to the breakthroughs of America's modern civil rights movement.[83]

Unfortunately, the lynching of a black boy in rural North Florida competed unsuccessfully for headlines with the exciting news from the battlefields of World War II. National attention focused on the atrocities overseas, making it easy to disregard the second-class treatment that African Americans faced on a daily basis. The same was true within the African American press; Howard's lynching seemed to pale in comparison with the fight for economic justice in the war industries, continued segregation in the armed forces, and attacks against black soldiers in uniform as they trained for and returned from war. The circumstances of Willie James Howard's lynching included none of the sensations that would have made his murder worthy of national headlines. The contested versions of his death pitted the words of three white men against that of one black man, which, in the 1940s, was not a dispute at all. There was no smoke from burning flesh or smoldering ashes. There was no indicting evidence or overwhelming public outcry. On the contrary, there was a conspiracy among the whites who controlled the mechanisms of justice in Suwannee County to suppress an investigation. Willie James was simply a boy who drowned in the depths of the Suwannee River while a powerless father, three hate-driven men, and the oaks stood quietly by. In the end, the surface of the Live Oak community remained as placid and unchanged as the river that carried Willie James Howard to his death, while the anger, fear, and sadness of the black community, deep and cold, flowed beneath.

*   *   *

"Lynchings," notes Jonathan Markovitz, "were intended to create collective memories of terror and white supremacy."[84] Moreover, events like the lynching of Willie James Howard often become the battlegrounds upon which hegemonic forces exercise their power to control both the contemporary narrative and the subsequent interpretation, or memory, of the incidents. Ever since the last moments of Howard's life unfolded on January 2, 1944, dueling sets of narratives have competed for legitimacy as the true version of events. Uncontested control over the pillars of society—courts, law enforcement officers, public offices, and the press—gave whites in Live Oak the ability to create and authorize the official records of such episodes. This was an old pattern, repeated time and time again throughout the South. The legal system routinely ignored the testimony of African Americans, giving it no weight or credibility. This is evidenced by the fact that James Howard lacked the power and the standing to independently present his account of the events that occurred at the banks of the Suwannee River that Sunday morning. Under threat of violence, he cosigned the affidavit submitted by Phil Goff, Seldon McCullers, and Reginald Scott, which described Willie James as jumping into the river on his own. That story contained elements that were nonsensical at best, but were accepted without question by those in power. Why would Willie James commit suicide if he was only being threatened with a whipping? During a period in American history when death was an acceptable punishment for a black male accused of the slightest offense against a white woman or girl, it is almost impossible to believe that he, upon realizing the gravity of his transgression, would have been unwilling to accept a whipping from his father for his misdeed or, even more implausibly, that he would have voluntarily jumped into a river and ended his life in order to avoid chastisement by his own father. And what of the location chosen to carry out the disciplinary session? Of the several wooded and secluded areas surrounding the already rural Live Oak, why did Goff, Scott, and McCullers feel the need to designate the banks of the Suwannee River to merely have the elder Howard "whip" his son? Feeling that they were justified in their actions, the party could just as easily carried out their wishes at the lumber company when they had both the father and son together. As easily as these explanations are dismissed, their utter incogitability redirects attention to the law enforcement officers who willingly and speedily accepted this version of events. Goff, McCullers, and Scott, with the cooperation of the sheriff, the chief of police, and other leading citizens, and the power of their standing in the Live Oak community, successfully insulated themselves from the legal ramifications of their acts.

What happened to James Howard—the attempt of whites in Live Oak to arrogate his voice in the official record of what happened to his son—represents an intentional use of the cultural weapons of dissemblance and denial by the white power structure to control perceptions of authenticity and credibility for the purposes of creating silence and erasure. This particular expression of white supremacy attempts to echo its power into history, extending its hegemonic control of public and private discourses into perpetuity. African Americans in the South, like many marginalized populations throughout time, have contended with representatives of white hegemonic structures and the ability they have to erase through intentional omission the perspective of outsiders, while simultaneously validating and preserving for posterity the authorized version of the truth. This is what the historian W. Fitzhugh Brundage has noted as the difference between what is "willful[ly] recalled" and "deliberately forgotten."[85]

The erasure is seldom complete, but it creates segregated discourses that coexist and compete through time for primacy, obscuring and blurring facts, and illegitimating truths. It is a psychic extension of the material contest embodied by Jim Crow policies that effectively curtailed and contained competition by African Americans for physical spaces, economic resources, social status, and political power, among other things. This was the situation faced by the Howards. Thwarted but not defeated, once safely outside of Suwannee County the Howards articulated what they witnessed leading up to their son's demise. Likewise, activist groups like the NAACP emptied their pens and raised their voices demanding an investigation and justice. Still, their eyewitness accounts and righteous outrage carried little weight, and would not overturn the account given by three white men.

At the same time, despite attempts to suppress discussion of the incident in the African American community, blacks kept these stories alive, sharing and retelling the tale in churches, in living rooms, in schools, on front porches, and in the fields. Published accounts from the most available sources—the instruments of public discourse in court records, official correspondence, and newspaper accounts—are tainted by this racial bias and, as a result, are only moderately reliable. These realities create a power struggle within the territory of memory for what is accepted as the authentic version of events. As in the case of the lynching of Willie James Howard and other such tragedies across the color line, historians reconstructing these events from fragmented, segregated pieces must rescue and integrate the remembrances and words of those contemporary but marginalized observers in formulating a more complete recollection that more closely approximates the truth.

In the years since Willie James Howard's death, the retelling and recycling of the events surrounding his lynching have resulted in an obfuscated narrative born to serve different purposes. This resulted in two interpretations that are notably incongruous, and the differences in remembrance in the communities—one black, the other white—are significant. In this second version of events, a private discourse crafted and maintained by blacks in Live Oak, Willie James Howard emerged as the unwitting victim, innocent of any significant racial transgression. Saying that Howard gave Goff the lyrics of a love song instead of a love letter brought Willie James safely back across the color line. He was thereby less responsible for foolishly penning his feelings for his white coworker. He becomes, in effect, blameless, while his murderers become more reprehensible for murdering a young boy for what seemed to be youthful indiscretion—at most, a trivial violation. The validity of this variation in the community's memory of the Howard incident, however, is significant for what it represents, as opposed to whether or not it can be substantiated. Willie James Howard emerges from this narrative of communal memory as a blameless and tragic victim of white brutality and inhumanity. The black community, replacing a psychic victory for the justice denied to them by their local criminal justice system, needed to reclaim his memory as the jovial, innocent boy his friends and family remembered him to be, not as the budding rapist closing in on his first victim who was stopped by a preemptive strike carried out by her chivalrous protectors. Barbie Zelizer, in reflecting on the experiences of Holocaust survivors, notes that collective memories "allow for the fabrication, rearrangement, elaboration, and omission of details about the past, often pushing aside accuracy and authenticity so as to accommodate broader issues of identity formation, power and authority, and political affiliation. Memories in this view become not only the simple act of recall but social, cultural, and political action at its broadest level."[86]

Perhaps as tragic as the lynching of Willie James Howard itself is the forced silence under which the community, especially those members of his family and the black community in Live Oak, suffered. Willie James's body was rapidly interred, along with any hope of justice. His parents vanished from the community. It was as if they had never lived at all, except in the memory of those who knew and loved them. Other scholars have noted a reluctance to speak about the Howard incident today.

"The reaction from the white community," Tammy Evans reflected, "was a rather bizarre mixture of denial and anger. These individuals unanimously dismissed the program as an utter fabrication. 'Nobody killed that boy,' one man told me. 'They scared him real good, but they didn't kill him.'" "Live Oak," Evans writes, "is after all, a product of the larger South; so if silence continues to dominate the town, it means that—like their predecessors more than fifty years ago—residents today are well versed in the rhetoric of southern silence and the particular ideology characteristic of it."[87]

Suppression of the Howard murder in 1944 was a dress rehearsal for the trial of Ruby McCollum in 1952. McCollum, an African American woman, shot Dr. Leroy Adams, a prominent white Live Oak physician and state senator-elect, after years of suffering physical and sexual abuse at his hands. The undeniable evidence of their affair took the form of a racially mixed child that she had already given birth to, along with the one she was carrying in her womb when she shot Adams. While the relationship between McCollum and Adams, along with innumerable forbidden interracial liaisons, existed in the shadows of the South, the bullets from McCollum's gun thrust not only her relationship but all the others like it into the spotlight. However, unlike in the case of Cynthia Goff, in which the mere suspicion of a black boy's attraction to a white girl proved enough to warrant his death at the hands of that girl's male protectors, Ruby McCollum would not, and perhaps could not, have her honor redeemed by her protectors, the men of her community. Black men, lynching proved, could not even fully protect themselves. In her own way, McCollum and other African American women who protested and fought back against their attackers and the institutions that supported them "reclaimed their bodies and their humanity by testifying about their assaults," and "fought for bodily integrity and personal dignity."[88]

Just as in the case of Willie James Howard, however, the power structures and the community at large in Live Oak moved to minimize and marginalize the matter. Doing so proved more difficult in this case. The dead body of Dr. Adams and the living body of his mixed-race daughter could not be concealed in the same way that the dead body of Willie James Howard had been. Also, unlike in the Howard case, the attention of the national media was intense and undeniable. Still, the city fathers removed

McCollum from the public eye, suppressed her ability to speak for herself—as Tammy Evans thoroughly documents—and quickly disposed of
McCollum between the wheels of justice to a speedy trial, a quick conviction, and long imprisonment in the Florida State Hospital for the Insane
at Chattahoochee. Tammy Evans rightfully notes that "acts of silence in
the South . . . often work to negate the stories of minority groups, such
as African-Americans and women, and by doing so, foreground stories
steeped in southern myths that have historically worked to advance individuals in positions of power. . . . If silence is a unique way of 'doing
things with words' in the South, it is also a powerful force that masks
physical violence or mental trauma suffered by individuals who challenge
these southern myth-fictions." There was also a silencing that accompanied lynchings. "Lynching," notes the historian Bruce E. Baker,

> was a self-effacing event. First it silenced an alleged offender; then
> the anonymity of the mob and the silence of local public discourse
> muted any attempt to name the lynching as a crime and to exact
> justice. The effect was amplified when . . . all the lynching victims
> were black, all the mobs were white, and whites exercised nearly
> complete control over public discourse for several decades after the
> lynching.[89]

These two events—the lynching of Willie James Howard and the ordeal
of Ruby McCollum—in Suwannee County vividly illustrate the hypocrisy
surrounding race and sex in the segregated South during the twentieth
century. They each represented echoes of racial dynamics that had been
established in colonial America during the seventeenth century that, on
the one hand, continued the criminalization and emasculation of black
manhood, and, on the other, sullied and devalued black womanhood. In
their position at the apex of power and privilege in southern society, white
men enjoyed sexual access to the black female body but brutally attacked
black men—or in the case of Howard, a boy—who dared to approach the
"dead line" between white women and black men. Breeching that line,
from one side or the other, virtually guaranteed the erasure—perhaps
physically, perhaps in memory, perhaps both—of the perpetrators. In the
void is silence.

There have been efforts in recent years, however, to penetrate the silence. Aired nationally in 2001 on PBS, the documentary film *Freedom Never Dies: The Legacy of Harry T. Moore*, in recounting the life and works of Moore, covered in great detail the lynching of Willie James Howard and sent ripples through Live Oak.[90] Since that time, Douglass Udell, the director of a local funeral home and a onetime county commissioner, has taken a great deal of interest in Howard's story. On January 16, 2005, sixty-one years after Howard's death, he held a program at Springfield Missionary Baptist Church, at which I was invited to be the keynote speaker.[91] It was the first time that I had spoken publicly about my research, and I remember the mournful feeling in the church that afternoon. The audience included older residents, young people, and some relatives of the Howard and Figgs families. The sole white person in the congregation was a reporter from the local paper. I could hear open sobbing in the room as I read James Howard's affidavit in which he recounted his son's last words. Afterward, Udell led a motorcade from the church to the Eastside Cemetery, where generations of my own family members are buried. That day Udell installed a headstone near the one that had been laid near the original marker where Willie James Howard was buried. It read:

Willie J. Howard
BORN—7-13-28
DIED—1-2-44
Murdered by 3 racist [*sic*]

A great unburdening took place that day. James Howard, at long last, was able to have his say. Willie James was publicly and properly mourned. His murderers were named. African Americans in Live Oak were able to shift the burden of Willie James's lynching from the shadows of memories into an open and public forum. He had not been a specter of their imaginations.

The reaction of the local newspaper, however, illustrates that the battle for communal memory in the case was not over. Despite the substantial historical record that had been accumulated and published in scholarly works of history and film, the obfuscation continued. Summarizing the ceremony for her readers, a reporter for the *Suwannee Democrat* surmised that "the circumstance around Howard's death appear clear to some, to others it's not." Despite her skepticism, the fact that the event was covered at all, and then reported on the front page of the newspaper, represented a great leap forward. Young people in Live Oak, of all races and creeds, would now know the name and the story of Willie James Howard and the men who lynched him.

STILL AT IT

The Lynching of Jesse James Payne, Madison County, 1945

On January 2, 1945, Millard F. Caldwell was sworn in as the governor of Florida. He could not have imagined then that the lynching of a black sharecropper in Madison County would haunt him for practically his entire term as governor. The murder of Jesse James Payne on October 11, 1945, resulted from an argument with his landlord. Payne was kidnapped, hunted, shot, and accused of attempting to rape a five-year-old girl. His only crime may have been attempting to stand up for himself at a time when that could cost a black man his life. The truth will never be known because Payne was taken from jail and killed before he could be brought to trial.

Even after death, however, Payne would not simply disappear. As reports of his lynching spread around the state and nation, the calls for justice became impossible to ignore as citizens demanded action from state and federal officials. When their investigations proved fruitless, the demands for action transformed into sharp criticism, directed mainly at Millard Caldwell. The tenor of that castigation gave birth to a libel suit that lasted for three years. In the end, Caldwell was victorious, but it came at a high price for him and the reputation of the state of Florida.

Caldwell, a man of traditional southern values, was caught off guard by a normally complacent white public that had begun to question the way black citizens were treated. A storm of letters flooded his office from around the country and as far away as Canada. Those critical of Caldwell often used language and rhetoric that revealed how the experience of World War II had expanded their understanding of democracy's meaning and value as the United States sought to secure its footing as a leader in global politics. America had helped win the war, but it now needed to win the peace by combating the influence of Communism around the globe. Payne's lynching and other instances of racial violence ran the risk of diminishing America's authority with the international community.

*   *   *

Madison County was established on December 26, 1827, and later, in 1838, Madison, the county seat, was founded, both named in honor of the country's fourth president, James Madison. As true of other areas in north-central Florida, white migrants from Georgia and South Carolina and their enslaved workers settled Madison County. By the mid-nineteenth century, it had become one of the most populated counties in Florida, with a population of 2,802 whites and 2,688 enslaved blacks in 1850. By 1860, the county's population increased to 7,779, of which 4,249 were enslaved. Their labor fueled the local economy, primarily through the cultivation of Sea Island cotton and sugarcane.[1]

The conclusion of the Civil War and the defeat of the Confederacy brought about drastic social change to Madison County. After emancipation, freedpeople in the area exercised their new status by establishing schools and participating in local politics, including organizing local branches of the Lincoln Brotherhood and the Union League, activities that local whites found objectionable and actively resisted.[2] Additionally, African Americans in the area were able to enjoy the fruits of political participation. Between 1867 and 1879, blacks in Madison County were elected to several positions, with five black men serving on the county commission and nine as justices of the peace. Seven black men served as councilmen in Madison during the same period. Local blacks also sent representatives to the Florida House of Representatives and Senate.[3] This success, however, did not come without a price. Racial violence was an unfortunate reality of the postbellum political struggle. In 1871, the sheriff of Madison County stated that of thirty-seven unsolved murders for the year, thirty-four of the victims were black. Incidents like these eventually eroded the gains blacks made after the war, and Democratic victories in state and local government after 1876 began the process of returning political control to southern whites. The passage of a new state constitution in 1885 signaled the death knell of civil rights for blacks in the state, and race relations continued to deteriorate over the decades.[4]

Through much of the late nineteenth and early twentieth centuries, blacks comprised a significant portion of Madison County's population. In 1885, they outnumbered whites, 8,432 to 6,073. By 1940, whites outnumbered blacks only slightly, 8,460 to 7,730.[5] Regardless of race, the majority of people in Madison County derived their livelihood from the red clay beneath them. Many were able to capitalize on the plentiful yellow pine that grew in the area, which could be cut for wood or tapped for turpentine. Lumber magnate George Franklin Drew made his home and a small fortune in Madison County, operating the largest sawmill in the state in the town of Ellaville, located on the western bank of the Suwannee River. Notably, after being elected governor in 1876, Drew established the state's convict leasing system, leasing prisoners to work on farms and in turpentine camps around the state.[6]

Over time, the county's economy continued to thrive on the production of cotton and the black labor that made it possible. The majority of blacks worked as paid laborers, both on and off the farm. As the devastation of the boll weevil reached Florida in the late 1910s, local farmers began to diversify their crops in attempts to fortify the faltering economy. As the cotton economy faded, Madison County farmers turned to tobacco. The first crops of shade tobacco were harvested in 1907, and subsequently the Florida Sumatra Leaf Tobacco Company established its presence in the area. Others followed its lead; the Friedman-Goldberg Leaf Tobacco Company came to Madison in 1920, and shortly thereafter, the Tampa Star Cigar Company established a cigar factory.[7]

As in other areas of the South, segregation defined nearly every arena of black life in Madison County. Not only did it relegate blacks to low-paying, menial jobs, but it also determined the location of their homes, the quality of their schools, and even when they had to go home. Black residents remember that a bell rang downtown each evening notifying them that it was time for them to return to their neighborhoods.[8] But within those communities they called home, blacks created havens of security and self-affirmation. Some of the earliest institutions in Madison's black community were churches. Damascus Baptist Church, one of the county's oldest black churches, was founded shortly after the Civil War, as was the New Zion Baptist Church in Greenville.[9]

Despite their progress, blacks in Madison County remained vulnerable to the white power structure and were routinely deprived of protection under the law and their right to due process. In addition to the threat of vigilante violence, law enforcement officers and the judicial system worked against black residents; without the power to vote, they could do little to change the situation. One resident recalled that her father, a sharecropper, spent six months in jail for simply disagreeing with the landowner.[10] In all, there were some fifteen lynchings in Madison County between 1894 and 1936. All of the victims were black men.[11]

*   *   *

Jesse James Payne was born in 1918 to William and Lucy Payne, the third of six children—two girls and four boys.[12] Those who knew him describe Payne as a man of average height and medium build and distinguished by his jet-black skin. During his early life, he traveled along the eastern seaboard—sometimes with his family, sometimes alone—laboring as a

FIGURE 5.1. Jesse James Payne was lynched on October 11, 1945, in Madison County, Florida, after being falsely accused of attempting to rape a five-year-old white girl. Courtesy of the Payne family.

seasonal migrant worker. Payne lived in Fort Lauderdale for one year, and then moved on to Belle Glade, then out of the state to Richmond, Virginia, and on to Cambridge, Maryland, where he worked for the Phillips Canning Company. In late 1943, he returned to Virginia, this time settling briefly in Norfolk. During his many migrations, Payne had a few brushes with the law, once serving time in a county work camp for possessing a firearm.[13]

Sometime late in 1944, Jesse Payne returned to Madison County, where his life took on some normalcy when he married Lillie Mae Wiley, a native of neighboring Jefferson County, and she gave birth to their child, a baby girl, in the spring of 1945.[14] To support his family, Payne worked on the farm of Willard Hambrey. From there, in December 1944 he began working with Daniel Levy Goodman, a white farmer in Greenville, as a sharecropper. As was customary, Payne cultivated a total of twenty-seven acres of Goodman's land, growing tobacco, cotton, peanuts, watermelons, corn, and okra, the proceeds of which he split with Goodman, minus any expenses. As a part of the deal, Goodman provided a home on the property in which Payne and his wife and child; his widowed mother, Lucy Ann; and his sister, Lucy Mae Anderson, and her husband, Edwin, lived. To help him maintain his large crop, Payne hired Dallas Grant, John Carlen, and Lonnie Livingston to work alongside him.[15]

The summer of 1945, like so many before it in Madison County, marked the beginning of the tobacco-harvesting season. Payne and his partners had the arduous task of "cropping" the leaves, hanging them in the barns, and using fire to cure them in preparation for sale. The process was time-consuming and labor intensive, but the rewards of the crop could not be reaped soon enough for Payne. That summer he suffered the hardships of the sharecropping cycle: living on credit until the bounty and profit of the crop could be cashed in. His family's needs were acute, especially with a wife, a new baby, and his mother at home to feed and clothe. He had already extended his account with the local merchant with whom he normally did business. In addition, Payne needed cash to pay the hands he had hired to help bring in the crop.[16]

The combination of these harsh realities led Payne to approach Goodman for an advance on his share of the crop on June 23. An unsympathetic Goodman, however, refused, and an argument ensued between the two men. Frustrated, Payne threatened to sell his crop to the government and warned that he might tell government officials that Goodman had not only overplanted his tobacco allotment but also had planted a crop for Sheriff Lonnie T. Davis, Goodman's brother-in-law. This would have endangered Goodman's government subsidy payment. The conversation, while heated, did not come to blows, but the confrontation marked the beginning of the tragic events to come.[17]

By the next week, the showdown between Goodman and Payne seemed to have blown over. Breaking from a hard week at work, on Sunday, July 1, Payne and his family visited Lonnie and Josephine Livingston on the farm of Arch Goodman, Daniel's father. While at the Livingston residence, Daniel Goodman and his two sons, Robert and David, came to the Livingston residence seeking Payne. When he appeared, the men demanded that he come with them. When the group protested, Goodman pulled a gun on Payne and forced him to the car. Once inside the car, the four men sped away.[18]

Goodman had not taken kindly to being threatened by his black tenant the week before. Jesse James Payne had forgotten his place and needed to be taught a lesson. The car eventually stopped in a secluded wooded area in the swamps. Goodman forced Payne out of the car and onto his knees. "I am going to teach you how to put the government on my land," Goodman told Payne. He aimed his gun at Payne, and there was a loud snap. The gun misfired. Seeing an opportunity, Payne sprinted into the swamp, fleeing for his life.[19]

Thus began the manhunt for Jesse James Payne. Inevitably, members of his family became targets for the whites who were desperate to capture him. During their five-mile walk home after Payne's kidnapping from the Livingston home, Lucy Ann and Lillie spotted a mob of whites and wisely took precautions to avoid the group. This was only a forecast of the encounters they would have with whites determined to find and punish Jesse Payne. While Payne managed to elude his captors, whites began to threaten his family members with beatings, attempting to intimidate them into revealing information about Payne's whereabouts. The day following Payne's abduction, Sheriff Davis forced Lucy Ann Payne, clad only in her nightgown and without shoes, to ride along as he searched for her son. Davis, a tall and intimidating man serving his third term in office and with a reputation for being hard on blacks, could not be refused. He drove her to the home of John "Bubba" Perry, a relative of the Paynes, in Monticello, the county seat of Jefferson County. Once there, Davis demanded to know if Perry had seen Payne. Perry said that he had not. After concluding his search, Davis took Lucy Ann Payne back home and gave her strict instructions to contact him if Jesse returned.[20] Another officer of the law, state trooper Simeon H. "Simmie" Moore, aware of the high likelihood of violence, began his own search for Jesse Payne. He also warned members of the Payne family to keep a low profile, lest they end up as targets of violence.[21]

The next day Sheriff Davis prevented Lucy Ann, Lillie, and the baby from boarding the bus from Madison to Monticello at 2:00 p.m. Two hours later, he returned and allowed them to board the bus with assurances that they were only going to neighboring Monticello to visit relatives. In Monticello, however, the women learned that they were not the only members of the family being harassed by law enforcement officers. The police had arrested two of Payne's relatives, Susie and John Perry, and jailed them. During the process, one of the officers hit Susie Perry in the arm and seriously injured her. John Perry was later released on $1,000 bond.[22] According to great-nieces of Lucy Mae Anderson, their aunt later recounted horrific stories of being held with a shotgun to her head, then being tied to a buckboard and beaten by captors who wanted to know her brother's whereabouts. She claimed that her mother, Lucy Ann, had been subjected to similar treatment.[23]

During this time, word of the conflict between Goodman and Payne spread through the white community. Local white men gathered at a watering hole, Shorty Jones's bar, to learn more about the incident. Before long, a posse of about fifty men, many armed and with their hound dogs in tow, met at Shorty's. Goodman, as the ringleader, focused the frenzy of the group. No matter who caught him, Goodman pronounced, Jesse James Payne would never go to trial—the black man, he now claimed, had attempted to rape his five-year-old daughter, Lavone. To achieve his aim of eliminating Payne as a threat, Goodman cleverly invoked a classic southern justification for murder of a black man that would quickly inspire the bloodlust of the community and rally white men to his side. As the group began to discuss finding and killing Payne, some, put off by the idea of taking the law into their own hands, declined to participate. All the while, Sheriff Davis sat and listened as his brother-in-law provoked the crowd.[24]

While the mob plotted to find him, Payne emerged from his hideout in the swamp shortly after sunset on July 3, at the home of his cousin Bubba Perry in Monticello. Scared, hungry, and dressed in rags, Payne begged Perry for money, food, and a change of clothes. Perry let him know that Sheriff Davis had already been there looking for him. Eager to send Payne on his way, Perry gave him money. When Payne repeated his request for food, Perry told him that he did not have time. Payne left but on his way out, desperate for nourishment, he burst a watermelon in the far end of the field and ate from it.[25]

The watermelon proved to be one of Payne's last meals as a free man. On the afternoon of Independence Day, Payne encountered the posse that had been pursuing him. They spotted him and ordered him to stop. In the distance ahead of him, Payne saw a group of men working on the state road. Remembering Goodman's prior attempt to take his life, Payne ran toward the workmen, hoping they would protect him from his pursuers. As he began to run, the sound of gunfire cracked the air. Payne fell to the ground, shot in the arm and shoulder. The mob had their man.[26]

After his violent capture, the officers who were with the posse took Payne into custody and transported him to the Jefferson County jail in Monticello. A crowd of about fifty men, presumably the same group that had pursued Payne, surrounded the jail. It was evident that the event flared the passions of the community, placing Payne's life in danger. Then Officer Moore received orders from his superiors to transport Payne to the Florida State Prison at Raiford for his protection. As Moore left the jail with Payne, some members of the crowd demanded to know where he was taking Payne. He assured them that he was only taking him to the doctor to have his gunshot wounds treated. They would be back, he told them. Moore's deception was strategic; if they knew Payne would be beyond their grasp, they might have attempted to take him from Moore's custody.[27]

Within days after Payne's capture and removal from Madison County, word spread of the accusations against him. Although the entire situation—the kidnapping, the attempted murder, the posse chase, and the shooting—was the result of a conflict between Goodman and Payne, Daniel Goodman alleged publicly that Payne attempted to rape his five-year-old daughter, Lavone, and had infected her with a venereal disease. That was why, Goodman claimed, he had attempted to kill Payne, and why

Payne needed to be brought to justice. In reality, Goodman knew that this type of accusation against a black man would surely generate the community support needed to justify Payne's murder.[28]

After Goodman accused Payne of attempted rape, the local court system took action. On July 12, a little more than a week after he had been captured, based on the sworn testimony of James Davis, uncle of the alleged victim and brother of the sheriff, Judge J. R. Kelley issued a warrant for Payne's arrest for the attempted rape of a minor under the age of ten. O. O. Edwards, assistant attorney general for the state of Florida, traveled to Raiford to take a statement from Payne. Edwards began the session by informing Payne of his rights, although he failed to mention that Payne had the right to an attorney. During the questioning, Edwards asked Payne about his relationship with Lavone Goodman. Payne denied knowledge of any crime committed against the girl. When asked about his contact with her, he recalled that the child played around the barns where he worked. She liked to climb the fences and push her baby stroller, and sometimes she played with his guitar. He noted that her mother always kept a close eye on the child and that they had never been alone. While Edwards's primary interest in Payne was as a criminal suspect, Payne made him aware of the crimes committed against him. He informed Edwards of Goodman's actions, the argument between them, the kidnapping, and Goodman's attempt to kill him. Despite Payne's accusations, Edwards did nothing to hold Goodman accountable for his actions.[29]

After his statement was taken, Payne remained at the Raiford prison for three months recuperating from his wounds and awaiting his day in court. On October 9, Deputy Sheriff Alexander Wade, of Madison County, traveled to Raiford to retrieve Payne and return him to Madison to face the grand jury. Still worried about more attempts on Payne's life, Wade later admitted that he traveled a roundabout route in case he had been followed. The next day in court, Payne pleaded not guilty to the charges against him, but the grand jury indicted him nonetheless. The court set his trial date for October 16. While it was still early in the case, there were indicators that the trial would be a "legal lynching," in which the primary objective of the jury was to convict those who were accused and sentence them to death, as had been the case with Cellos Harrison. In a glaring violation of due process, James Davis, the uncle of the alleged victim, served as a member of the grand jury that brought charges against Payne.[30]

After the arraignment, instead of returning Payne to Raiford for safe-keeping, Sheriff Davis held him in the Madison jail. This proved to be a fatal mistake. On the evening of October 10, Deputy Wade made the last inspection of the jail at about 6:30 p.m., at which time he turned the inside lights off and the outside lights on before he left for the night. It was general practice to leave the jailhouse unguarded; the sheriff's home was attached to the jailhouse, so it was assumed that his presence would deter any attempts to break into the facility or escape from it. From the outside, the jail seemed nearly impenetrable. A high, spiked metal fence with a locked gate surrounded the perimeter of the jail, which was constructed of brick and cement. Within the jail, two locked metal doors secured the entrance to the cells, to which only the sheriff held the keys. The cellblock, with separate cells for black and white prisoners, usually remained unlocked.[31]

In the jail that night, the inmates talked among themselves until about 10:00 p.m. Sometime later, prisoners in the white cellblock awoke to muffled sounds coming from the other side of the jail where the black prisoners were held. In the darkness, they were unable to see anything; after the noise stopped, they went back to sleep. When they awoke the next morning, they discovered that Payne was gone.[32] At about the same time, seven miles out of town, a truck driver spotted the buckshot-riddled body of Jesse James Payne on the side of the road.[33]

*   *   *

The residents of Madison County awakened the next morning to news of Payne's lynching. It was a remarkable break from traditional forms of extralegal violence, conspicuously absent of ceremony and spectacle. The killers had acted in seemingly complete secrecy. While whites in the area had turned out by the dozens to participate in the manhunt for Payne, and again stalked outside the Monticello jail once word of his capture spread, the persons who ultimately killed him did so with quiet and deadly efficiency. They had entered the jail and kidnapped the victim without waking the other prisoners or the sheriff who slept next door.

After the discovery of Payne's body, the authorities assembled a coroner's jury to investigate the events. The members viewed the deceased's body that morning and met again two days later, on October 13. With no clues pointing to the culprits of the crime, the jury determined that Payne met his death "at the hands of unknown person or persons." While the citizens of Madison County were satisfied that justice had been served, the public reaction to the verdict indicated that many were unwilling to accept what they viewed as a "whitewash" of the situation.[34]

As news of the jury's verdict spread, appeals for investigation poured into Governor Caldwell's office from around the country. The lynching of Jesse James Payne was the first, and subsequently the only, such event recorded in the United States that year. The reaction of the Florida press reflected an increasing impatience with such horrendous crimes. The day after Payne's murder, the *Jacksonville Journal* ran an editorial entitled "Judge Lynch Again," claiming "that sinister figure whom conscientious Southerners are striving to banish from their realm stalked through the little Florida town of Madison on Wednesday night." The editors accused Payne's lynchers of having "no concern for the South's reputation as a haven of law and order. Their acts are an injury to all their fellow citizens, as well as an outright crime in themselves."[35] The *Miami Herald* struck a similar note, calling Payne's lynching a disgrace to the state of Florida. Further, the paper placed the onus on Governor Caldwell to investigate the crime and prosecute those responsible. "Governor Caldwell," it claimed, "owes it to this nation, to this state, to the honor of the White people of Florida to bring the lynchers to justice. . . . Nothing should deter him from pursuing a complete and exhaustive search to assure final vindication of the law and its enforcement."[36] The *St. Petersburg Independent* also expressed its opposition to mob violence. "The mob doesn't think at all and thus denies the human intelligence which alone differentiates man from the dumb beasts of the field," it argued. "That is why thoughtful lawyers have always classified the mob as the deadliest enemy of society—or government by law rather than by the caprice of arbitrary men."[37]

Other state newspapers joined the chorus of criticism that arose after the Payne lynching; nearly all condemned the actions of the mob in strong language that highlighted the inconsistencies between the lynching and the wartime rhetoric about democratic values. Under the headline "Fair Trials for Nazis, Japs But Lynch Law in Florida," a *St. Petersburg Times* editorial condemned the Madison lynchers as traitors to America's cause. "The lynching at Madison," the editorial fumed, "is an example of how to flout the very ideals for which our army has been fighting."[38] The *Lakeland Ledger* expressed concern over the perception that "law and order" had failed in Florida, and frowned on the lawlessness represented by the incident. It claimed that

> no person who commits such a crime should go unpunished, but before the penalty is meted out the evidence should be heard by a jury in a duly established court of law, and if the prisoner is found guilty, the penalty should be inflicted by the state, not by a mob. In this American democracy there is a legal provision that every individual shall be presumed innocent until proved guilty in a court of law. A group of angry men on a mission of murder cannot calmly weigh evidence. They are not even seeking evidence. They are seeking vengeance.[39]

In light of the growing fervor, Florida's public officials dreaded the increasing public scrutiny and began to offer Governor Caldwell advice on dealing with the situation. W. T. Davis, a Florida senator, voiced support for local government in Madison County. In response to the criticism of Sheriff Davis, he sent a telegram to Caldwell in late October to discourage him from calling for a special grand jury to investigate the incident and to voice support of Sheriff Davis. "[The] [g]rand jury is made up of as good and honorable men as can be found in the county," he told Caldwell. "I believe that the sheriff is being done a gross injustice."[40] Southerners outside of Florida, however, wrote Governor Caldwell to express grave concern about the implications of Payne's lynching. Hatton W. Sumners, chair of the judiciary committee for the U.S. House of Representatives, was on the front lines of the southern battle against the passage of antilynching legislation. He was worried that this incident and others like it would be used to support the drive for the passage of such legislation. Sumners reminded Caldwell that the defense against a federal antilynching law was predicated on the South's ability to protect and deal fairly with its black citizens. "It is this sort of thing," he wrote to Caldwell, "which makes it so difficult for those of us who have the responsibility of trying to protect the South against those who are actuated by sectional prejudice as well as by those who feel no respect for the sovereignty of the states in our scheme of government." Sumners concluded his letter with a call for positive action on Caldwell's part. He warned him that the incident was "not a mere question of this man who was killed, or the sheriff, but it is a question as to whether or not the southern states will demonstrate a capacity to handle their problems of this sort without federal interference."[41] Caldwell also received correspondence from Representative Sam Hobbs, of Alabama, requesting more information on the case so that he could convince "others who do not have such implicit faith in the Governor's conclusions." Hobbs, like Sumners, was preparing to circle the wagons in anticipation that the Payne lynching would be used to argue for the passage of a federal antilynching bill.[42]

Civil rights leaders in Florida also took the opportunity to demand positive action from the governor. Edward Davis, president of the Marion County NAACP, questioned why whites had been so unwilling to grant Payne a fair trial. Framing his appeal in the rhetoric of wartime sacrifice, he warned the governor of the damage this incident would have on race relations in the state. "We as Negroes feel that this is, to say the least, a *VERY STRANGE WELCOME* to the hundreds of thousands of Negro soldiers returning to this country after giving their best to help save our country and make the world safe for Freedom, *Democracy*, and *Justice*."[43] As with other instances of lynching during the decade, Harry T. Moore, president of the Florida State Conference of the NAACP, also expressed his concern over Payne's murder to Governor Caldwell. "This is the third time within the space of twenty-seven months that Florida's record has been marred by the brutal lynching of its helpless Negro citizens," Moore informed Caldwell. Furthermore, he continued, "the lynching of Payne again reveals that type of carelessness that seems to be so prevalent among our local officers when the lives of Negro prisoners are at stake." Both Davis and Moore encouraged Caldwell to take a firm stand on the matter.[44]

In addition to encouraging an investigation, Moore also advocated on behalf of Payne's relatives, who, fearing for their own safety, had moved to Sanford, just outside of Orlando. Moore recorded the statements of Payne's wife, mother, and sister about Payne's kidnapping by Goodman, as well as the nature of the conflict between the two men. The women told of the abuse they and their family members experienced before leaving Madison County. Moore forwarded their affidavits to Governor Caldwell in the hope that he would intervene. In response, Governor Caldwell encouraged the Payne family to return to Madison County and present their information before the grand jury investigating the murder. Moore, however, warned Governor Caldwell that his request might expose the family to danger, making them potential targets of violence. "You will note that some of Payne's relatives were threatened and handled roughly by local officers and members of the mob when this trouble started last July," he reminded Caldwell. "Those of us who have never been in the hands of such a mob cannot fully appreciate what an experience it is."[45]

After news broke that the coroner's jury was unable to determine who was responsible for Payne's death, the media focused their attention on Sheriff Davis for his negligence in protecting his prisoner and criticized his failures in strong language. The *Tampa Morning Tribune* spoke frankly on the matter: "When, especially in that section of the state, a Negro is charged with attacking a white woman or girl, there is always danger of a lynching. Sheriff Davis knew this full well [and] should be immediately suspended by the Governor for obvious negligence and failure to do his official duty."[46] Sheriff Davis's pronouncements on the situation did not help his image. At the inquest a tearful Davis acknowledged that the incident had "put me on the spot," but he denied claims that he was responsible or had cooperated with the murderers. "If I had wanted to kill him," Davis continued in his defense, "I could have shot him in jail. I wouldn't have had to engineer a deal like this."[47] This statement did little to inspire confidence in his commitment to law and order, which had already come into question a few months before Payne's murder. A Madison County resident wrote to the governor complaining that Sheriff Davis allowed gambling to go on unchecked in the area. In turn, Governor Caldwell wrote to Sheriff Davis asking him to reply to the allegations. The state beverage department also expressed its frustration in working with Sheriff Davis in its attempts to prosecute bootleggers, with the department's director accusing Sheriff Davis of severely hindering his office's prosecutions in Madison County.[48]

While many of the state's major newspapers expressed the view that Sheriff Davis bore the most blame for the lynching, they increasingly criticized Governor Caldwell for his reluctance to suspend the sheriff for his failure to protect his prisoner. It was up to the governor, they argued, to send the message that neither professional negligence on the part of law enforcement officers nor mob violence would be tolerated. Only firm and direct action, they argued, could restore Florida's damaged reputation. Governor Caldwell should "demonstrate his devotion to the concept of government by law by immediately suspending and publicly reprimanding Sheriff Davis for gross negligence of duty," one paper proclaimed.[49]

The timing of Payne's lynching created a tragic irony. "With the Payne lynching coinciding with the preparations for the Nuremberg trials," one historian noted, "Americans read about the atrocities of Nazi Germany and the Madison affair on the same pages of the same newspapers."[50] It was difficult to ignore the striking inconsistency and hypocrisy of America's claim of democratic supremacy that this parallel presented. It was an ideological chasm that Communist organizers especially used to their advantage. The *New York Daily Worker*, the outlet of the Communist Party of America, spoke plainly in its assessment: "It is frequently asserted that the difference between Hitler's wholesale lynchings in Europe and such fascist manifestations as that at Madison is that Hitler's crimes were engineered and sanctioned by the state." "We know of no way whereby a state may disassociate itself from such fascist acts except by condemning them openly and seeking out the guilty," it claimed. "Florida has done neither."[51] The Jacksonville branch of the Congress of Industrial Organizations (CIO) echoed the sentiment and called on the FBI to "help end the Hitlerite lynching[s] that have cropped up too often in our great state."[52]

Caldwell seemed more annoyed than concerned by the Payne lynching. A transplant from Tennessee, Caldwell began his political career in his new home of Santa Rosa County, Florida, serving as city attorney in 1926, in the Florida House of Representatives in 1929, and in the U.S. Congress in 1933. While in Congress, Caldwell voted against antilynching legislation. When he became governor in 1945, Caldwell planned to focus his administrative energies on promoting the state of Florida as an attractive place to live and work in postwar America. Lynching, however, did little to bolster Florida's image as an American paradise. Caldwell's handling of Payne's lynching reflected his failure to appreciate the enormity of the situation. The *Orlando Reporter-Star* quoted him as saying that Payne's lynching was "just one of those things." Despite his attempts to downplay the incident, the extensive press coverage and protest letters became nearly impossible to evade. In an effort to address the criticism and satisfy the calls for justice, Governor Caldwell requested that Florida attorney general J. Tom Watson go to Madison and investigate the circumstances surrounding the kidnapping and murder.[53]

Watson arrived in Madison on October 19. Once there, he interviewed Sheriff Davis to learn more about the incident and ascertain how the kidnappers had obtained Payne from the jail. After inspecting the jail with the sheriff, Watson found no indication that the kidnappers broke into the jail. "On the contrary," he reported to Caldwell, "the evidence all pointed to the fact that [Payne] had been removed by the use of keys used to unlock a gate to the jail yard and to unlock two doors to the jail . . . one outer and one inside."[54] Based on the information he gathered, Watson recommended the temporary suspension of Sheriff Davis. He also reported to the governor problems with the grand jury. The jury that had been called up for that term of court was the same jury conducting the investigation. That meant that the group of people who indicted Payne were also responsible for investigating the circumstances of his death. Furthermore, James Davis, uncle of the alleged victim and brother of the sheriff, sat as a member of that body. The revelations forced Caldwell's hand; he ordered that a new grand jury be impaneled and banned Sheriff Davis from participating in the investigation any further.[55]

Following Watson's recommendation, Caldwell called Judge R. H. Rowe, of Madison County, and requested a new grand jury to investigate Sheriff Davis for negligence and to attempt to locate Payne's murderers. Meeting again on October 27, the specially impaneled grand jury predictably found that Sheriff Davis was not negligent in executing his duties as sheriff. Further, they were unable to identify Payne's murderers. In concluding their work, the jury sarcastically requested that Governor Caldwell "be extended the thanks of this Body for his splendid cooperation in assisting the Grand Jury in its efforts."[56]

*　*　*

The verdict confirmed what many people across the state and nation already believed: Payne's murderers would not be brought to justice. Criticism of Governor Caldwell and Sheriff Davis reverberated through the press. One paper characterized the situation as a "whitewash." "The Grand Jury had handed the whitewash brush to Governor Caldwell," it posited, sarcastically. "Will he too use it?"[57] Disturbed by the lack of action on the part of local officials, the International Labor Defense and the Southern Negro Youth Congress joined together to offer a reward of $1,000 for any information leading to the arrest, prosecution, and conviction of anyone involved in the Payne lynching.[58]

In time, Caldwell's administration began to crack under the pressure to seek justice in the Payne affair. Apparently displeased with the course of events in Madison, Attorney General J. Tom Watson wrote to the governor about his concerns. A few weeks after he submitted his report to the governor, it became clear that Caldwell was not following his recommendations. Watson complained to Caldwell about not being kept abreast of the governor's handling of the case. The developing rift between Caldwell and Watson eventually made its way into the paper and fueled the impression that the governor was not doing everything in his power to correct the situation.[59]

Caldwell also requested that William Gasque work among the people of the community in an attempt to gather information. In a report dated November 7, Gasque delivered his findings to Caldwell. Based on his interactions with the residents, Gasque found that "95% of the people were glad the lynching took place." Despite the seemingly overwhelming support for Payne's execution, Gasque did happen upon one cooperative witness. N. T. Langston, a local farmer, told Gasque what he knew about the incident because he had been present at Shorty Jones's bar on July 4 when Goodman was organizing other whites to go out and search for Payne. Langston planned to participate until the conversation turned to killing Payne. While he declined to participate, Langston told Gasque that Sheriff Davis had witnessed the entire discussion. Both Gasque and Langston testified to these facts before the special grand jury, but the jury remained unswayed.[60]

While revealing little new information, Gasque's investigation, like that of Watson's, did not reflect well on Sheriff Davis. When inquiring about the security of the jail, Gasque discovered that Sheriff Davis kept the keys to the jail either in a box on the floorboard of his unlocked car or on a nail in his kitchen, a fact that was common knowledge in the area. Later, when confronted by Gasque about his presence at Shorty Jones's bar while the posse was meeting, Sheriff Davis would neither confirm nor deny the accusation. In concluding his report, Gasque advised the governor that while he generally believed Sheriff Davis to be "ignorant," he was not convinced that his negligence was malicious. Even if he was involved, Gasque continued, "no Grand Jury you might be able to get would indict or make any presentments."[61] That plainspoken truth encapsulated one of the main reasons lynchers throughout Florida, as well as throughout the South, were able to go undeterred for as long as they did. Regardless of the cause and form of extralegal violence, this familiar pattern of community sanction via silence and inaction could be found in nearly every case. Law enforcement officers—whether a party to the plot or not—would not take sufficient action to protect the accused or investigate the subsequent murder. Likewise, members of the local community were silent, tacitly endorsing the lynchers and their deeds. Any effort by state and federal officials to act against lynchers would be negated by these circumstances. Even if the perpetrators could be identified, a local grand jury composed of men from the same community as the accused lynchers would not indict or convict their neighbors.

Given the media attention created by the Payne lynching and the ensuing uproar, branches of the federal government also instituted their own investigations. Since the 1942 lynching of Cleo Wright in Sikeston, Missouri, the nation's leaders began to pay more attention to extralegal violence and the propaganda these episodes provided for America's international enemies. The horrific public spectacle, and the subsequent failure to prosecute, forced President Roosevelt to respond. He ordered the Department of Justice (DOJ), with the cooperation of the FBI, to investigate every reported instance of lynching and prosecute when possible.[62]

While unsuccessful in bringing Payne's lynchers to justice, the act of investigating sent a clear message that the federal government would involve itself in the fight to stamp out lynching violence. Turner L. Smith, head of the Civil Rights Division of the DOJ under newly appointed U.S. attorney general Tom Clark, took a very proactive stance on the issue.[63] On October 15, 1945, after learning of the incident, he wrote to the assistant attorney general for the Criminal Division, Theron Lamar Caudle, and FBI director J. Edgar Hoover to request an "immediate investigation" into the circumstances surrounding Payne's death. From initial reports, Smith suspected that there was a "possible violation of Section 52, Title 18, United States Code." The law held officers responsible if they used the "color of law"—their influence because of their official responsibilities—to deprive a citizen of his or her civil rights, in this case, the right to due process. The U.S. Supreme Court had recently handed down a decision in the *Screws v. United States* case confirming the conviction of a Georgia sheriff, Claude Screws, for beating Robert Hall, a black man he had arrested, to death. The case set a precedent for the prosecution of law officers who were involved in violating the civil rights of blacks. Moreover, given the odds against being able to successfully identify and charge Payne's lynchers, holding Sheriff Davis responsible held the best chance of success.[64]

Per Smith's request, the Miami office of the FBI dispatched Agent James B. Hafley to Madison County to investigate the situation. Most of the information included in his report came from news reports and a conversation with John T. Wigginton, executive secretary for Governor Caldwell. The lack of physical evidence and the refusal of local citizens to assist the investigation rendered Agent Hafley's attempts futile. With the news that a Madison County grand jury had failed to indict anyone for the crime, DOJ interest dwindled. Without proof that Sheriff Davis had somehow aided or abetted the situation, the DOJ had no grounds for prosecution. As a result, Turner Smith closed the investigation.[65]

Dismayed by the numerous failed investigations, the American public flooded the DOJ with letters urging state officials to take more concrete action. While many individuals were personally moved to action, much of the correspondence was encouraged by the Southern Negro Youth Congress, based in Birmingham, Alabama, and the International Labor Defense (ILD), under the leadership of Vito Marcantonio. Leaders of both organizations wrote to Attorney General Tom Clark and encouraged others to do the same. Because of its connection to the labor unions, the ILD created the greatest uproar over the matter. The organization also published and circulated a leaflet outlining the circumstances of the deaths of not only Payne but also Moses Greene in South Carolina and Sam McFadden in Suwannee County, Florida, and directed supporters to contact the U.S. attorney general and demand action. The pamphlet highlighted the fact that both Greene and McFadden were veterans, which was sure to rile the consciences of many Americans. Several labor organizations sent resolutions and telegrams, representing the voices of more than 360,000 individuals, condemning both the murder and the lack of prosecution in Madison County.[66] The *Chicago Defender* joined in the campaign, echoing the demand by the Southern Negro Youth Congress that the federal government protect the civil liberties of blacks in America, just as it had for the people of Germany and Japan.[67]

Ultimately, all of the news articles, telegrams, phone calls, and other expressions of outrage and appeals for justice came to naught. After two separate investigations, two grand juries found insufficient evidence to

This leaflet published by

INTERNATIONAL LABOR DEFENSE

HON. VITO MARCANTONIO . . . . *President*
DOXEY A. WILKERSON . . . . *Vice-President*
LOUIS COLMAN . . . . *Secretary*
ROBERT W. DUNN . . . . *Treasurer*
DOROTHY LANGSTON . . . . . . *Field Secretary*
MILTON BECKER . . . . *Director, C.I. Rights Bureau*

112 East 19th Street   New York 3, New York

STOP

LYNCHINGS AND LYNCH-MURDER

THE DEPARTMENT OF JUSTICE HAS A DUTY TO PROSECUTE IN THE THREE CASES DESCRIBED IN THIS LEAFLET.

YOU Have a Duty Too

REPORT ON THE CASE OF L. C. AKINS, OF DALLAS, TEXAS

L. C. Akins, Negro worker of Dallas, Texas, was sentenced to die in the electric chair on October 6, 1945. He had been convicted of murder because after a white policeman had shot him without provocation, Akins tussled, turned the gun on his assailant, killing him. The United States Supreme Court had turned down Akins' appeal. In mid-september, the International Labor Defense, supporting the local efforts of the Dallas Branch of the National Association for the Advancement of Colored People, launched a national campaign in defense of Akins.

Akins' sentence was commuted to life imprisonment.

In a letter dated October 20. Governor Coke Stevenson himself told the reason. "The number intervening on behalf of L. C. Akins totals more than 15,000," he wrote in a letter on that day. "The great majority of these are from out of the State."

There is no reason why Akins should serve a life sentence. Neither you nor the ILD can accept that verdict for an innocent man. Now that Akins' life has been saved, plans are being developed for a nation-wide campaign which will set him wholly free.

FIGURE 5.2. The International Labor Defense (ILD) was instrumental in raising public awareness of miscarriages of justice against blacks in the 1930s and 1940s. This circular detailed the circumstances surrounding the deaths of Jesse James Payne, Moses Greene, and Sam McFadden, and urged Americans to write to the attorney general to force an investigation. Interestingly enough, two of the three instances occurred in North Florida, within thirty miles and a few days of each other. Source: U.S. Department of Justice Classified Subject Files.

THE UNITED STATES GOVERNMENT CAN STOP THIS!

On October 11, Jesse James Payne, a Negro lad, was taken out of the jail at Madison, Florida, and lynched. The jail had been left unguarded over night. *The Sheriff had the only key to the jail.* He admitted it was constantly in his possession. He said he did not know about the lynching until next morning. *Whoever took Payne out used a key.* The circumstances were so shocking even State's Attorney General J. Tom Watson urged suspension of the Sheriff pending clearing up of the case.

Two Madison County Grand Juries have refused to act on the case. Governor Millard F. Caldwell has refused even to suspend the Sheriff.

War Veteran Moses Greene, a Negro, was wantonly murdered by two deputy sheriffs on his farm near Ellenton, S. C., on September 9. The two left the scene without any explanation to Greene's widow or to another eyewitness, for their action. It is clear, however, that they expected—and received from the state — immunity from punishment because they were deputies, and their victim was a Negro.

In this case there was not even an investigation, an inquest or any other formal action taken by state or county authorities. Police told an undertaker to go out and pick up the body of a man they had killed, and bury it.

War Veteran Sam McFadden, a Negro, was lynched by three men, one a local police chief, on October 21, in Suwanee County, Florida. No direct motive for this lynching is known, but County Judge Rowe told a Grand Jury composed of 18 landowners and businessmen, in presenting the case: "Generally, we find when some major crime is committed, that selfish property interests are involved." An investigator for the Governor of the state presented a clear case against three men to the Grand Jury.

On November 13, the Grand Jury refused to return any indictment for this murder.

Under a recent ruling of the United States Supreme Court (Screws v. U. S., 65 Sup. Ct. 1031) the Department of Justice is bound to take action leading to prosecution in these three cases. The lynchers are guilty under the Federal Law. In the past the Department has weaseled out of such prosecutions on the excuse it lacked jurisdiction. That excuse can no longer be made. The lynch-murderers can be prosecuted under the Federal Civil Rights Law, imprisoned for from one to ten years, fined from $1,000 to $5,000.

Florida and South Carolina have refused to act.

YOU CAN MAKE THE DEPARTMENT OF JUSTICE ACT!

Immediately, thousands of communications from organizations, individuals, must pour in on

ATTORNEY GENERAL TOM CLARK
Department of Justice
Washington, D. C.

Demanding that his Department act NOW to stop these lynchings and lynch murders, the number of which grows daily, by full prosecution and punishment under Federal Law of all those responsible for the lynch-deaths of Jesse James Payne in Madison, Fla., of Sam McFadden in Suwanee County, Fla., and of Moses Greene at Ellenton, S. C.

MAKE THE POWER OF THE PEOPLE FELT IN WASHINGTON—FOR JUSTICE

Published by INTERNATIONAL LABOR DEFENSE, 112 East 19th Street, New York 3, N. Y.

FIGURE 5.3. International Labor Defense (ILD) antilynching flyer (*back*).

connect any individual with the death of Jesse James Payne. Anticipating more criticism, Governor Caldwell issued a statement to the press on November 8, 1945, attempting to salvage his own reputation and that of Florida. He was also becoming keenly aware of the national and international import of the events in Madison County, as letters and telegrams from around the nation and world poured into his office. Governor Caldwell was stuck in a difficult position between the parochial traditions of race relations and the evolving understanding of the meaning and scope of American democracy, both domestically and internationally. His attempt to maneuver between these two realities resulted in an uninspiring display of finger-pointing and name-calling. He characterized Payne's death as a "disgraceful occurrence," but placed the responsibility mainly on the people of Madison County. He blamed them for the failures of the local justice system, which resulted in bringing national scrutiny to the state, arguing that "a system can be no greater than is the desire for efficiency on the part of the citizenship." He also explained his decision not to remove Sheriff Davis from office. "Although Sheriff Davis has in this case proven his unfitness for the office," Caldwell stated, "he was, nevertheless, the choice of the people of Madison County. Stupidity and ineptitude are not sufficient grounds for the removal of an elected official by the Governor." Governor Caldwell concluded by warning other law enforcement officers that if situations similar to the Madison case should arise, "I expect the highest degree of care to be exercised."[68]

Predictably, the press did not suffer Caldwell's renouncements well. They argued that what the governor characterized as carelessness reflected "upon Florida's good name [just as if] the sheriff had been guilty of active participation."[69] Others believed that Caldwell's statements left "a hollow feeling." Since no one was punished for Payne's murder, "how much effect will the governor's warning have for the future?" another paper asked. If Sheriff Davis's actions were not enough to warrant removal from office, "to what extent can official stupidity, ineptitude and fatal neglect of duty go before the official involved becomes unworthy of holding office?"[70]

Some Floridians, however, thought that Governor Caldwell was unfairly singling out Sheriff Davis and voiced their support for the sheriff. A telegram sent from "Voter" in Greenville and dated one day after Caldwell's criticism of Sheriff Davis was meant to send a clear message to Caldwell. "We were ignorant in voting last election," it read, "but not on the sheriff's office." Others accused Caldwell of being unduly sympathetic to blacks. One anonymous writer thought that Caldwell was "just twice as stupid as Sheriff Davis. . . . I can't help but think you are just a 'Negro lover.'" Another letter writer claimed Caldwell and Attorney General Watson "must be Negro lovers" and accused them of "prying" into local affairs. "I think no one should complain at what happened to the Nigger," wrote Vernon L. Tyson, of Miami. "I think the people of Madison County are to be congratulated for seeing Justice carried out and for saving the state and county the expense of a trial."[71]

Other commentators aimed their ire at the North, linking the meddlesome influence of the liberal, northern press to the racial amelioration that seemed to flow from FDR's New Deal policies, and especially the antiracism activities of his wife, Eleanor. As southern defenders of white supremacy during the World War II era, they felt themselves and their way of life under attack by northern "fascists." "We never had such until Eleanor Roosevelt buted-in and placed herself on equality with the low-down negros and CIO Jew crooks from Russia. . . . Thank God Eleanor is out of the White House. . . . All this labor trouble is caused by the Eleanor Roosevelt kind. . . . The sooner we tell Russian to go straight to hell the better off we will be. We won two wars to get rid of dictatorship and now we are an allie with the bigest one of them all." The writer continued by endorsing the lynching of Jesse James Payne: "In regards to your Madison case, I don't think the men should be indicted. They should be given a medal even though you could not make such public."[72] Another letter writer praised Caldwell as "a gentleman who upholds white supremacy in our Southland.[73] "It has always occurred to me," penned another correspondent, "that the Southern Governors could do a great deal by being somewhat active in combatting this 'propaganda,' I call it. . . . If we had any organization 1/10 as active as the NAACP, I think there would be a great deal of good accomplished."[74]

*   *   *

The lynching of Jesse James Payne and the controversy surrounding it took on a life of their own, despite Governor Caldwell's efforts to put the incident behind him. The next round in the debate was sparked, innocently enough, by a research project. In mid-December, R. B. Eleazer, of Tennessee, wrote to Caldwell. He was in the process of completing the entry on lynching for *Encyclopedia Britannica*'s 1945 yearbook, and wanted clarification on the governor's statement on the Payne murder to include in his report.[75] Governor Caldwell wrote back to Eleazer three days after Christmas. In the letter, he included the text of his November 8 statement. Beyond that, he explained to Eleazer that he took issue with classifying the incident as a lynching, writing that "whether or not the killing of Jesse James Payne was a lynching must depend upon one's definition of that term. My personal opinion is that the crime did not come within any recognized definition of lynching." In the next part of his statement, Caldwell borrowed from the decades-old excuse for lynching violence: the chivalric protection of the white female. Caldwell explained to Eleazer matter-of-factly,

> The ordeal of bringing a young and innocent victim of rape into open court and subjecting her to detailed cross-examination by defense counsel could easily be as great an injury as the original crime. This fact probably accounts for a number of killings or lynchings which might otherwise be avoided. Society has not found a solution to this problem.

In closing, Caldwell reiterated his belief that the people of Madison County were accountable for handling the situation.

> My comment on the case in which you are interested is in line with my policy of holding the citizens of a county responsible for the officials they elect to office. It is my intention to awaken a sense of civic responsibility in our citizens. To that end, I have refused to do their work for them on the theory that when they have found that they must act or take the consequences they will act. Paternalism softens and deadens civic responsibility and it is my intention to stimulate the people to action and make democracy work.[76]

Governor Caldwell continued with this line of defense into the new year. In January, he openly rejected the Tuskegee Institute's report that listed Payne's death as the only lynching recorded the previous year. Members of the press were baffled by Caldwell's conclusion. In an editorial entitled "Pedagogue Caldwell," the *St. Petersburg Independent* taunted the governor's theoretical acrobatics, observing that he "evidently dislikes having his official conduct questioned and is willing to indulge in far-fetched

FIGURE 5.4. This crude cartoon reflects one segment of the public opinion against Governor Caldwell for his failure to seek justice in the Payne lynching. Cartoons like this, Caldwell argued, reflected the damage done to his reputation by the *Collier's* magazine editorial. Source: Caldwell Civil Case File.

verbal gymnastics as a means of rationalizing his position." The *Chicago Defender* wrote about the controversy using the tagline "Dixie Tangles with Dictionary." Others admonished that his words could be misconstrued as support for lynching. Caldwell's constituents also wrote to him, criticizing his seemingly callous attitude toward the Payne lynching. "I have been profoundly shocked and disappointed at your attitude on the Madison lynching," chided one writer from Daytona Beach. "Nor am I alone! Everywhere, in circles of people who think, the same disappointed is being expressed."[77]

The warnings proved prophetic. On January 7, *Time* magazine published an article entitled "Two Governors." In the piece, the editors compared Governor Caldwell's handling of the Payne murder with the actions of Governor Gregg Cherry, of North Carolina. Cherry had recently stayed the execution of a black teenager accused of rape, instead commuting his sentence to life in prison. *Time* was impressed not simply because of the action taken by Governor Cherry but also because of the reasons behind it. Cherry argued that it was hypocritical to deal so heavy-handedly with people whose criminal behavior was a result of the deprived living conditions and inferior education available to blacks in that state. *Time* then juxtaposed Cherry's benevolence with Caldwell's attitude toward the Payne murder. The magazine characterized Caldwell as condoning the lynching, using the statement that Caldwell himself issued to Eleazer and, subsequently, the press.[78]

Caldwell protested *Time's* characterizations of his words. He immediately contacted the magazine's editors and demanded an apology. The editors reconsidered their position in the January 7 piece, and determined that it was indeed unfair to Caldwell. *Time* issued an apology and retraction in its subsequent issue. Commenting on *Time's* backpedaling, the *Jacksonville Journal* agreed that *Time* had misinterpreted Caldwell's statement but urged the governor to better explain himself to prevent future mishaps.[79]

Caldwell, however, refused to acknowledge his own contribution to the situation. Instead, he began to publicly attack the press. On February 12, while speaking at the Governor's Day luncheon in Tampa, Caldwell criticized the press, specifically *Time* magazine, for intentionally misrepresenting his words. He also took issue with papers within the state for maligning the state's reputation.[80] Caldwell's statements only encouraged the wrath of the state's larger newspapers, and they responded with predictable ire. They accused the governor of "quibbling" and splitting hairs, pointing out that Caldwell had created the problem with his failure to act and with his own words. "Despite the governor's quibble as to whether the Madison killing was perpetrated by one person or a dozen," noted the *Jacksonville Journal*, "with or without 'noise and confusion,' the nation's verdict is going to be that it was a lynching, and it would be much better to face up to it on that level. And what difference does it really make? A man was snatched out of jail and killed without legal process."[81]

The *St. Petersburg Independent* responded to the governor's accusations with acidic derision:

> The Independent, along with other sane newspapers in the state, has not seen eye to eye with Governor Caldwell. This has hurt his feeling [sic] rather badly. In fact, he has used the occasion of the annual Governor's day luncheon at Tampa to take a swipe at the newspapers in the Tampa bay area for publishing such facts. He said that this nullifies the money being spent by the state on advertising. . . . The job of any newspaper is to print all the news that is newsworthy. We are sorry if this pains the govenor [sic]; but we have not the slightest intention of failing in our public duty. Furthermore we shall continue to differ with his policies if and when our considered judgement leads us to the conclusion that he might be mistaken. And whenever we feel that his policies deserve praise, we shall gladly grant him an accolade of three full paragraphs.[82]

With the problems surrounding his public image compounding, Caldwell and his staff developed an offensive strategy to fight the attacks on his administration and his personal character. Having staked his ground by rejecting Payne's murder as a lynching, the governor needed facts to substantiate his claim. Caldwell first wrote to the Tuskegee Institute Department of Records and Research, requesting the institute's criteria for listing a murder as a lynching. Jessie Guzman, then the acting director of the division, responded to the governor and outlined the criteria agreed upon in 1940 by all agencies that tracked the incidents: "1. There must be a dead body. / 2. Which met death illegally. / 3. At the hands of a group. / 4. Acting under pretext of service to justice, race, or tradition." Based on the criteria they outlined, the governor and his staff devised grounds on which to contest the Tuskegee Institute's characterization of the Payne murder as a lynching.[83] John Kilgore, who coordinated the move, explained the approach to Caldwell, asserting, "I am looking at this, not as a letter, but as a clynching [sic] argument for newspaper release. Liberals like St. Pete Times, etc., worship [Jessie Daniels Ames] and the [Association of Southern Women for the Prevention of Lynching

(ASWPL)] is certainly an outstanding white authority. Putting a complete argument in this letter makes it an offensive against Tuskegee . . . not a defense inside State."[84] The governor's administration planned to exploit the difference of opinion between the two organizations, based on their varying criteria for what constituted a lynching. The approach had the advantage of leveraging the respect, prestige, and whiteness of the ASWPL to discredit the Tuskegee Institute's assessment of Payne's death.[85]

Writing again to Tuskegee in March, Governor Caldwell spelled out his objection to Tuskegee's listing of Payne's death as a lynching. First, Caldwell insisted that there was no evidence that Payne met his death "at the hands of a group." That fact alone, he argued, should have excluded Payne's name from the lynching roll. According to Caldwell, the issue of motive was also important. All definitions he had encountered characterized lynching as a form of punishment. In the Madison incident, he argued Payne's killer or killers "acted with revenge as a motive and from personal interest, by reason of blood or family relationship or friendship with the victim and not under a pretext of service to society or racial group."[86]

While Caldwell debated semantics with Tuskegee and recovered from the blow dealt by *Time*, another national magazine was preparing to issue a similar assessment of the Cherry/Caldwell comparison. On February 13, *Collier's* magazine's forward edition was distributed to the nation's newspapers. In it was an article entitled "Two Governors on Race Problems." The article sounded a note nearly identical to the *Time* article, if not with a sharper edge. "Caldwell," the article claimed, "expresses the old, narrow view which has been about as harmful to Southern white people as to Southern Negroes. We can only congratulate North Carolina on its governor, and hope that Florida may have similar gubernatorial good luck before long."[87]

Incensed, Governor Caldwell immediately contacted William L. Chenery, publisher of *Collier's*. Was he not aware, the governor inquired, that *Time* had printed a similar statement only to retract it? Chenery told the governor that he would look into the matter, but there was nothing he could do. Nearly three million copies of the magazine were printed and shipped, and on February 23 would be released to the public.[88] After the magazine was released with the unaltered article, Caldwell's patience expired. He informed *Collier's* that he intended to sue the magazine for libel, seeking $500,000 in damages, which, in the event of a successful judgment, he would turn over to the Florida Agricultural and Mechanical College for Negroes (FAMC) in Tallahassee.[89]

Upon learning of Caldwell's plan to sue, former governor Spessard Holland, who had to contend with lynchings during his own term in office, wrote the current governor to applaud his action. He blamed "up country publishers" for using instances like the Payne incident to stir up racial prejudices that, in his view, were the real source of bloodshed in the region. "It is an obsession, abetted and aided by the radical whites and half whites to use force and violence—and Colliers hands are not clean in this," Holland asserted.[90] Other Floridians wrote Governor Caldwell to show their support for him and included copies of the letters and cancellation notices they had sent to *Collier's* in protest. "When your wife or sisters or daughters come down to Florida for a vacation," one correspondent wrote to the *Collier's* editors, "we will do our utmost to see that they are properly respected by everyone, and in no manner molested by the few brute-type Negroes who are in our midst. . . . [Blacks] have to be controlled by force and knowledge that if they do molest any white woman they will be executed."[91]

After a delay of a year, the libel trial against *Collier's* began in February 1947 in the court of Dozier Devane in Tallahassee. John T. Wigginton, Julius F. Parker, and Leo L. Foster represented Governor Caldwell. Chester H. Ferguson, Pat Whitaker, and J. Lewis Hall represented Crowell-Colliers Publishing Company. Initially, lawyers for the defense argued that the trial should be moved because of the undue influence that Governor Caldwell, in his role as the head of the state, exercised over people and politics in the Tallahassee area. The judge denied the defense's request for a change of venue; instead, he simply asked that state employees recuse themselves from jury duty.[92]

During the trial, Caldwell's attorneys worked to cast the governor as a victim. Key to Governor Caldwell's case was proving that his reputation had been damaged by the *Collier's* article. During his testimony, when asked how the editorial affected his job duties, Caldwell cited difficulty with negotiating regional educational matters, specifically when he had to engage with his black constituents. During negotiations, Caldwell stated that "I felt on the part of the Negroes of this state they felt I was not dealing fairly with them, not in good faith attempting to approach the subject

FIGURE 5.5. Cartoons like this one drew attention to the lawlessness that continued to plague the South, and particularly Florida, during the 1940s. This cartoon was submitted by lawyers for Governor Millard Caldwell in his libel suit against *Collier's* in the aftermath of the lynching of Jesse James Payne. Source: Caldwell Civil Case File.

of education." Additionally, Caldwell claimed that he experienced greater difficulty in working with the legislature over the past year.[93]

The defense, on the other hand, focused on Caldwell's handling of Jesse James Payne's murder. On the witness stand, Caldwell continued to deny the incident was a lynching.[94] The defense then asked Caldwell why he did not suspend Sheriff Davis. Caldwell argued that removing the sheriff would have had no long-term impact. "In the first place," he stated, "[the] suspension would not have been confirmed by the Senate and the sheriff would have become a martyr in the eyes of some people." "In the next place," he continued, "[Davis] would have been vindicated by re-election at the next election."[95] Caldwell's statements were revealing because they showed that he seemed more concerned with the political outcome of the Payne investigation than the immediate goal of justice and legal due process.

Despite Caldwell's concern about his reputation, he and his attorneys knew that there were other underlying issues involved in the case. In the end, Caldwell's attorneys based their appeal on age-old sectional mistrust and southern disdain for northern interference in local affairs. John Wigginton argued just that in his closing statement. "Are you going to let people sitting up at 250 Park Avenue in New York tell us down here the kind of man we ought to have to run our state?" he asked the jury. He then singled out *Collier's* editor Henry LaCossit: "I believe, from talking to [LaCossit] that he has the idea that we live half like savages, with at least one-third of our people, the colored people, constantly in fear and trembling, which all of us, including you men, know is not true."[96] In his closing argument, Pat Whitaker attempted to counter Wigginton by sounding a patriotic note. He argued the First Amendment rights to freedom of speech and the press. He encouraged the jury to avoid making a judgment based on passion or personal feelings. Further, he tried to portray Governor Caldwell as thin-skinned. "When a man assumes public office," Whitaker argued, "he takes on the burden, the responsibility of taking criticism, having the public disagree with him."[97]

On March 10, 1947, after closing arguments, the jury retired to deliberate. Three hours later, they returned with a verdict that awarded Governor Caldwell $237,500, reportedly the most ever granted in a libel suit in the United States.[98] Writers for the *Tampa Tribune* called the award excessive and disputed the claim that Caldwell's reputation had been damaged. Instead, they argued the reverse: "[He] enjoys today much higher esteem, confidence and respect from the people of Florida than he did in the early days of his administration."[99]

Vindication by the jury did not mean that blacks in Florida were willing to forget the governor's unwillingness or inability to punish those responsible for Payne's death. Nor did the promise of money for FAMC ease the pain of living without the full protection of the law. Harry T. Moore told Caldwell shortly after the verdict,

> We wish to make it clear that we shall not consider this as a gift
> to the Negroes of Florida. If Florida A. & M. College is not getting

sufficient financial support to make it measure up to the standards maintained at the University of Florida at Gainesville and Florida State University at Tallahassee, it is the fault of our State Government, and not the responsibility of Florida Negro citizens. . . . Such a gift will not soothe the wounded feeling of Florida Negro citizens.

Furthermore, Moore suggested that the money would be better put to use in support of the Payne family—his wife, young daughter, and mother.[100] The decision did not mark the end of the battle, as Collier's immediately filed an appeal and was granted a retrial on the grounds that Judge Dozier DeVane should have cautioned the jury to disregard attorney Wigginton's appeal to sectional loyalties. The new trial was held two years later. The jury reached the same conclusion, but lowered the amount of the damages to $100,000. Shortly thereafter, attorneys for both sides came up with a compromise. LaCossit had already announced that he planned to take the case as far as he could, given his belief in the First Amendment. Now out of office, Caldwell had nothing to gain from a protracted legal struggle, and he and his attorneys were not necessarily interested in seeking a larger judgment to enrich FAMC. Aside from that, Caldwell had proven his point. He was victorious over the Yankee slanderers of his good name and the reputation of his state. The parties reached a settlement for $25,000, lawyers' fees, and court costs.[101] Nearly four years after the lynching of Jesse James Payne, the dust finally settled, and Caldwell received a hollow victory.

While Caldwell did his best to evade responsibility, Payne's lynching is a dramatic illustration of the failure of law enforcement officials and politicians in Florida to actively protect the lives and rights of African Americans in the state. In the end, Caldwell seemed more concerned with the classification of Payne's murder than with the injustice of the murder itself, or the culpability of those who executed him. For those reasons, he spent more time defending the public perception of his administration and the reputation of the state of Florida than he did investigating Payne's murder.

Despite Sheriff Davis's unwillingness to act, there was sufficient evidence that he and his deputies knew that Payne's life was in danger, yet he was never made to answer whether he was present while the posse was organizing with the intention of killing Payne. Other officers were aware of the threat and took appropriate safeguards: Patrolman Moore outwitted the mob that waited on Payne outside the Monticello jail, and Deputy Wade took precautions when transporting Payne between Madison and Raiford. All were aware that Payne had been shot when he was being captured, and Payne informed authorities of Daniel Goodman's attempt to kill him. Above all else, the nature of the crime Payne was eventually accused of, the attempted rape of a five-year-old white girl, was sure to inspire vengeance.

To his credit, Caldwell made some effort to solve the crime. His request for a second special grand jury charged with determining if Sheriff Davis was negligent was certainly a step in the right direction. That was, however, as far as he was willing to go. His actions were in line with the measures taken by the previous governor, Spessard Holland, when acts of lawlessness occurred during his tenure. The main problem that Caldwell faced was a significant shift in public opinion when it came to extralegal violence; even he acknowledged that the lynching's significance "transcends the borders of both the county and state and draws unfavorable attention to Florida."[102] The prism of World War II changed and possibly heightened appreciation of democracy. People were no longer satisfied with the semblance of justice and inconclusive investigations that held no one accountable. The public reaction to Payne's lynching indicated that an increasing number of white Americans were unwilling to look the other way while citizens, black or white, were denied due process and the full protection of the law. More important, they were concerned with the way it made their country look. Caldwell's failure to take decisive action showed his divided loyalties between southern tradition and progress, a challenge many other southern politicians would face in the postwar world. The governor, and others in the South, learned an important lesson: the region could "no longer sidestep the lynching problem through semantics," and "lynchings were no longer synonymous with mob justice, and quiet executions at the hands of the unknown would not escape the record books or national scrutiny."[103]

CONCLUSION

World War II drastically altered the moral landscape of both the United States as a whole and the South in particular. Internationally, the specter of Adolf Hitler, his ideology of Aryan supremacy, and the tragic results of its implementation on the Jewish people of Europe forced Americans to face the uncomfortable truth about their own racist philosophies. With the advent of the Cold War and the ensuing battle for global preeminence, America's swaggering claims about the benefits of democracy seemed like false advertising when it came to the treatment of African Americans. In the quest for world power, credibility was everything. Claims about the benefits of American-style democracy and capitalism rang hollow in light of rampant racial discrimination, economic exploitation, and unchecked lynching, especially to nations of brown and black people recently liberated from their own racist colonial masters. Writer, folklorist, and Florida-native Zora Neale Hurston, in an essay entitled "Crazy for This Democracy," mocked President Franklin Roosevelt's claim that the nation would be an "arsenal of democracy":

> I heard so much about "global" "world freedom" and things like that, that I must have gotten mixed up about oceans. . . . I thought when they said Atlantic Charter, that meant me and everybody in Africa and Asia and everywhere. But it seems like the Atlantic is an ocean that does not touch anywhere but North America and Europe. . . .

I accept this idea of Democracy. I am all for trying it out. It must be a good thing if everybody praises it like that. If our government has been willing to go to war and to sacrifice billions of dollars and millions of men for the idea, I think that I ought to give the thing a trial.[1]

As one scholar on race relations during this era phrased it, "To become the world's reformer, the United States has first to democratize its domestic social and political institutions—to harmonize them with its self-proclaimed global aspirations—for it was not possible, to use the famous phrase, 'to make the world safe for democracy' as long as America itself was not genuinely democratic."[2]

During the postwar years, a series of horrendous racially motivated murders took place in the United States. In 1946, Columbia, Tennessee, witnessed a bloody race riot. Later that same year, whites in Monroe, Georgia, lynched two African American couples, including a war veteran and a pregnant woman. White law enforcement officers in Batesburg, South Carolina, attacked army sergeant Isaac Woodward after a verbal argument with a Greyhound bus driver. A police officer gouged out both of his eyes, leaving him permanently blind. All told, between June 1945 and December 1946 as many as sixty blacks were estimated to have been murdered by southern whites, often with participation by law enforcement officials.[3] America's international enemies made good use of instances of lynching and racial violence, reprinting photographs of lynchings in their newspapers. John Sengstacke, publisher of the *Chicago Defender*, made this point clear in writing to Governor Caldwell after the lynching of Jesse James Payne: "All the world now knows about Columbia, Tennessee, Monroe, Georgia, and Athens[,] Alabama[,] as well as innumerable instances which have come to the light of day. . . . Unless immediate action is taken we stand before the world as making mockery out of democracy. Our pleas for world unity at Paris are but empty words."[4]

If Americans were sent overseas to fight fascism in Europe, what was the government doing to fight the oppression of a segment of its own population? If Hitler's ideas of white supremacy were wrong, was not racism in America wrong? "As long as we tolerate such vicious nonsense," William H. Hastie wrote in his resignation as civilian aide to the secretary of war, "we can be respected neither by the forces of fascism which we condemn nor by the forces of democracy which we assume to lead."[5] During World

War II, federal officials were forced, both by diplomatic realities as well as an increasingly militant and politicized black population, to take steps to end the extralegal murder of America's black citizens and preserve the nation's reputation. With the intensifying belief that racial discrimination was wrong, the United States demonstrated a new willingness to act on that feeling.

The condemnations of Payne's lynchers by activists across the nation, along with the subsequent criticism of the failure to bring the guilty parties to justice, demonstrate a clear change of public opinion on the subject of extralegal violence that was fostered by the experience of World War II. Letters sent to the Department of Justice (DOJ) encapsulated Americans' growing sensitivity to racial injustice. Writing in December 1945, David Brown, of Swarthmore, Pennsylvania, declared that "as a citizen and as a voter I am much concerned with the apparent break-down of democratic processes here at home at the precise moment in history we fight world-wide wars to save freedom on the earth."[6] Shamas O'Sheel, of New York City, believed blacks deserved equal treatment under the law because of their contributions and sacrifices in the global fight for democracy during World War II, and also because of the risk of damage to the nation's reputation. He argued:

> The American people gave blood and treasure in the prosecution of the Second World War because they believed it to be a war to prevent the triumph of repulsive claims of racial superiority, and to extend the bounds of human freedom. Millions of Negro Americans fought and served nobly and bravely during the war. The logic of history, the logic of our national evolution as well as the logic of the Negro's destiny, call for reward of these services by further and very substantial extension to our Negro citizens of those rights, those assurances against discrimination, those securities, which theoretically have been theirs for 80 years. It is a realization of this which causes viciously reactionary elements in our population deliberately to increase outrages against Negro citizens at this time. If they are allowed to go unpunished, serious dangers lie directly ahead for our country.[7]

William B. Stevenson struck a similar note when he wrote to U.S. attorney general Tom Clark:

Our memories cannot be so short that we have already forgotten that we have just fought and won a costly, bloody war to prevent the world from being dominated by the bestial, inhumane rule represented by Fascism. In the name of those millions of Americans, of all racial and national backgrounds, who suffered the cruelties and pains of war, who risked and lost limb and life, who worked in all fields to contribute toward winning the war; in their name we ask that you, as Attorney General, use your power to see that the Department of Justice acts NOW, under the Federal Civil Rights Law, to punish those responsible for the specific crimes named above, as well as to prevent similar occurrences in the future. LET US NOT FAIL TO MAINTAIN AT HOME IN PEACE-TIME THOSE PRINCIPLES OF HUMAN DECENCY FOR WHICH WE FOUGHT A WAR ABROAD.[8]

Some of the most moving calls for action came from veterans of the war, many of whom had served with black troops during the conflict. One such veteran was John Gilman. In an open letter that was published in the *Chicago Defender* under the title "Put Lynchers on Trial with Nazis, Asks DSC Hero," Gilman pointed out to Clark that

the same crimes that Hitler . . . and all the other Nazi criminals have enacted are *now going on right before your eyes.* . . . I have just returned from a foreign war. I fought consistently for 270 days on the front line. . . . There were millions of other G.I.'s, colored and white, Jewish and Italian, Polish and Russian, and every other nationality who did the same. For what? To come back to an America that lynches people? To come back to an America that has race hatred and civil strife? . . . I am the holder of the Silver Star, awaiting award of the Distinguished Service Cross and the Bronze Star. *These medals won't mean a thing to me or this nation if these acts go on without punishment being meted to the men responsible.*[9]

Another veteran who had served in World War I wrote to Governor Caldwell to express his disappointment that Nazi-like atrocities were happening in America: "And now look what is going on in the south, the brutal lynchings of Negroes. I fought side by side with Negroes, who were nice boys, many died for our rich beautiful America. I have Negro neighbors who are the finest neighbors I have. Is there anything that can be done to stop the brutal, Hitler Lynchings?"[10]

HITLER IS HERE! by Bill Chase (from Amsterdam News)

FIGURE C.1. The image of a black man dying on the blade of "Southern Fascism" depicts a tragic reality faced by black Americans during the era of World War II. Printed shortly after the June 1943 lynching of Cellos Harrison in Marianna, Florida, this cartoon shows that parallels were being drawn between Hitler's atrocities and the violence committed by whites against blacks in America. It represents the goals of the "Double V" campaign waged by blacks during World War II, and their desire to win democracy and equal protection under the law at home while fighting for democracy abroad. Source: *Baltimore Afro-American*, July 10, 1943.

While many across the nation pressured both the Roosevelt and Truman administrations to investigate instances of lynching and racial violence, that encroached on a perilous and well-guarded border between states' rights and federalism. As one historian observed, "the most sacred and jealously guarded right of the Southern states is undoubtedly the right to lynch Negroes; consequently, any Federal law seeking to limit this right will be promptly construed to be an infringement upon the sovereignty of states."[11] The federal government also knew that interfering with southern affairs would invite comparisons to the era of Reconstruction. FDR avoided supporting federal antilynching legislation for years as not to rupture this barrier.

Nevertheless, in the face of public relations nightmares such instances of violence created, the federal government became increasingly responsive to calls for justice. During his first two administrations, President Roosevelt became more sensitive to the dilemma. He had painted an image of a world in which *all* people could enjoy the "Four Freedoms": freedom of speech and expression, freedom of religion, freedom from want, and freedom from fear. Despite Roosevelt's optimism, continued lynching meant that a significant segment of the nation's population could not claim the last of these. Frank Coleman, special assistant to the U.S. attorney general, recognized the quandary facing the president and the nation. "Stories of lynching and police brutality against individuals of racial and religious minorities in the United States," he warned, were "welcome ammunition to the Axis enemies in their campaign to discredit the self-appointed champions of the 'Four Freedoms.'"[12] As the historian Christopher Waldrep noted, it was during these years that the federal government, through the Civil Right Division of the DOJ, completed an about-face in its approach to lynching violence, relating that these "local" crimes could impact international perceptions of the United States.[13]

The shocking lynching of Cleo Wright in Sikeston, Missouri, in January 1942 provoked Roosevelt to take action, mandating that the DOJ investigate reports of lynchings. The decision represented a new departure in the federal government's handling of such cases. As a result of their newly found antilynching fervor, the FBI and the DOJ convicted the murderers of Howard Wash in October 1942, who was lynched in Laurel, Mississippi. This victory represented the first federal indictment for lynching in forty years. J. Edgar Hoover, however, criticized what he called "an iron curtain" within the region that made it impossible for his agency to effectively investigate these crimes.[14]

Despite the spate of attacks against African Americans during the war, Hoover chose to use the power of his agency to investigate alleged sedition in the black press. He was able to convince President Roosevelt that the black press needed to be reined in, but Attorney General Francis Biddle, well known for his dedication to civil liberties, refused to pursue prosecution. Hoover's apprehension was embodied in a 714-page report released in September 1943, "Survey of Racial Conditions." In a stunning example of tone-deafness, the field reports from Florida, coming from Jacksonville, Tampa, and Miami, pinpointed the harmful "outside influence" of the northern black press and northern black soldiers stationed near these communities as a dangerous and inflammatory element.

J. Edgar Hoover's concerns were partially based on facts. Certainly the African American press had grown tremendously; the circulation of black newspapers trebled between 1933 and the end of the war, from 600,000 to over 1,800,000. Collectively, black newspapers with national circulations like the *Chicago Defender, Baltimore Afro-American, Pittsburgh Courier,* and *Amsterdam News*—and, to a lesser degree, Florida-based papers like the *Pensacola Colored Citizen* and *Florida Tattler* out of Jacksonville—were responsible for drawing attention to racial discrimination, such as the decision by the American Red Cross not to accept blood from black donors and the mistreatment of African American soldiers, as well as continuing to report on instances of racial violence across the nation. Black journalists sought to expose the Roosevelt administration for failing to desegregate the military, and some promoted the 1941 March on Washington Movement's fight against racial discrimination in war industries. The *Pittsburgh Courier* demonstrated the power of the black press to influence blacks across the nation when it instituted the "Double V" campaign in 1942. By July 1943, persistent lobbying by black newspaper publishers earned them a meeting with representatives within FDR's administration, including Vice President Henry Wallace, Attorney General Francis Biddle, and War Manpower Commission chairman Paul McNutt. The group of editors used the meeting to articulate a litany of requests on behalf of African American citizens and soldiers, including placing advertisements in their papers to announce training programs related to war industry jobs and the listing of casualties of war by race. Through their headlines, articles, and editorials, black newspaper publishers and editors drew attention to continuing racial injustices and told inconvenient truths with which Roosevelt and Hoover did not wish to contend. The soundness and validity of their perspective, however, could not easily be denied.[15]

The pressure faced by the federal government inevitably trickled down to the state level, forcing executives like Spessard Holland and Millard Caldwell to make difficult choices. Historically, state agencies were hesitant to intercede in instances of racial injustice, opting to leave investigations up to local law enforcement officials. In the case of civil unrest, the governor had the power to send in the National Guard, but only after the local sheriff requested assistance. These sheriffs, however, were "usually reluctant about calling for aid of this kind, and they often refused to believe that the danger is acute until some overt act [occurred]."[16]

In facing the challenge of lynching violence in Florida, the two governors in office between 1941 and 1945, Holland and Caldwell, both reacted with deliberate hesitation. They were political actors caught between tradition and change, with increasingly less room to maneuver politically. Any action they took was motivated by the threat or reality of negative press and protest. If communities failed to bring the lynchers to justice, the governors sent investigators to search independently for evidence. After receiving inconclusive reports, each made public statements that were the equivalent of wringing one's hands and shrugging one's shoulders at the same time. While they had the power to remove sheriffs from their positions if they believed them negligent, neither Holland nor Caldwell used that power. Their lack of action is indicative of their desire not to involve themselves in "local affairs," leaving the whites in a community to decide what course of action, if any, should be taken. Too much interference might have subjected them to political backlash.

Threatened by out-of-state influence in local matters, white Floridians organized to resist the threat of expanding nationalism. One group, the Florida Voters for Constitutional Government (FVCG), using the motto "Let's Keep America American," based its platform on four tenants: commitment to winning the war, upholding a constitutional government, preserving states' rights, and respecting southern tradition. In explaining the last of these, the group demanded the right of southern states "to the

FIGURE C.2. The transfer of responsibilities between Governor Spessard Holland (*left*) and Governor-elect Millard Caldwell on January 2, 1945, included responding to lynching that occurred in the state of Florida. While Holland managed to appease demands for justice by calling for investigations into such incidents, Caldwell's handling, or mishandling, of the 1945 lynching of Jesse James Payne would catapult him into the national spotlight. Courtesy of the State Archives of Florida.

preservation of their local, time-honored customs and traditions." Further, the group warned of a conspiracy to establish a "fanatical, socialistic, paternalistic, totalitarian system" that would "sacrifice our precious personal liberties" and make Americans "slaves to a dictatorial bureaucratic system that offers so-called security but robs us of our FREEDOM." The FVCG also accused these same cryptic forces of encouraging "class and race prejudices" in an effort to "break down local customs and traditions peculiar to certain sections," resulting in a "national situation that threatens our internal peace and security," citing as examples the rash of race riots around the nation.[17]

One Florida resident wrote to Governor Holland, encouraging him to disassociate himself from U.S. senator Claude Pepper, claiming that Pepper was "the only southern senator that was low, dirty, servile and traitorous enough to cause, condition and tradition of the South, to vote for the infamous [Fair Employment Practices Commission], which was designed with a view of *forcing* social equality on the South."[18] This conservative interpretation of international politics would come full circle during the Cold War era, when southerners succeeded in painting both progressive politicians and civil rights organizers as "Reds," forcing them into a defensive stance and regaining the high ground, at least temporarily, in the battle over civil rights. As one historian of the period notes, "white-supremacist southerners co-opted the anticommunist hysteria to defend segregation against all who dared to challenge it.[19]

The pressure placed on state executives in Florida sparked an evolution in their response to lynching violence. Spessard Holland, during his term as governor between 1941 and 1945, was in office during the Williams, Harrison, and Howard lynchings. While he did little to curtail lynching sentiment or hold law enforcement officials responsible for their inability to protect the prisoners in their care in these early instances, Governor Holland proved that he had learned from those examples. His test came in July 1944. Three young black men, Fred Lane, age nineteen; James Davis, age sixteen; and James Williams, age twenty-six—later dubbed the "Quincy Three"—were arrested and charged with kidnapping, raping, and shooting the twenty-year-old white wife of an army sergeant just outside of Quincy on July 30, 1944. According to reports, the woman had experienced car trouble while traveling from her job at the state mental hospital in Chattahoochee to Quincy for a hair appointment. While awaiting assistance, Lane, Davis, and Williams supposedly came upon her, forced her into their car, and drove to a secluded location. Once there, they allegedly raped her, shot her twice in the head, and left her to die, covering her under a thin layer of leaves and twigs.[20]

After their arrest, the Quincy Three were held in Tallahassee until their trial was scheduled to begin. On the morning the trial was to take place, however, state patrolmen encountered a mob of armed white men blocking the road to Quincy. While initial reports described the gathering as an angry lynch mob, others later disputed that account. Witnesses claimed that the group had been composed of businessmen who were there to prevent the kidnapping and lynching of the Quincy Three. Nevertheless, the activities of some whites in Quincy confirmed that danger was indeed brewing. In Quincy, there were reports that armed whites were selling pictures of the three accused men on the street, while others warned blacks to close their businesses, go home, and stay there for the night.[21]

Eager to prevent another outbreak of violence on his watch, Governor Holland reacted with unusual zeal to ensure that the Quincy Three were protected from mob violence. As a precaution, he called out 500 National Guardsmen to accompany the convoy transferring the accused from the Florida State Prison at Raiford to Gainesville for trial. Holland appeared on the steps of the Tallahassee jail with Major Albert Blanding, head of the state defense council; General Vivien Collins, state adjutant general; and J. J. Gilliam, director of the state public safety department, and explained that his action came from the belief that the men could not be tried in Quincy without bloodshed.[22]

What took place instead looked more like a legalized lynching. Lane, Davis, and Williams pleaded guilty in court in Gainesville on August 31, 1944, and Judge W. May Walker sentenced all three defendants to the electric chair. When their convictions and sentences were announced outside the courthouse, the news was met with applause and cheers. Their motion for a new trial was denied. The men desired to appeal the decision to the Florida Supreme Court, claiming that they had been beaten into confessing to the crime. The appeal also sought leniency for sixteen-year-old James Davis, arguing that he was too young to be executed. Lane, Davis, and Williams were able to find a lawyer to take their case, but he resigned after learning the Ku Klux Klan (KKK) threatened bodily harm to anyone responsible for a successful appeal for the Quincy Three. Although they were not represented by counsel, the Florida Supreme Court dismissed the appeal, and Governor Holland refused to stay their executions until they could secure representation. Despite a campaign to prevent their deaths, Lane, Davis, and Williams were electrocuted on October 9, 1944, just three months after they were arrested. James Davis became the youngest person in Florida's history to be executed.[23] Surely Holland must have felt a sense of satisfaction that Lane, Davis, and Williams had not been punished outside of the law at the hands of a mob; their trial and

executions, however, were hardly examples of due process in full operation. The fact remained that in the minds of those whites involved, the
three had to die; the only question was who was authorized to kill them.[24]

The change in attitudes about lynching violence in Florida that reflected
a sensitivity to national and international opinion was evident not only
in the governor's actions but also in the reaction of the press throughout
the state. "The governor knows lynchings are contrary to the principles for
which this nation stands," proclaimed the *Tampa Times*. "Fair-minded people are counting on the governor to continue his vigilance against possible
lynchings and feel sure that he will do his utmost to assure that law and
order and due processes continue to prevail."[25] Editors at the *St. Petersburg
Times* voiced their interpretation of the events with praise for Governor
Holland, casting the event in terms of international impact. Entitled "Law
and Order Starts at Home," the piece proclaimed:

> Organized society can not tolerate rape without inviting its own de-
> struction. . . .
>
> In the present ugly case in northwest Florida no delay of justice,
> no signs that established law and order was failing in its responsi-
> bilities can justify the mob. But ignorance and passion that subverts
> the law opens a crevice in the delicate fabric of world relationships.
>
> Japan and Germany use 10 and 20-year-old American lynch-
> ing pictures in their efforts to stir up the teeming millions of Asia
> against the whites, and to prove that democracy is a failure in that
> it can not even establish basic law and order. . . .
>
> The restoration of world law and order with justice based on the
> consent of the governed rests on the ability of every community and
> province to demonstrate that it can handle the unsocial outlaw in
> orderly fashion.
>
> We congratulate Governor Holland for living up to his oath of of-
> fice with such poise and courage.[26]

The global perspective of the editorial is undeniable. Because of the impact of World War II, southerners were forced to acknowledge that their
actions, whether positive or negative, would reflect not just on the region
but on the nation as well. Southerners argued for decades that lynching was a regional issue, one that was best left to them. For years, many

northerners accepted that excuse. However, with the rise of Hitler in Europe and the eventual outbreak of World War II, many Americans came to interpret the tragedy of lynching through an international lens. Extralegal violence had become fodder for the media elements of the nation's enemies. The behavior of white southerners, and especially their dealings with African Americans, were being carefully watched for incidents that could embarrass the United States before the world.[27]

In contrast to Holland, Governor Caldwell was less successful in confronting the challenges of lynching. In dealing with the Payne murder, Caldwell failed to take action when it was necessary, justified, and within the scope of his responsibility. Moreover, his decision to deny that Payne's murder was a lynching proved especially damaging to his public image. The public mood shifted during the war, and Caldwell failed to gauge this change, which had been brought on by the nation's experience during the war. During the course of the conflict, the United States underwent tremendous transformation, both internally and internationally. These years wrought dramatic developments in Florida—rapid population growth, intense militarization, and an expanding economy based on tourism and agriculture—which in turn ushered in a period of remarkable postwar expansion and development known as Florida's "Big Bang."[28] Despite the generally progressive developments in the regional economy, antiblack sentiment and the violence that accompanied it remained entrenched. The more that African Americans sought to use the spectacle of Hitler's disastrous policies of Aryan supremacy to advance their conditions within the United States and to leverage antiracist rhetoric in their favor, southerners redoubled their efforts to maintain racial boundaries as they existed.

In addition to demonstrating a change in public sentiment and response to lynching violence, the extralegal murders of Williams, Harrison, Howard, and Payne confirm trends about the decline and change in extralegal violence during the mid-twentieth century. Philip Dray noticed a change in the form of lynching during the Second World War that turned away from spectacle lynching to more clandestine affairs. The lynchings in Florida during the 1940s also follow this pattern. In the instances examined here, the lynchers operated with a high level of secrecy, fitting what W. Fitzhugh Brundage described as "private mobs." With the exception of the lynching of Willie James Howard, they came in the dead of the night, as opposed to the daytime, in order to maintain the element of surprise. Williams's and Harrison's kidnappers reportedly used masks to hide their identity, indicating that they were concerned with being identified.[29]

The change in the frequency and form of lynching that took place during the 1940s is also indicative of changing social attitudes about extralegal violence. This change in format also fits into Roberta de la Roche's theory about the role of partisanship in collective violence. According to this theory, when there is a conflict between two parties, influential third parties can be drawn to the side of the group with whom they share social closeness and superiority. These partners then collaborate against the party that is viewed as inferior and socially remote.[30] She correlated this to the partisan relationships between the whites who carried out lynchings, primarily against blacks, and the hegemonic power structures of the community, also controlled by whites—particularly governmental administrations, law enforcement officers, the courts, and the press— that shielded participants from punishment. This took place actively, with members of the power structure assisting in lynching directly or indirectly, or passively when the community and its leaders failed to identify, investigate, prosecute, or convict the participants. What is evident in the responses to the lynchings explored in this study is that the Florida partisans who had previously shielded lynchers were less willing to play that role. This was in no small part due to the efforts of groups like the NAACP, the Committee for Interracial Cooperation (CIC), and the Association of Southern Women for the Prevention of Lynching (AS-WPL), who targeted groups of the aforementioned partisans and discouraged their tacit support of lynching violence in their communities. Responses to Gallup polls on the question of antilynching legislation reveal increasing support among southerners for federal intervention. In 1943, 56 percent of respondents favored federal antilynching legislation, compared with 47 percent in 1937.[31] In addition to the changes in public opinion, by the 1940s the mainstream press in Florida routinely condemned lynchers and those who protected them as traitors to the state and nation. Likewise, state and federal officials increasingly signaled their displeasure through the press and also used the power of their offices to investigate the incidents. Walter Howard pinpointed this external pressure and "shaming" as a factor in the decline in lynching violence in Florida in the 1930s.[32]

While scholars can gain a great deal from understanding the trends of antiblack violence in the 1930s and 1940s, the narrow focus on the decline and eradication of lynching *as a specific class of acts* obscures continuing patterns of behavior that achieve the same goals. Ashraf Rushdy, in his work *The End of American Lynching*, makes this point very well. The AS-WPL spent the early 1940s eager to pin down the "end of lynching" or the "last lynching," with the belief that it would represent victory on its part and, more important, progress on the part of the South and the nation in the area of race relations. Groups and observers like the NAACP, however, understood lynchings as one of a cluster of violent, terroristic acts designed to continue the social, economic, and political oppression of African Americans. While the trends highlighted in this study are helpful in tracing the decline of lynching as one form of black oppression, it is important to appreciate the transition or fading of this one tradition in direct relation to the other forms of antiblack violence and oppression that replaced extralegal murder as a method of controlling the black population in the state. In the case of Florida, as well as other states in the South, the legal machinery of the criminal justice system—law enforcement officials, courts, and prisons—came to replace the extralegal means that had been used to ensure white supremacy.[33]

In this way, southerners began utilizing other legal avenues to punish black criminals; studies have shown that as lynchings decreased in the South, the rate of blacks who were executed or sentenced to long prison terms increased. These "legal lynchings" used the machinery of the courts, instead of extralegal violence, to achieve a predetermined outcome of death for the accused. While the means were different, both legal and extralegal executions served the purposes of retribution and reinforcing white supremacy. Statistics regarding the rate of capital punishment for black men during the latter half of the twentieth century delineate this trend. Between 1924 and 1964, the state of Florida executed 196 men, 131 of whom were black, representing 67 percent of those killed by the state. Between 1910 and 1950, African Americans represented 75 percent of those executed in the former slave states. When convictions for rape were taken into account, 95 percent (forty-one of forty-three) of those executed were black. In this way, extralegal violence was replaced by the more palatable practice operating through the court system, with similarly deadly results.[34]

On all fronts, the intersection of white supremacy and the criminal justice system created dangerous conditions for African Americans accused
of crimes. All the lynching instances described in this work share another
key factor: inadequate protection of potential lynching victims and, in the
event of a lynching, inadequate responses by law enforcement officers. In
his research on lynching in the 1930s in Florida, Walter Howard found that
the majority of the victims were kidnapped from police custody.[35] This
pattern continued into the next decade, as all but one victim was taken
from law enforcement officers. As one historian of lynching in Florida
pointed out, "lynchers expected and for the most part received immunity
from the law. Local officials, who were usually friends, neighbors or relatives of the lynchers, frequently condoned and even participated in these
sordid affairs. Police facilitated lynchings by handing over prisoners or
by looking the other way as the lynchers carried out their deed."[36] Three
victims, Williams, Harrison, and Payne, were kidnapped from jail. In all
three instances, there were sufficient reasons to suspect a lynching attempt, especially in the cases of Williams and Payne, who were accused of
the attempted rape of young white girls. With tragic consistency, Sheriffs
Luten, Gause, and Davis failed to take extra precautions to protect their
prisoners. While there is no conclusive evidence proving that the sheriffs
were intentionally negligent or working in collusion with the lynchers, it
is hard to believe these were uncoordinated coincidences.

While it would be unfair to assume that all law enforcement officials
in the South were racist or acted solely to ensure white supremacy, the
reality is that the majority of the law enforcement officers were the sons
of the South, and as such, were products of their environment. Many
were homegrown "good ol' boys," sharing a common background with the
people who elected them.[37] Law enforcement officers, whether sheriffs,
deputies, policemen, or constables, were more beholden to their white
constituents than to the letter of the law. This was especially true of small
communities. In their positions of authority, these individuals decided
what laws to enforce and when to enforce them. Because of these conflicts,
southern law enforcement officers existed in a type of sociopolitical para-
dox, negotiating between the demands of their public offices and the local
pressures of social codes and mores.

If Jim Crow was the law, there had to be someone to execute it. Southern law enforcement officers, as an essential function in their roles as

administrators of the public will, enforced segregation laws. Consequently, sheriffs, deputies, and constables constituted the front line in the battle to maintain white supremacy. Because of this, sheriffs were expected "to uphold the will of the superior race." As one anthropological study of southern culture noted:

> The ability to subordinate Negroes is for some positions a prime requisite, and such a reputation a political asset. [Maintaining] the caste system intact, "keeping the niggers in their place," is extremely important to the whites and is part of the informal obligation which the official assumes. The caste element is particularly important in the case of law-enforcement officers such as the sheriff and chief of police.[38]

The authority of southern law enforcement officers, in essence, reinforced the hegemonic systems that were foundational to maintaining the racial status quo in the region.[39] Conversely, the bad behavior of law enforcement officers sustained the vulnerability of the African American community and, further, bred an inherent distrust of the criminal justice system among blacks. Sheriffs frequently did not investigate adequately, if at all, acts of violence perpetrated against African Americans. At other times, sheriffs failed to protect blacks in their custody and, in the worst instances, were directly involved in extralegal violence or murder. In some situations, sheriffs benefited politically by remaining inactive during racial crises; being viewed lenient toward blacks invited attacks from electoral challengers who could portray them as weak or soft on African Americans. Communities rewarded candidates who successfully maintained the color line with their votes.[40] Conversely, because the vast majority of African Americans in Florida were disenfranchised, they could not effectively participate in electoral politics and hold law enforcement officers, or any other publicly elected official for that matter, accountable for their mistreatment of blacks. In a compounding tragedy, through their inactivity, sheriffs encouraged future violent attacks against blacks by sending the message that black lives were not valued or would not be protected.

In the war years, however, a slow evolution challenged these traditional arrangements. Indications of the change came about in 1943, when, on April 10, a federal grand jury in Macon, Georgia, indicted Robert Screws, sheriff of Baker County, and two other law officers for violating the civil rights of Robert Hall using the guise of their government position, sentencing each to three years in prison and a $1,000 fine. The officers had beaten Hall on January 23, 1943, and left him to die on the floor of a jail cell. Screws's lawyers appealed the decision to the U.S. Supreme Court, which ordered a new trial. However, at the second trial, the jury failed to convict Screws. While ultimately unsuccessful, the decision represented a major victory in the way of curbing the murder of blacks.[41] Thurgood Marshall referenced this as a positive development, commending "a few instances of courageous United States Attorneys in such places as Georgia who have vigorously prosecuted police officers who have used the power of their office as a cloak for beating up Negro citizens."[42]

While Robert Screws escaped justice, his case would set a precedent that became the basis of the conviction of another officer of the law, this time in Florida. In September 1945, Tom Crews, constable for Suwannee County, took Sam McFadden, a black army veteran, into his custody. In retaliation for what he viewed as disrespect, Crews whipped McFadden and then forced him to jump at gunpoint into the Suwannee River, where he drowned. It was the same body of water that had claimed the life of Willie James Howard the year before. While a local jury failed to indict Crews, a federal investigation found evidence that Crews had violated McFadden's civil rights under Section 52 of the U.S. Code, just as in the Screws case.[43] The federal appeals court of the Fifth District agreed with that interpretation, finding Crews guilty. Despite the legal precedent, the sentence, one year in prison and a $1,000 fine, was appallingly insufficient punishment for the horrific loss of a man's life.[44] It seemed, however, that at long last the federal government had found a way to use its prosecutorial power to address egregious abuses of power by law enforcement officers.

* * *

Black Floridians achieved incremental but significant progress on the political front in the years during and after World War II, with the indefatigable Harry T. Moore serving as a key orchestrator. Moore began his protest efforts with the Florida State Teachers Association; founded in 1937, this organization led the legal battle for the equalization of pay for black and white teachers in the state. As an active leader in the state's NAACP, beginning as president in 1941 and later taking the helm as executive secretary in 1946, he continually worked for justice on the part of lynching victims and their families. After all-white democratic primaries were declared unconstitutional in the *Smith v. Allwright* decision in 1944, Moore organized the Progressive Voters League (PVL). Hoping to lay claim to the opportunity for the franchise, Moore led the PVL in a massive voter registration campaign throughout the state. His goal was to leverage the power of the black voting bloc to pressure public officials to be more responsive to their black constituents. His was an unrelenting voice for racial advancement in the state. Moore wrote to political candidates and asked them to make plain their stance on civil rights issues, including antilynching legislation, sending the message that black voters held serious demands that they expected to be addressed.[45]

The PVL was one of several organizations encouraging African Americans to take advantage of the opportunities presented by the *Smith* decision. Communist organizers in Jacksonville also encouraged blacks to exercise their political rights, citing the recent murders in the state as motivation: "REGISTER DEMOCRAT BECAUSE Your registration is a protest against the lynch murder of two Negroes in Florida," the circular proclaimed. "Mr. Jesse James Payne of Madison County and Mr. Sam MaxFadden [sic] of Suwannee County will not have died in vain if you REGISTER DEMOCRATIC!"[46] In total, this effort alone changed the political calculus of electoral politics in Florida, a fact that would be borne out in the coming decades. In the 1946 Democratic primary, the PVL was responsible for the participation of some 30,000 blacks. By the 1950 gubernatorial election, 31 percent of all eligible black voters in the state, over 116,000, cast their vote for governor. Another important outcome of increased access to the franchise would be that African Americans, armed with the right to vote, would be better able to hold law enforcement officials responsible for their conduct, remedying a key factor in the endurance of lynching and other forms of racial violence.[47]

Aside from these conflicts, Florida continued to struggle to provide equal protection to its black citizens. This conflict between social code and the law was brought to life in Gadsden County in 1946. A white girl in the county received a letter allegedly signed by Leroy Bradwell, an African American veteran who had recently returned home. Within hours of this discovery, Sheriff Otha Edwards and Deputy E. Maples, of Gadsden County, began looking for him. They found him at his home, and, without arresting him, the sheriff requested that Bradwell come with him. It was the last time Bradwell was seen alive. Later, the two claimed that they had let Bradwell out of the car at the state line. Despite accusations of foul play, no charges were ever brought against them.[48] What is enigmatic about this incident is that there was no formal breach of the law, yet the sheriff sought to remove Leroy Bradwell from Gadsden County for his own "safety." However, the passing of a note from a black man to a white woman was definitely a social taboo, and Bradwell had clearly broken this code. More important, Sheriff Edwards, through his actions, effectively stated that he was either unwilling or unable to protect Bradwell in the event of a crisis. Subsequent handwriting tests conducted by the FBI concluded the note was not written by Bradwell.[49]

Other incidents of abuse and violence against African Americans continued to be reported around the state, many of them related to labor disputes. In 1945, the Workers' Defense League (WDL) led the call for a federal investigation of worker abuse in Lake County, in the central part of the state, carried out by law enforcement officers led by Sheriff Willis McCall, who earned a notorious reputation for his brutal handling of African Americans. Black and white workers, including some Bahamian laborers, reported being arrested, detained, and fined for no reason. The DOJ opened an investigation into the matter, although it was never able to charge McCall. One worker, Mack Fryar, claimed that Sheriff McCall cracked his skull and threatened to lynch him. The NAACP also called on the Florida attorney general to investigate the brutal death of a black sharecropper, Wyatt Trueblood, who had allegedly been shot and beaten to death in front of his two sons by his landlord, Ben Bryant, of Greensboro. The confrontation started after Trueblood attempted to claim his part of a batch of syrup.[50]

The next major incident of racial violence and murder in Florida occurred in 1949. In Groveland, on July 16, 1949, Norma Lee Padgett, a white woman, claimed she was kidnapped and raped by four black men. She later identified Sammy Shepard, Walter Irvin, Ernest Thomas, and sixteen-year-old Charlie Greenlee as her attackers. As news of the incident spread in the community, a white mob stormed the black section of Groveland in retaliation, shooting and burning homes. Before he could be arrested, Ernest Thomas fled the area, only to be shot to death by a white posse in Madison County. The remaining three young men, dubbed the "Groveland Boys," were indicted of the crime and awaited trial.[51]

The NAACP came to the aid of the Groveland Boys, urging investigation and providing lawyers. Despite its efforts, the three were found guilty, and the oldest two, Irvin and Shepard, were sentenced to die in the electric chair. Lawyers appealed the decision, claiming that the Groveland Boys were forced into confessing to the crime after being severely beaten while in police custody. While the Florida Supreme Court denied the appeal, the U.S. Supreme Court overturned the decision in April 1951, citing the lack of blacks in the jury pool and the inflammatory atmosphere in the community created by the press.[52]

The victory would be temporary, as the men were scheduled for retrial in November. On November 6, 1951, Sheriff Willis McCall transported Irvin and Shepard from the Florida State Prison at Raiford to Groveland to await trial. Along the way, McCall claimed he stopped twice to allow Shepard to relieve himself. On the second stop, he claimed, the two prisoners attempted to overpower him. He had no choice but to shoot them both. Unfortunately for Sheriff McCall, Walter Irvine survived the attack and told another version of the events. He told reporters that McCall had stopped the car, presumably to check the tires. After he exited the car, he pulled both Shepard and Irvin from the car and shot them. While pretending to be dead, Irvin heard McCall on the radio calling for help.[53] The events in Groveland spawned national and international reverberations. As did Holland and Caldwell before him, Fuller Warren found it difficult to confront the challenge of racial violence during his reign as governor of Florida. He was called to task in the press for not doing more to bring about justice in the Groveland case. As a result of this pressure, Warren arranged to meet a delegation of black leaders to discuss the issue. It was the first time since Reconstruction that such a meeting had taken place.[54]

Tragedy would also strike Harry T. Moore. Because of his skilled and dedicated work as an organizer, Moore became the executive secretary, and eventually president, of the Florida Conference of the NAACP. Throughout the 1940s, Moore tirelessly advocated the arrest and prosecution of those who were responsible for lynching in the state. In language that was at the same time eloquent, damning, and demanding, Moore wrote to governors, as well as to the DOJ and Florida congressional representatives, pressing for positive action. In addition, after Howard and Payne were lynched, Moore worked with their survivors, taking affidavits from them and forwarding them to investigators. Moore's penchant for writing caustic protest letters caused Governor Caldwell to inquire as to the source of his continuing irritation.[55]

The governor was not the only one who considered Harry Moore an irritant. He became the first NAACP officer to be assassinated in the organization's history when his home in Mims, Florida, was bombed on Christmas Day in 1951. Moore died from his injuries within a few hours. His wife, Harriett, died a few days later. While no one was ever charged with the bombing, it is widely believed that the KKK was responsible for the murder of the Moores. The assassination of the Moores sparked national and international protest. The Civil Rights Congress, under the leadership of William Patterson, included the incident as one of dozens of grievances it sought to present before the United Nations. The petition, entitled *We Charge Genocide*, urged the international body to intervene and place pressure on the U.S. government to do more to identify those responsible for the Moores' death, as well as the death of Samuel Shepard and the wounding of Walter Irvin. After the killings, Channing Tobias, representing the United States in Paris, complained that "the American delegation [was] . . . confronted daily [with] a recital of racial violence," from ambassadors from the U.S.S.R. as well as from representatives from nonwhite countries. By March 1952, the White House had received over 6,000 telegrams demanding that more be done to solve the case.[56] The outcry placed the Truman administration in a difficult position, especially when it came to international politics. "The focus of American foreign policy was to promote democracy and to 'contain' communism," notes Mary Dudziak, "but the international focus on U.S. racial problems meant that the image of American democracy was tarnished."[57] Continued racial violence in Florida had the overall effect of hampering these global imperatives.

The violence, and shifts caused by the experience of World War II, also had repercussions in Florida, causing more African Americans to reevaluate their position in society. The four communities that were touched by lynching were all a part of rural northern Florida, where blacks had been accustomed to the sway that whites held over their lives. But there was an increase in militancy among blacks after World War II. More than one million blacks served their country in that conflict; after their sacrifices, they returned to the United States determined to stake their claim to full and equal citizenship. This new attitude translated into the feeling that they would not accept being discriminated against or pushed around by the white power structure. The viciousness and senselessness of these lynchings encouraged blacks in these communities to come together to advocate for and protect themselves. The growth of NAACP chapters in North Florida is evidence that more blacks were beginning to organize to work for better living conditions. Between 1944 and 1945, the organization's presence in the state increased from thirty-three branches with 2,850 members to forty-eight branches with 7,226 members. In the communities examined in this study, chapters of the NAACP were chartered within a few years. Blacks in Suwannee County established a chapter in 1944, the same year Willie James Howard was killed. In 1946, three years after the lynching of Cellos Harrison, blacks in Jackson County founded a chapter. African Americans in Madison County formed their organization in 1947, two years after the Payne murder.[58] Tired of the bloodshed and encouraged by the nation's response to violence in their state and the cracks in southern society created by the New Deal and World War II, African Americans in rural Florida organized in defense of themselves in order to experience democracy's promises at long last.

STRANGE FRUIT, BITTER SEEDS

The Echoes of Lynching Violence

The lynchings of Arthur C. Williams, Cellos Harrison, Willie James Howard, and Jesse James Payne were more than isolated incidents. The survivors—both members of the family and the black community—lived with the ever-present threat of white violence that lynching represented. Not only did they lose loved ones, but these individuals had no recourse in the way of either emotional or legal satisfaction. Moreover, because of the nature of segregated society, blacks could place little faith in police protection or the judicial system. As one scholar has noted, lynchings were "as much a crime against Black families and households as against Black bodies."[1] As the decades passed, for many blacks who experienced lynchings the recollection of these incidents remained shrouded in silence and secrecy, serving as sources of painful memories and tragic parables.

One consistent factor in the aftermath of all the lynchings examined in this study was the displacement of the remaining family members. The families of the lynching victims were often compelled by a combination of tragic circumstances to abandon their homes and flee their communities. Most left for fear they would be killed, as the immediate family members would be the ones most interested in seeking justice for the murder of their loved ones. They served as visual reminders of the event. For the perpetrators, this meant that the silence necessary to conceal their activities and escape prosecution was incomplete; the survivors were potential witnesses whose testimonies could stand in opposition to their own versions of the truth. They might also be able to convince sympathetic whites in powerful places to intervene on their behalf. They could write letters to the press and government officials urging investigation, or influence sympathetic whites in the local community to intervene. Such was the case of Mary Turner after a mob lynched her husband in Valdosta, Georgia, in 1918. After learning of her criticism of their acts and her threats to have them prosecuted, she became their next victim. Turner was lynched and had her unborn fetus cut from her charred body, only to be crushed to death.[2]

One painful example of the price paid by African American women in the aftermath of a lynching comes from Lillie Mae, Lucy Ann, and Lucy Mae Payne, the wife, mother, and sister, respectively, of Jesse Payne. The three women had been brutalized and held against their will by whites during the search for Payne. Left without a protector or provider after Payne's murder, two of them were forced into exile, leaving Madison for Sanford in Seminole County. Lucy Ann lived there for the remainder of her life, along with her daughter, Lucy Mae, and her son-in-law. Evidence points to their destitution. Appeals from the family's advocates and supporters almost always include a request for financial support or indemnity for Payne's mother, widow, and infant daughter. The women also sought compensation for the crop on Daniel Goodman's land that they were forced to abandon.

The other Payne siblings also faced significant changes in the aftermath of their brother's murder. Upon leaving the U.S. Navy after serving in the Pacific theater during the war, his brother Amos Payne settled in Sanford along with his sister and mother. Lucy Mae and her husband continued to labor as migrant workers, but ultimately she chose to remain, without her husband, in upstate New York. Another Payne sibling, Leroy, after leaving the Marines, moved to Detroit and changed his name, leaving both his identity and family behind. He kept the family legacy alive, however, by naming his children after the relatives he left behind in Florida. Because of the separation and the secrecy, it has taken Amos's and Leroy's children generations to put the broken pieces of their family tree back together. Two sets of cousins, some in Sanford and some in Detroit, grew up knowing practically nothing about the others. The sole link, Aunt Lucy Mae, hardly ever talked about her brother's lynching, but when she did the memories drove her to tears. Her stories about her experiences in faraway Florida, especially the violence she had personally endured, and their murdered uncle haunted her nieces. They also heard stories about another uncle, Stephen, the oldest boy, who also died under mysterious circumstances in 1933.[3] Not until later research did they learn about another aunt, Ruby, the first-born daughter of William and Lucy Ann, who was unknown to them.

The lynching of Jesse James Payne and the subsequent displacement of the family, however, severed some ties completely. During the turmoil after the tragedy, the family lost contact with Jesse James Payne's widow, Lillie Mae, and the baby daughter the couple shared. Even her name has been lost to time. The family that remains hopes to one day identify their long-lost cousin, meet her, and share with her the family's history of tragedy and survival.

In Live Oak, the Howards sold their home and fled to Orlando within a matter of days after their son was killed, amid threats that if they sought justice, they would be killed as well. Bessie Harrison, the wife of Cellos Harrison, actually left for New York after her husband was rearrested in May 1943, a few weeks before he was killed. Soon thereafter, Harrison's mother left Jackson County for the North also. Hattie Williams fled north to Illinois, where her sister lived, with her two youngest children, leaving behind her husband and another son. Because of Arthur C. Williams's lynching, this family was forever shattered, as they never reunited as a family.[4]

The survivors of lynchings, even after moving away from the scene of the murders, experienced severe economic and emotional repercussions. Some families experienced significant financial losses without their primary breadwinner, as did the relatives of Jesse James Payne, who left twenty-seven acres of agricultural products unharvested in the wake of their exodus. The Payne family members also told authorities that their former landlord, Daniel Goodman, withheld from them a government check that had arrived in the mail. Payne's wife, Lillie Mae, was left as the sole provider for the couple's daughter. Aside from financial hardship, the emotional scars inflicted after this type of loss remained with family members for years after the event. Compounding the problem was the stress and alienation of being uprooted from one's home community and moving to another, the anger that naturally stems from knowledge of such an injustice, and the grief of losing a loved one under such brutal circumstances. Distance and time did little to erase the pain. Family members describe witnessing the survivors experience bouts of depression and anxiety as well as other mental and behavioral changes that in today's society would be classified as post-traumatic stress disorder (PTSD).[5]

The experience of Ann Flipper, the younger sister of Arthur Williams, testifies to the trauma families lived with after the lynching of a relative. Only nine years of age at the time of her brother's murder, Flipper's entire world changed when she was separated from her home, her father, and her brothers. Her mother, Hattie Williams, made arrangements to leave Florida and join her sister in East St. Louis, Illinois. However, the sister only had enough money for two bus tickets, one for Hattie and one for Ann, the only girl. The others, she remarked, could "hobo" their way to Illinois. Resentful, Frank Williams stayed behind with the boys—Rufus, the twins Freddie and Eddie, and Frank Jr. Young Ann was devastated by the separation. At one of the Greyhound bus stops, she left her mother and tried to run away to make it back to Quincy to be with her father. It was a childish and foolhardy attempt by a young girl who, already traumatized by the death of her brother, now was being separated from her father and remaining brothers. While the elder Williams did eventually make it to East St. Louis, he decided to return to Quincy to live, rendering the temporary separation of the Williams family a permanent one.[6]

As a result, Ann was forced to grow up fatherless. Her only remaining parent was consumed by grief. Together, mother and daughter shared the bitter memories of the lives that had been lost. Though Hattie Williams and her youngest children made new lives for themselves in East St. Louis, the nightmare of Arthur's lynching never faded from Ann Flipper's memory. In speaking of her emotional journey, she recalled,

> It was hard. For one reason, Florida was our home. To pack up and leave our friends and . . . we all was born there. . . . When I was growing up I really had a lot of hatred in my heart towards the white[s]. I really did. And as I grew and got older, I realized that all of them [were] not the same. These people that I know now didn't do that. I had to, I had a lot of hatred in my heart. And now I don't but it took years for me to get over that. Now I find myself, sometimes as I talk about it, I find myself crying because of the way that they did my brother.[7]

Flipper's statement is representative of the resentment and anguish experienced by members of the victims' families and communities, which lasted years beyond the lynchings themselves.

Another survivor of racial violence is Allie Mae Neal, daughter of

Claude Neal, whose lynching was the last major spectacle lynching to take place in Florida in 1934. She was three years old at the time of her father's murder, and remembered fleeing through the woods with her pregnant mother. The trauma of that night would scar them both, not just mentally but physically. Allie Mae suffered a back injury that has hampered her ever since. Her mother lost the child she was carrying. As she grew up in Marianna, Neal describes suffering from sadness and depression caused by the void of her father's death. "Just every little thing that go on I'd say, I wish I had a daddy," she recalled. "If my daddy was living, so and so. If I had a daddy, I could go such and such a place. I kept that up all the time. My daddy wouldn't let this happen. My daddy wouldn't let that happen. . . . I never had a father to take me to a school party or nothing. I never had the joy of a daddy. Never did." Neal also admitted that she occasionally still experiences nightmares.[8]

Several black residents of these communities testified about the inability to speak openly, whether to inquire about or much less protest lynchings. There was a real fear that if one talked too freely, one might become the next target of violence. During the course of my researching these lynchings, more than a half-century after they had taken place, some interview subjects reacted with suspicion, hostility, or fear when asked about instances of racial violence in their communities. Cellos Harrison's widow, Bessie Harrison, when contacted by phone, flatly refused to talk about her husband's murder. Lula Howard, the mother of Willie James Howard, has also remained adamant about not speaking of her son's death. Even for those relatives who do remember, the horrific memories and all-consuming anger, even today, are disabling. A close relative of Willie Howard broke several scheduled interviews because she did not care to relive such painful memories. Another interview subject agreed to talk with me after being convinced by her son, but later had him contact me and withdraw her permission to use what she told me. This was despite that fact that I had offered to use a pseudonym to avoid using her real name. This woman's desperate fear, near fifty years after the events in question, confirmed the lasting power of racial violence and how well the lessons of white supremacy had been learned in that one community.

In traditional treatments of lynching, the focus remains on the victim and the immediate aftermath of the incident, often losing sight of those left to grieve the loss of their loved ones. Given the fact that most victims were black males, their deaths frequently created serious voids in the lives of the women they left behind—mothers, wives, sisters, and daughters. During the era of Jim Crow, black women in the South were arguably among the most vulnerable people in American society. Devalued and marginalized by American society in general, they survived either with the limited protection that they could find on their own terms or, most frequently, in union with a black man. However, the limited ability of African American men to protect themselves from random violence, particularly in the South, translated to a continued assailableness on the part of black women, whether physically or economically, or both. Additionally, in the aftermath of a lynching, family members, regardless of gender, were potential targets of intimidation or retribution, as any knowledge they may have relating to the violence made them potential witnesses.[9]

Researchers have noted similar effects of lynching on the historical landscape of a community. Writing about his experiences researching in Lauren County, South Carolina, Bruce Baker made several significant discoveries about the power and purpose of community memory in the aftermath of lynching violence. He discovered that, for members of the black community, remembering was a part of extracting justice from an unjust situation. Retelling the stories of past injustices gave them the power of accusation, which, while a poor substitute for legal prosecution of the perpetrators of such crimes, allowed blacks to claim moral superiority. Baker found that while stories of lynching tended to become less accurate over time, the primary focus was on the content, message, and moral value of these episodes. They also served as warnings for younger generations of blacks about the dangers present in the racism and discrimination that permeated American society. Thus, tragic memories became a method of socializing black children, especially black males.[10]

The interpretation and retelling of lynching legends within the African American community demonstrate an effort to exercise control over, and extract cultural value from, the memory of instances of white brutality. In developing and fortifying their own interpretations of these stories, blacks rejected the white-controlled public discourse about these lynchings and replaced them with their own authentic versions of events. These stories and their retelling kept alive the tales of injustice, the loss of land and profit, and the tragedy inflicted on the families. They confirmed the innocence of the victims and the treachery of the murderers. Behind closed doors they named names, identifying and remembering the perpetrators and conspirators. At times these tales took on an element of karmic justice through tragedy, with lynchers suffering long illnesses, painful deaths, or the loss of their own loved ones. As Jonathan Holloway notes about the spaces between archives, memory, silence, and forgetting in his work *Jim Crow Wisdom*, "black collective memory is a memory of the forgotten, a memory of those whose very presence made the rest of the country white, a memory of those who lived lives struggling against a denial of their citizenship so that others would know how to claim their stake in America."[11]

Additionally, oral histories conducted for this study of lynching in Florida between 1941 and 1945 appear to confirm that lynching created a long-lasting climate of fear in black communities. As Baker posited, the recollections of many individuals who lived through lynching episodes collected in this study reveal an inclination to "stack" memories, a process in which the details of separate lynchings are merged into a singular account, which is valued more for the accuracy of lessons or warnings contained in the recounting rather than the actual exactness of the memory itself. This proved to be especially true in communities that had experienced multiple lynchings within a generation. Before Arthur C. Williams's lynching in 1941, another black man, Will "Bull" Larkins, had been lynched in 1929 in Quincy. When asked about the Williams lynching, some subjects said that his body had been dragged around the courthouse square. This detail, however, was only true of Larkins's lynching. In Marianna, although Cellos Harrison had been killed more recently, the details of Claude Neal's lynching in 1934 were more prominent in many people's memories. At least one subject, when asked about the Harrison murder, retold a story of a white man showing off Harrison's amputated toe in a store in downtown Marianna. This description, however, corresponded with accounts of activities after Neal's lynching. Further, official reports on the condition of Harrison's body stated that his body had not been mutilated. In both Quincy and Marianna, the prior lynchings were more dramatic and made deeper, more lasting impressions on the community's memory. The bodies of both Larkins and Neal had been placed on display for the public to see. In each instance, the recollections of people who lived through these dreadful events were merged by the remembrance of emotions, fear of racial violence, and anger about racial injustice.

Control of memory also has redemptive properties. In interviewing numerous subjects, it appears that in their remembrances and retellings, members of the black community could, when necessary, craft the details surrounding a lynching to cast the situation in a different, more favorable light. This may have been the case in the Howard lynching. As noted previously, the recorded history, told primarily from the point of view of whites, differs greatly from the recollections of Live Oak's black community. On the one hand, Howard was accused of breaking a social taboo by making romantic advances toward a white girl. On the other hand, Howard was the unwitting victim of a misinterpreted gesture, the innocent words of a love song written down by request. In some ways, the origin of the divergence is less important than the result. In the eyes of the black community, Willie James Howard remains the innocent victim, not the transgressor or potential sexual aggressor, as the cultural stereotypes about black males portray.

By the end of the twentieth century, while lynchings have become more representative of times past than the present, the recountings of lynching stories have become less frequent and seem to have faded, in all but the rarest cases, from community discussion and folklore. As legal segregation and inequality have faded, warnings about the dangers of interracial interaction have become unnecessary. Yet, while submerged, memories of lynching and racial injustice continue to haunt the collective consciousness of black communities throughout the South; with the right set of circumstances, these ghosts reemerge. As discussed in the introduction, the case of Ray Golden's contested death illustrates that the burden of memory—in this case, the memories of the horrors of lynching—still fuel an inherit distrust of the American legal and judicial system on the part of many blacks. Understanding the root of these attitudes and beliefs is the first step in the attempt to destroy the barriers of resentment that continue to divide communities nationwide along racial lines. In order to do this, more attention to the long-term psychological and social effects of lynching, racial violence, and unequal protection under the law in the United States is necessary.

NOTES

Introduction

1. "Was It Suicide or Murder?" *Palm Beach Post*, July 27, 2003.

2. Ibid.

3. Abby Goodnough, "A Suicide or a Lynching? Answers Sought in Florida," *New York Times*, July 29, 2003; "King's Sons Coming to Glades to Investigate Hanging Death," *Palm Beach Post*, August 4, 2003.

4. Susan Eastman, "Death and Doubts," *Broward–Palm Beach New Times*, October 30, 2003.

5. "Inquest into Hanging Death Ends; Lynching Ruled Out," *Palm Beach Post*, July 30, 2003; "Civil Rights Commission to Probe Hanging of Florida Man after Inquest Calls Death a Suicide," *Jet*, August 18, 2003, 49–50.

6. "Inquest into Hanging Death Ends; Lynching Ruled Out," *Palm Beach Post*, July 30, 2003.

7. The impact of lynching violence on communities is taken up by Sherrilyn A. Ifill in *On the Courthouse Lawn*. Jonathan Markovitz also offers a broad look at the impact of lynching on American film, popular culture, and public memory, arguing that "lynching has become a metaphor for racism and that collective memories of lynching have been mobilized and reconstructed in order to understand and either to contest or to further various racial projects." Markovitz, *Legacies of Lynching*, 137–48.

8. See Stampp, *Era of Reconstruction*; Litwack, *Been in the Storm So Long*; Rabinowitz, *Race Relations in the Urban South*.

9. Kharif, "Refinement of Racial Segregation in Florida"; Shofner, "Custom, Law and History," 277–98. For a discussion on racial violence in Florida during this period, see Newton, *Invisible Empire*; Peek, "Aftermath of Military Reconstruction," 123–41; Peek, "Lawlessness in Florida," 164–85. For recent scholarship on Reconstruction-era violence in Jackson County, see Weinfeld, *Jackson County War*.

10. The landmark U.S. Supreme Court decision in *Plessy v. Ferguson* established the constitutionality of "separate but equal," which would become the basis of so-called Jim Crow laws in the South and legal segregation in other areas of the nation.

11. Sydnor, "Southerners and the Laws," 9–10.

12. For a comprehensive examination of the black experience during Reconstruction in Florida, see Richardson, *Negro in the Reconstruction of Florida*; Shofner, *Nor Is It Over Yet*; Brown, *Florida's Black Public Officials*; Ortiz, *Emancipation Betrayed*, 10.

13. Ortiz, *Emancipation Betrayed*, 62.

14. Ibid., 80–81.

15. Ibid., 37–39, 64.

16. Wells, *A Red Record*, in Royster, *Southern Horrors and Other Writings*, 75–80; Schechter, *Ida B. Wells-Barnett*, 112; Zangrando, *NAACP*, 9; Litwack, *Trouble in Mind*, 121.

17. Wells-Barnett, *Southern Horrors* (1892). *A Red Record* (1894). *Mob Rule in New Orleans* (1900); Schechter, *Ida B. Wells-Barnett*; Wells-Barnett, *Crusade for Justice*.

18. Zangrando, *NAACP*; Dray, *At the Hands of Persons Unknown*, 58, 60; Fox, *Guardian of Boston*.

19. Emmons, "Flame of Resistance," 18–24, 58–61.

20. Colburn and Scher, *Florida's Gubernatorial Politics*, 222.

21. NAACP Division of Research and Information, "Anti-Lynching Legislation, 1921–1945," NAACP Papers.

22. Ortiz, *Emancipation Betrayed*, 227.

23. Ibid., 205–28.

24. Jones and McCarthy, *African Americans in Florida*, 81–84; Jones et al., "Documented History."

25. Mary Talbert, National Director of the Anti-Lynching Crusaders, NAACP Papers; Lerner, *Black Women in White America*, 211–12; Zangrando, *NAACP*, 78, 81; Hall, *Revolt against Chivalry*, 165–66.

26. Jones and McCarthy, *African Americans in Florida*, 60–63, 72–74.

27. Jones, "'Without Compromise or Fear,'" 479–80.

28. Dunn, "New Deal and Florida Politics," 179–89.

29. Pilkington, "Trials of Brotherhood," 55–80; Kneebone, *Southern Liberal Journalists*, 47–51.

30. Egerton, *Speak Now against the Day*, 123, 302; Johnson, *Reforming Jim Crow*, 48–65.

31. Southern Commission on the Study of Lynching, *Lynchings and What They Mean*; Raper, *Tragedy of Lynching*; Kneebone, *Southern Liberal Journalists*, 77–96.

32. Cash, *Mind of the South*, 248; Heflin, "A Segregationist Discusses Interracial Marriage," in Newby, *Development of Segregationist Thought*, 127; Hall, *Revolt against Chivalry*; Hall, "'The Mind That Burns in Each Body'" in Snitow, Stansell, and Thompson, *Powers of Desire*; White, *Rope and Faggot*, 56; Feimster, *Southern Horrors*, 62–86.

33. Davis, Gardner, and Gardner, *Deep South*, 25.

34. Hall, *Revolt against Chivalry*, 146–49; Myrdal, *American Dilemma*, 561; Howard, *Lynchings*, 73–80.

35. Hall, *Revolt against Chivalry*.

36. Kimberley Johnson argues that these activists have not received the proper credit for the work they undertook and the results it provided. See Johnson, *Reforming Jim Crow*, 64.

37. Ames, *Changing Character of Lynching*.

38. Ibid., 15.

39. Jonathan Daniels, "A Native at Large," *Nation*, September 14, 1940, 219.

40. *New York Times*, May 10, 1940.

41. Waldrep, "War of Words," 75–100; Waldrep, *Many Faces of Judge Lynch*, 127–50.

42. For more on the cultural transition in the African American community during the era of the Great Migration and World War I, see Lewis, *When Harlem Was in Vogue*; Schneider, "*We Return Fighting*"; Harrison, *Black Exodus*; Marks, *Farewell*. On the black military experience in World War I, see Patton, *War and Race*; Nalty, *Strength for the Fight*.

43. Voogd, *Race Riots and Resistance*.

44. Sitkoff, *New Deal for Blacks*, 3–33; Cronon, *Black Moses*; Stein, *World of Marcus Garvey*.

45. Gerald Horne offers an articulate summary of the international interests of African Americans during the late nineteenth and early twentieth centuries in "Race from Power," 437–61; see also Layton, *International Politics*.

46. Plummer, *Rising Wind*, 16.

47. Kearney, "Japan," 117–28; Kearney, *African American Views of the Japanese*.

48. With great opposition from the ruling classes in the region, Communists organized African American labor in the South through the National Textile Workers Union, the American Negro Labor Congress, and the Red International Labor Union. See Gilmore, *Defying Dixie*, ch. 2; Carter, *Scottsboro*.

49. Several issues of *Crisis* magazine in the spring of 1932 took up the debate over the value of Communism in the struggle for black equality, with responses that ran the spectrum of opinion, both for and against. See "Negro Editors on Communism," *Crisis* (April 1932): 117–19; Solomon, *Cry Was Unity*.

50. Roman, *Opposing Jim Crow*, 125–53; Gilmore, *Defying Dixie*, ch. 4.

51. Gilmore, *Defying Dixie*, ch. 4.

52. Kapur, *Raising Up a Prophet*; Plummer, *Rising Wind*, 57.

53. Sakashita, "Lynching Across the Pacific," in Carrigan and Waldrep, *Swift to Wrath*, 181–214; Borstelmann, *Cold War*, 35–37; Gallicchio, *African American Encounter*, 58–60; White, *Man Called White*, 68–69.

54. Gilmore, *Defying Dixie*, 161.

55. W. E. B. DuBois, "As the Crow Flies," *Crisis* 40 (September 1933): 197; Sitkoff, "African Americans, American Jews, and the Holocaust," in Chafe, *Achievement of American Liberalism*, 181–203.

56. *Washington Tribune*, April 9, 1938. An informative analysis of responses in the black press to Hitler can be found in Lunabelle Wedlock, "The Reaction of Negro Publications and Organizations to German Anti-Semitism," *Howard University Studies in the Social Sciences* 3, no. 2 (1942): 91–115, reprinted in Adams and Bracey, *Strangers and Neighbors*.

57. For a thorough account of the Shoemaker lynching and the attacks on his compatriots, Eugene Poulout and Dr. Samuel Rogers, see Ingalls, *Urban Vigilantes*, 163–204.

58. Ibid., 185.

59. *Miami Herald*, November 24, 1937.

60. Ibid.; Ingalls, *Urban Vigilantes*, 163–204; Newton, *Invisible Empire*, 99.

61. Howard, *Lynchings*, 113–16; Pinar, *Gender of Racial Politics and Violence*, 155.

62. Jones, "'Without Compromise or Fear,'" 479–80.

63. Sitkoff, *New Deal for Blacks*.

64. U.S. Department of Agriculture, Bureau of Agricultural Economics, Division of Program Surveys, "Plans and Attitudes of Winter Vegetable Growers in Palm Beach and Broward Counties, Florida," July 21, 1943, quoted in Kryder, *Divided Arsenal*, 221–22. These conflicts are also mentioned in Johnson, *To Stem This Tide*, 25–27; Katznelson, *When Affirmative Action Was White*, 27–52.

65. Tyler, "'Blood on Your Hands': White Southerners' Criticism of Eleanor Roosevelt during World War II," in Feldman, *Before Brown*, 102–5.

66. Logan, *What the Negro Wants*, 8.

67. For a description of the inspiration for the proposed March on Washington and the passage of Executive Order #8802, see Sitkoff, *New Deal for Blacks*, 314–25; Quarles, "A. Philip Randolph: Labor Leader at Large," in Franklin and Meier, *Black Leaders of the Twentieth Century*, 139–66; Pfeffer, *A. Philip Randolph*, 39–43.

68. Washburn, *African American Newspaper*, 143.

69. A. Philip Randolph, "Keynote Address to the Policy Conference of the March on Washington Movement," September 26–27, 1942, in Broderick and Meier, *Negro Protest Thought*, 201.

70. Wynne, *Florida at War*, 13; Mormino, "World War II," in Gannon, *New History of Florida*, 323–43 (this essay details Florida's transition during World War II); Mohl and Mormino, "The Big Change in the Sunshine State," in Gannon, *New History of Florida*, 418; Mormino, *Land of Sunshine*, 2, 9–10.

71. Mormino, "GI Joe Meets Jim Crow," 23–42.

72. Lichtenstein, "'We at Last Are Industrializing,'" in Cassanello and Shell-Weiss, *Florida's Working-Class Past*, 184–87.

73. Newton, *Invisible Empire*, 104.

74. For a more complete treatment exploring the impact of the New Deal on the South and the role southerners played in FDR's administration, as well as how matters of race were handled within these bounds, see Egerton, *Speak Now against the Day*; Mormino, "GI Joe Meets Jim Crow," 23–42; Ward, "A War for States' Rights," in Kruse, *Fog of War*, 126–35.

75. Nearly 83 percent took place on southern soil, and almost 73 percent of the victims were black. White victims of lynch mobs tended to be outsiders because of their ethnicity (foreigners) or their political beliefs (socialists and Communists). "Lynchings, by States and Race, 1882–1951," in Guzman et al., *Negro Year Book*, 1952, 277.

76. Tolnay and Beck, *Festival of Violence*, 38; NAACP, *Thirty Years of Lynching*, 35; Ames, *Changing Character of Lynching*, 2.

77. Paul Ortiz identifies the tenets supporting the myth of "Florida's exceptionalism" in his afterword in Winsboro, *Old South, New South, or Down South?*, 220–34.

78. Newton, *Invisible Empire*, 73, 100–104.

79. Ingalls, *Urban Vigilantes*.

80. Brundage, *Under Sentence of Death*, 17–45.

81. Brundage, *Lynching in the New South*, 28–30.

82. McGovern, *Anatomy of a Lynching*.

83. Pfeifer, *Rough Justice*; Wyatt-Brown, *Honor and Violence in the Old South*; Ayers, *Vengeance and Justice*. Gonzales-Day provides another regional perspective in *Lynching in the West*.

84. Howard, *Lynchings*, 138.

85. Ibid., 133.

Chapter 1. Lynched Twice: Arthur C. Williams, Gadsden County, 1941

1. Borstelmann, *Cold War*; Anderson, *Eyes Off the Prize*.

2. Howard, *Lynchings*, 91–112.

3. Sitkoff, *New Deal for Blacks*; Egerton, *Speak Now against the Day*.

4. Dunn, "New Deal and Florida Politics," 287.

5. Claude Pepper was a dedicated New Dealer but toed the line on segregation. As Roosevelt's programs became more unpopular in the South, Pepper found himself increasingly ostracized at home. His efforts in the campaign to repeal Florida's poll tax in 1938—the holy grail of white supremacy—won him few friends. His senatorial campaign in 1950 was torpedoed by his competitor in part because of accusations of Pepper's racial liberalism. Later in his career Pepper became a supporter of civil rights, and, according to Robert Zangrando, the experience during the 1937 filibuster changed his view on civil rights matters. See Clark, *Red Pepper and Gorgeous George*, 13–14; *U.S. Congressional Record*, 75th Congress, 1st Session, 8756–58; Zangrando, *NAACP*, 149. Tensions surrounding issues of race and politics in the South are discussed in Gilmore, *Gender and Jim Crow*, 91–118; Ferber, *White Man Falling*, 34–43.

6. Howard, *Lynchings*, 108–32.

7. Ames's announcement came shortly after a conference between representatives of the ASWPL, the NAACP, and the Tuskegee Institute to find consensus for a single definition of lynching to govern reporting. While initially giving her consent, Ames later rejected the guidelines. Waldrep, *Many Faces of Judge Lynch*, 145–50; Waldrep, "War of Words," 75–100; Walter White, "Lynching Still Goes On," *New York Times*, May 17, 1940.

8. Tebeau, *History of Florida*, 413; Evans, "Weathering the Storm"; Revels, "Blitz-krieg of Joy," in Wynne, *Florida at War*, 11–18.

9. Compromises were made with southerners to exclude certain classes of agricultural and domestic laborers, a field dominated by black workers, from the Social Security Act of 1935. Similarly, southerners also managed to exclude these same groups of laborers from the minimum wage protections established in the Fair Labor Standards Act of 1938. Sitkoff, *New Deal for Blacks*, 102–38; Egerton, *Speak Now against the Day*, 82–98, 104–10; Kennedy, *Freedom from Fear*, 257–73, 344. Where legislative and political maneuvering failed, whites in Florida resorted to extralegal violence and intimidation to keep the black workforce in check. See Shofner, "Legacy of Racial Slavery," 411–26. For more on the anxieties of southerners over labor changes and urbanization, see Daniel, "Going among Strangers," 886–911.

10. The threat of the March on Washington and the subsequent creation of the Fair Employment Practices Commission (FEPC) represented the success of a social movement to create international tension to effect a domestic result. Other civil rights organizations would follow similar strategies in the coming years. See Garfinkel, *When Negroes March*; Ruchames, *Race, Jobs, and Politics*; Kessleman, *Social Politics of FEPC*.

11. The success of the teacher pay equalization case by the Florida State Teachers' Association represented a key element in the rejuvenation of the civil rights movement in Florida and the growth of the state's NAACP membership. Porter and Neyland, *History of the Florida State Teachers Association*; Emmons, "Flame of Resistance," 85–108.

12. White House News Release, August 21, 1941, http://avalon.law.yale.edu/wwii/atcmess.asp; Hart, "Making Democracy," 55.

13. Hart, "Making Democracy," 81.

14. U.S. Senate, Congress, Senate, Subcommittee of the Committee on the Judiciary, *Hearings (H.R. 801)*, 76th Congress, 3rd session, 58–59, 75–79 (February 6–7, March 5, 12–13, 1940).

15. Borstelmann, *Cold War*, 36.

16. McGuire, *Taps for a Jim Crow Army*, xliv.

17. Sullivan, *Days of Hope*, 136; Nalty, *Strength for the Fight*, 164.

18. Letter from "A Soldier" to the *Chicago Defender*, January 9, 1944, quoted in McGuire, *Taps for a Jim Crow Army*, 88.

19. The quote is attributed to a black student at a southern college debating with his professor, which was later recounted to Walter White of the NAACP. White, "What the Negro Thinks of the Army," 67–71.

20. In 1863, there were 4,193 slaves and 5,202 whites in Gadsden County. Avant, *Illustrated Index*, 54.

21. Ibid., 87–100, 137–40; Rivers, *Slavery in Florida*, 36–37; Baptist, *Creating an Old South*.

22. Chestang, "Shade-Grown," 24; Richardson, *Negro in the Reconstruction of Florida*; Ortiz, *Emancipation Betrayed*.

23. In Cuba, "shade" tobacco grew under the shadow of trees, shielding the plants from direct sunlight and improving the quality of the leaf. Farmers in Gadsden County constructed cloth and board structures to simulate the shade phenomenon. Avant, *Illustrated Index*, 155; Pando, "Shrouded in Cheesecloth"; Stoutamire, Helfenstein, and Kierce, *Tobacco Growing in Florida*.

24. Avant, *Illustrated Index*, 151.

25. Tisdale, *Tobacco Diseases*, 108; Avant, *Illustrated Index*, 171.

26. Avant, *Illustrated Index*, 173.

27. Florida State Planning Board, *Statistical Abstract of Florida Counties* (hereafter cited as *Stastical Abstract*).

28. Ibid.

29. Chestang, "Shade-Grown," 108.

30. Cox, "Lynching and the Status Quo," 584.

31. Dixie interview.

32. Chestang, "Shade-Grown," 18.

33. Litwack, *Trouble in Mind*, 137.

34. Ibid., 121.

35. Kelley interview.

36. Summers interview; Kelley interview.

37. Thompson and Waldorf, *Historical and Architectural Survey*, 13.

38. "Negro Rapist Meets Death at Hands of Angry Mob Sat. Night," *Gadsden County Times*, November 14, 1929; "Quincy Negro Killed by Mob," *Daily Democrat*, November 12, 1929.

39. "Quincy Negro Killed by Mob," *Daily Democrat*, November 12, 1929.

40. Editorial, *Gadsden County Times*, November 14, 1929.

41. Summers interview.

42. In interviews and conversations with African Americans in Quincy, explanations of Larkins's lynching vary a great deal. Some say that Larkins was having an affair with a white woman. Others infer that he simply touched a white woman's leg. Muhammad, "Justified Southern Punishment."

43. Testimony of Dan Davis, transcription, "Investigation into the Seizure of A. C. Williams" May 12, 1941, 10–12, Holland Papers (hereafter cited as Seizure Investigation). This investigation was conducted by Orion C. Parker, state attorney for the Second Judicial Circuit of the state of Florida.

44. Ibid.

45. Ibid.

46. Testimony of M. P. Luten, transcription, Coroner's Inquest on the body of A. C. Williams, Quincy, Gadsden County, Florida, May 13, 1941, 25–26, Holland Papers (hereafter cited as Coroner's Inquest). This investigation was conducted by Orion C. Parker, state attorney for the Second Judicial Circuit of the state of Florida.

47. Davis, Seizure Investigation, 3.

48. "Governor Holland Awaits Reports on Quincy Negro Slaying," *River Junction Tribune*, May 6, 1941.

49. Testimony of M. P. Luten, Seizure Investigation, 32.

50. Ibid.

51. Ibid.

52. Testimony of Maria Bell, Seizure Investigation, 28–29.

53. Testimony of Annie Bell, Seizure Investigation, 24.

54. Ibid., 24–27.

55. Testimony of Thelma Bell, Seizure Investigation, 18–23.

56. Dr. Wilhoit had also examined the twelve-year-old victims in the Larkins rape case in 1929. Maurice Tripp to Governor Spessard Holland, May 24, 1941, Holland Papers. (Tripp's correspondence hereafter cited as Tripp Report); "Negro Rapist Meets Death at Hands of Angry Mob Sat. Night," *Gadsden County Times*, November 14, 1929.

57. Ann Flipper is the sister of Arthur C. Williams, the youngest child and the only daughter of Frank and Hattie Williams's fourteen children. Arthur was the oldest. Flipper interview.

58. Frank Singleton is the brother of Sam Singleton, a member of the party that attempted to transport Williams to Tallahassee. Sam Singleton, now deceased, relayed an account of the events to his brother after the incident. Singleton interview.

59. "Luten, Bassett Take Office Tuesday," *Gadsden County Times*, January 9, 1941.

60. Luten, Coroner's Inquest, 28.

61. Testimony of S. E. Wilhoit, Coroner's Inquest, 2–5; Singleton interview; Testimony of Will Webb, Coroner's Inquest; Luten, Coroner's Inquest.

62. The presence of another car is mentioned in this report but not in the testimony given by Webb at the Coroner's Inquest on May 13, 1941. Tripp Report, 3.

63. Testimony of Rufus Williams, Coroner's Inquest, 48.

64. Tripp Report, 6.

65. Coroner's Inquest.

66. Webb, Coroner's Inquest, 10–12.

67. Ibid., 13–14.

68. Testimony of Will Webb, Sam Singleton, Horace Courtney, Rufus Williams, Jessie Lee Hill, Coroner's Inquest, 8–23, 39–43.

69. Orion C. Parker to Governor Spessard Holland, May 19, 1941, Holland Papers.

70. Tripp Report, 6.

71. Testimony of Ed Wynn, Coroner's Inquest, 24–25.

72. Tripp Report, 5.

73. "Holland Studies Williams Case Reports," *River Junction Tribune*, May 23, 1941.

74. George F. Hoffman, U.S. Attorney, Pensacola, Florida, to the Office of the Attorney General, Washington, D.C., July 14, 1942, Holland Papers.

75. Wendell Berge, Assistant Attorney General, U.S. Department of Justice, to George Earl Hoffman, U.S. Attorney, July 23, 1942, Holland Papers.

76. Between 1921 and 1930, the ASWPL recorded 277 lynchings, compared with 114 between 1931 and 1940, a decrease of 59 percent. According to NAACP statistics, in the time periods previously indicated, the number of lynchings decreased from

290 to 130, showing a 45 percent decrease. Ames, *Changing Character of Lynching*, 11; "Lynchings in the United States, 1921–1946," NAACP Papers.

77. The ASWPL shared this sentiment. Although ASWPL members campaigned vigorously throughout the 1930s for the end of lynching, the group refused to endorse federal antilynching legislation, citing its belief in the predominance of states' rights. See Hall, *Revolt against Chivalry*, 244–48.

78. "Wounded Negro Attack Suspect Seized, Killed," *Tampa Morning Tribune*, May 14, 1941; "Once Again, Lynch Law!," *St. Petersburg Times*, May 14, 1941; "Westbrook Pegler Lynches a Community," *Daily Democrat*, May 20, 1941; "Masked Men Slay an Accused Negro," *New York Times*, May 14, 1941; "Negro Is Killed by Lynchers on Second Attempt," *New York Herald Tribune*, May 14, 1941.

79. Pegler's heated condemnation of the Quincy lynching was quite interesting, in that in 1933 he found himself in the midst of controversy after writing a column in support of lynching when two whites were lynched in California for kidnapping and murdering a college student. See Platt, *Pegler*, 119–23; Westbrook Pegler, "Fair Enough," *Tampa Tribune*, May 19, 1941.

80. "Westbrook Pegler Lynches a Community," *Daily Democrat*, May 20, 1941.

81. Ibid.; "Holland Studies Williams Case Reports," *River Junction Tribune*, May 23, 1941; Harold Colee to *River Junction Tribune*, May 30, 1941.

82. LaMar Watts, "Here's a Letter from the Editor," *River Junction Tribune*, May 23, 1941; W. Robert Hopkins, Madison, Tennessee, to *River Junction Tribune*, May 30, 1941; W. Pooser, Marianna, Florida, to *River Junction Tribune*, May 30, 1941.

83. T. R. Smith to *River Junction Tribune*, May 23, 1941.

84. "Upper House Flays Pegler for Writings," *Florida Times-Union*, May 29, 1941.

85. "Attacks on Quincy Show That Community Isolation Is a Relic of the Past," *River Junction Tribune*, May 23, 1941.

86. Gill and Jenkins, "Nazis and the American South," 670–76.

87. Zangrando, *NAACP*, 19.

88. "Churchman Asks Ouster of Sheriff in Lynching Case," *Tampa Morning Tribune*, May 15, 1941.

89. Sanford May, Quincy, Florida, to Governor Spessard Holland, May 15, 1941, Holland Papers.

90. Jessie Daniel Ames to Governor Spessard Holland, May 29, 1941; Mrs. L. W. Alford, Chairman of the Mississippi Council of the ASWPL, to Governor Spessard Holland, June 2, 1941; Alma L. Richardson, Virginia Council of the ASWPL, to Governor Spessard Holland, May 23, 1941; Mrs. T. W. Koster, Alabama Conference of the Woman's Society of Christian Service, May 24, 1941, all in Holland Papers.

91. Hall, *Revolt against Chivalry*.

92. Jane Havens, Chairman of the Florida Council of ASWPL, to Governor Spessard Holland, May 26, 1941, Holland Papers.

93. Julia Barnwell, Madison, Florida, to Governor Spessard Holland, May 18, 1941; Alice Cramer, Tampa, Florida, to Governor Spessard Holland, May 16, 1941; Mrs. J. T. Feaster, Miami, Florida, to Governor Spessard Holland, May 15, 1941; Dorothy

Zeuch, Vero Beach, Florida, to Governor Spessard Holland, May 19, 1941, all in Holland Papers.

94. Signed petition to Governor Spessard Holland, May 23, 1941, Holland Papers.

95. Miami Negro Youth Council to Governor Spessard Holland, May 29, 1941; Peter Landon, Harlem Peoples Club, to Governor Spessard Holland, May 17, 1941, both in Holland Papers.

96. Roy Wilkins, Assistant Secretary of the NAACP, to Franklin D. Roosevelt, May 16, 1942, NAACP Papers.

97. "Year's Fifth Lynch Case Stirs Action," *Chicago Defender*, May 24, 1941.

98. *Baltimore Afro-American*, May 24, 1941.

99. *Pittsburgh Courier*, May 24, 1941.

100. *Pensacola Colored Citizen*, December 5, 1941.

101. M. P. Luten to Governor Spessard Holland, May 14, 1941, Holland Papers; "Masked Men Slay an Accused Negro," *New York Times*, May 14, 1941.

102. Cox, "Lynching and the Status Quo," 580.

103. Dixie interview.

104. *Baltimore Afro-American*, May 24, 1941.

105. Florida Department of Agriculture, *Sixth Census of the State of Florida*; *Baltimore Afro-American*, May 24, 1941; Singleton interview; Summers interview.

106. The only other evidence discovered that supports this is the 1935 census report, in which Arthur Williams is not listed as a member of the Williams household. Flipper interview.

107. In Mississippi in 1955, Emmett Till, a fourteen-year-old African American youth and Chicago native, was accused of whistling at or flirting with a white woman. The woman's husband and brother-in-law kidnapped Till and coordinated his brutal murder. His murder is frequently cited as a catalyst of the modern civil rights movement. See Whitfield, *Death in the Delta*.

108. Summers interview.

109. *Baltimore Afro-American*, May 24, 1941.

110. Kelley interview.

111. Flipper interview.

112. Ibid.

113. Muhammad, *Condemnation of Blackness*, 35, 50; Tonry, *Punishing Race*, 7, 101–3; Belknap, *Federal Law and Southern Order*, 2.

114. Brundage, *Under Sentence of Death*, 61.

115. Singleton interview.

Chapter 2. A Degree of Restraint: The Trials of Cellos Harrison, 1940–1943

1. Shofner, *Jackson County, Florida*, 23.

2. Stanley, *History of Jackson County*, 233, 235, 243.

3. Ibid.

4. Richardson, *Negro in the Reconstruction of Florida*, 188; Brown, *Florida's Black Public Officials*, 144–48, 162–63.

5. Shofner, *Jackson County, Florida*, 279–93; Richardson, *Negro in the Reconstruction of Florida*, 169–72; Weinfeld, *Jackson County War*.

6. Stanley, *History of Jackson County*, 263.

7. Ibid., 263–65.

8. Ibid.; Myrdal, *American Dilemma*, 236.

9. Bryant interview; Wilson interview; Shofner, *Jackson County, Florida*, 403–4, 465–68.

10. Shofner, *Jackson County, Florida*, 465; Bryant interview; Wilson interview.

11. Shofner, *Jackson County, Florida*, 465–68.

12. The lynching victims were identified as follows: Simmons Simpson, killed March 29, 1890, in Marianna; John Sanders and an unknown black person, killed June 10, 1910, in Sneads; Doc Peters, killed July 1, 1905, in Cottondale; Edward Christian and Hattie Bowman, killed September 2, 1910, in Graceville; and Galvin Baker, killed March 5, 1911, in Marianna. With the exception of Baker, who was accused of making threats to kill, the victims were suspected, complicit, or accused of committing murder. NAACP, *Thirty Years of Lynching*, 53–56.

13. See McGovern, *Anatomy of a Lynching*.

14. Ibid.

15. Ibid.

16. Wilson interview; E. Pittman interview; Bryant interview; Robinson interview.

17. Municipal Court Records, City of Marianna, 1939–40.

18. Lease record, May 30, 1939, Jackson County Courthouse; Robinson interview; Pender interview.

With the passage of the Twenty-First Amendment in December 1933, officially marking the end of Prohibition, the Florida legislature approved the sale of beer and light wine, but the production and sale of moonshine continued throughout the state. The illegal sale of hard liquor and the failure to pay federal taxes on its production and consumption created a very active underground economy in Florida. Many law enforcement officers in Florida were accused of accepting bribes in order to turn a blind eye to bootlegging operations within their jurisdictions. See Guthrie, *Keepers of the Spirits*, 109–29.

19. *State of Florida v. Cellos Harrison*, June 23, 1941; Coroner's Inquest into the Death of Cellos Harrison, June 16, 1943, Marianna, Florida.

20. Coroner's Inquest into the Death of Cellos Harrison, June 16, 1943, Marianna, Florida.

21. *State of Florida v. Cellos Harrison*, June 23, 1941.

22. There is conflicting evidence as to who actually discovered Johnnie Mayo on the morning that he was attacked. The local newspaper, the *Jackson County Floridan*, reported that Ira Johnson, truck driver for a local grocery store, discovered Mayo lying on the floor of the service station. But Reiff, not Johnson, gave testimony at Harrison's trial. *Jackson County Floridan*, June 6, 1941.

23. *State of Florida v. Cellos Harrison*, June 23, 1941.

24. Interview with Joe Sims in FBI Investigation, August 19, 1943, Department of Justice, Classified Subject Files, Record Group 60, National Archives and Records Administration II, College Park, Maryland (hereafter cited as DOJ Files).

25. Testimony of Dr. C. D. Whitaker, *State of Florida v. Cellos Harrison*, 1941.

26. Ibid.

27. *Report of the Secretary of State of the State of Florida* (Tallahassee, Fla.: Office of the Secretary of State, 1933), 274, 281.

28. Governor Fred Cone to J. P. Gause, January 25, 1937, Cone Papers.

29. FBI Investigation, July 5, 1943, DOJ Files; Robinson, "Law and Order."

30. *State of Florida v. Cellos Harrison*, June 23, 1941; *Legacy*, 109; R. Pittman interview.

31. *Jackson County Floridan*, June 6, 1941; Testimony of Lawrence Swilley, *State of Florida v. Harrison*, 1941.

32. Marriage Records, Jackson County Courthouse, Marianna, Florida; *State of Florida v. Cellos Harrison*, June 23, 1941.

33. *State of Florida v. Cellos Harrison*, June 23, 1941.

34. Seizure Investigation, 36–39.

35. Ibid.

36. *Cellos Harrison v. State of Florida*, February 19, 1943.

37. Ibid.

38. FBI Investigation, September 15, 1943, DOJ Files.

39. Testimony of Cellos Harrison, *State of Florida v. Harrison*, 1941.

40. Ibid. J. Tom Watson, Florida attorney general, disputed this claim in his brief for the appeal before the Florida Supreme Court.

41. Ibid.

42. Ibid.

43. Ibid.

44. Kinsolving interview.

45. *Jackson County Floridan*, June 13, 1941.

46. *Jackson County Floridan*, June 20, 1941; Testimony of Jack McMullian, *State of Florida v. Harrison*, 1941.

47. Trial Transcript, *State of Florida v. Cellos Harrison*, 1941.

48. Jackson County Circuit Court Minutes, *State of Florida v. Luke Coleman*.

49. Ibid.

50. Trial Transcript, *State of Florida v. Cellos Harrison*, 1941.

51. Ibid.

52. Ibid.

53. Ibid.

54. Ibid.

55. *Jackson County Floridan*, June 27, 1941.

56. *Jackson County Floridan*, July 4, 1941.

57. Trial Transcript, *State of Florida v. Cellos Harrison*, 1941.

Chapter 3. The Failure of Forbearance: The Lynching of Cellos Harrison, Jackson County, 1943

1. *Jackson County Floridan*, July 18, 1941.

2. Brief of the Appellant, *Cellos Harrison v. State of Florida*, September 18, 1941.

3. *Chambers et al. v. Florida*, 309 U.S. 227 (1940).

4. *Cellos Harrison v. State of Florida*, 1941.

5. *Jackson County Floridan*, June 5, 1941.

6. *State of Florida v. Cellos Harrison*, 1942.

7. *Jackson County Floridan*, June 5, 1942.

8. Carter, *Scottsboro*; Cortner, *Mob Intent on Death*.

9. Kinsolving interview.

10. *Cellos Harrison v. State of Florida*, December 18, 1942.

11. FBI Investigation, July 5, 1943.

12. *Cellos Harrison v. State of Florida*, December 18, 1942.

13. *Cellos Harrison v. State of Florida*, February 19, 1943.

14. Ibid.

15. Ibid.; *Jackson County Floridan*, May 14, 1943.

16. Manley and Brown, *Supreme Court of Florida*, 108, 122–26.

17. Ibid., 126.

18. "Petition for Clarification of Opinion," *Cellos Harrison v. State of Florida*, filed March 2, 1943.

19. *Jackson County Floridan*, May 28, 1943; Minute book of the Fourteenth Circuit Court, Jackson County Courthouse, Marianna, Florida. Similar legal transformations had been taking place throughout the state, as St. Petersburg began allowing African Americans to sit on juries in December 1941. Arsenault, *St. Petersburg and the Florida Dream*, 301.

20. *Jackson County Floridan*, June 4, 1943.

21. Statement of Clyde Atkinson, FBI Investigation, July 5, 1943, DOJ Files.

22. FBI Investigation, June 11, 1943, DOJ Files.

23. Ibid.

24. Ibid.; Statement of D. W. Wells, FBI Investigation, August 19, 1943, DOJ Files.

25. Statement of D. W. Wells, FBI Investigation, August 19, 1943, DOJ Files.

26. Ibid.

27. Robert Hadley, who was incarcerated at the Marianna jail the night Harrison was kidnapped, described this version of the events. FBI Investigation, July 5, 1943, DOJ Files.

28. FBI Investigation, February 9, 1944, DOJ Files.

29. Ibid.

30. Ibid.

31. Ibid.

32. Robinson interview.

33. FBI Investigation, July 5, 1943, DOJ Files; FBI Investigation, August 19, 1943, DOJ Files.

34. FBI Investigation, July 5, 1943, DOJ Files; FBI Investigation, March 15, 1944, DOJ Files.

35. Coroner's Inquest into the Death of Cellos Harrison, June 16, 1943, Marianna, Florida.

36. Ibid.

37. FBI Investigation, July 5, 1943, DOJ Files.

38. Ibid.

39. W. H. Gasque to Ralph Davis, June 16, 1943, Holland Papers.

40. *Daily Democrat*, June 16, 1943; *Tampa Morning Tribune*, June 17, 1943.

41. Escobar, *Race, Police, and the Making of Political Identities*, 233–53; Mazón, *Zoot-Suit Riots*.

42. *Baltimore Afro-American*, June 16, 1943; Burran, "Violence in an 'Arsenal of Democracy,'" 39–52; Olson and Phair, "Anatomy of a Race Riot," 64–72.

43. *Baltimore Afro-American*, June 26, 1943; Capeci and Wilkerson, *Layered Violence*, 3–31.

44. *Atlanta Daily World*, n.d.; *Baltimore Afro-American*, July 3, 1943; Johnson, "Gender, Race, and Rumours," 259.

45. Marjorie McKenzie, "Pressure Should Be Directed to Passage of Anti-Lynch Bill," *Pittsburgh Courier*, June 26, 1943.

46. "NAACP Says Riot Calls for Lynch Bill Act," *Atlanta Daily World*, June 22, 1943.

47. *Atlanta Daily World*, July 8, 1943.

48. Cliff Mackay, "Repression Rears Its Ugly Head," *Atlanta Daily World*, June 20, 1943.

49. *New York Age*, June 26, 1943.

50. Pearl S. Buck, American Civil Liberties Union, to Governor Spessard Holland, June 17, 1943, Holland Papers.

51. Pearl S. Buck, "The Asiatic Problem: The Colored People Are Still Waiting, Still Watchful," February 10, 1942, *Vital Speeches* 8, no. 10 (1942): 303–5.

52. Harry T. Moore, President of the Florida Conference of the NAACP, Mims, Florida, to Spessard Holland, Governor, State of Florida, Tallahassee, July 12, 1943, DOJ Files.

53. George Hayes and James Myers, Federal Council of the Churches of Christ in America, to U.S. Attorney General Francis Biddle, Washington, D.C., June 17, 1943, DOJ Files.

54. See Capeci, *Lynching of Cleo Wright*; Coleman, "Freedom from Fear," 425–26.

55. Wendell Berge, Assistant Attorney General, Department of Justice, to George Earl Hoffman, U.S. Attorney for the Northern District of Florida, Pensacola, June 17, 1943, DOJ Files.

56. George Earl Hoffman to Wendell Berge, June 25, 1943, DOJ Files.

57. Robert Hill explores J. Edgar Hoover's racial views and their impact on the activities of the FBI in his introduction to *FBI's RACON*, 9.

58. The following is a list of the FBI agents who investigated the Harrison lynching and the dates of their reports: Clare Franklin Carter and Joel D. Colglazier (July 5, 1943); Charles Williams Johnson (September 15, 1943); Jack Borden (August 19, November 17, 1943, and February 9, 1944); Elmer Francis Vickers (March 15, 1944), DOJ Files.

59. Jackson County, Deed Records, 1939, Jackson County Courthouse; *Cellos Harrison v. State of Florida*, February 19, 1943, Records of the Florida Supreme Court, Florida State Archives, Tallahassee; for a description of *bolita*, see King, *Devil in the Grove*, 77–79.

60. Statement of Jess Meeks, August 6, 1940, Cone Papers.

61. Governor Fred P. Cone to L. F. Cawthon, State Prison Supervisor, May 21, 1940; L. F. Cawthon to Governor Fred P. Cone, May 24, 1940; Governor Fred P. Cone to L. D. McRae, State Attorney, May 27, 1940; Governor Fred P. Cone to Nathan Mayo, Commissioner of Agriculture, October 12, 1940, all in Cone Papers.

62. FBI Investigation, July 5, 1943, DOJ Files.

63. FBI Investigation, February 9, 1944, DOJ Files; Statement of B. L. Solomon, FBI Investigation, November 17, 1943; Statement of Mary Harrison, FBI Investigation, July 5, 1943, DOJ Files.

64. FBI Investigation, July 5, 1943, DOJ Files.

65. Ibid.

66. Statement of James Finlayson, FBI Investigation, July 5, 1943, DOJ Files.

67. Ibid.

68. FBI Investigation, July 5, 1943, DOJ Files.

69. FBI Investigation, August 19, 1943, DOJ Files.

70. Charles M. Guyton to Governor Spessard Holland, January 6, 1943, Holland Papers.

71. FBI Investigation, July 5, 1943, DOJ Files.

72. Ibid.

73. Ibid.; Shofner, *Jackson County, Florida*, 523.

74. FBI Investigation, February 9, 1944, DOJ Files.

75. FBI Investigation, March 15, 1944, DOJ Files.

76. FBI Investigation, July 5, 1943, DOJ Files.

77. Gause "stated that prior to the original trial Harrison had been taken by him to the jail of Chipley, Florida, for his own protection and that this appeared to have resulted in the Supreme Court's language impliedly reprimanding the local authorities for such transportation. He said this may have influenced the Judge in his decision to leave Harrison in the Marianna jail, also." Ibid.

78. In a letter to Governor Holland, he explained, "I employed one Tom Belser [*sic*] as a sepcial [*sic*] night watchman to be up and on the alert at night while Harrison was in jail." W. Barkley Gause, Marianna, Florida, to Governor Spessard Holland, Tallahassee, Florida, June 24, 1943, Holland Papers.

79. Statement of R. T. Gilmore, FBI Investigation, November 17, 1943, DOJ Files.

80. FBI Investigation, April 11, 1944, DOJ Files.

81. Coroner's Inquest; FBI Investigation, April 11, 1944, DOJ Files.

82. O'Brien, *Color of the Law*, 185.

83. J. Edgar Hoover to Tom C. Clark, July 3, 1944, DOJ Files; Tom C. Clark to J. Edgar Hoover, July 10, 1944, DOJ Files.

84. Wilson, interview; FBI Investigation, June 26, 1944, DOJ Files.

85. Statements of B. Skipper, Mrs. Phillips, and Mrs. Lewis, FBI Investigation, July 5, 1943, DOJ Files.

86. Vandiver, *Lethal Punishment*; Clarke, "'Without Fear or Shame.'"

87. Brundage, *Lynching in the New South*, 209, 242–44; Howard, *Lynchings*, 142–47.

Chapter 4. "A Very Cheap Article": The Lynching of Willie James Howard, Suwannee County, 1944

1. Lucius Harper, "Mississippi Adds Another 'Freedom' To List," *Chicago Defender*, October 17, 1942; Enoc, "Mississippi Mob Hangs Two Youths, 14, from Bridge," *Baltimore Afro-American*, October 17, 1942; Waters, "Two Lynched Boys Were Ace Scrap Iron Collectors in Mississippi Town," *Chicago Defender*, March 6, 1943; Whitfield, *Death in the Delta*.

2. Suwannee History Committee, *Echoes of the Past*, 1–4.

3. Ibid., 5–6. The largest plantation in the county belonged to T. D. Dexter, a white man who owned fifty-three slaves. Unlike Dexter, the majority of slaveholders in the county only owned a few slaves. Of the ninety-three whites who owned slaves, the majority (fifty-seven) owned fewer than ten slaves.

4. Tully C. Denham, Lewis Fields, Berry M. Gardner, Nathan Goodman, Nelson M. Kerby, Samuel McIver, George Manker, Caleb Simpkins, and Frank Stockton served on the county commission during these years. Another African American, Robert Allen, served as justice of the peace between 1876 and 1877, and Thomas L. Thompson served as a city councilman for Live Oak in 1878. Suwannee 2000 History Committee, 8–9, 17–18; Curry, "History of Suwannee County"; Suwannee History Committee, *Echoes of the Past*, 50, 206; Brown, *Florida's Black Public Officials*, 181.

5. Suwannee History Committee, *Echoes of the Past*, 8–9, 17–18.

6. Ibid., 70.

7. While the majority of whites (43 percent) were either farm owners or managers, only around 17 percent of blacks held the same positions. The majority of blacks were either farm laborers who earned wages (20 percent) or laborers in other areas besides agriculture (21 percent). It was a comparatively poor county, with the effective buying income per capita for the residents half the statewide mean, $343 per capita as opposed to $685 per capita for the state. Blacks made up only about one-third of the county's population (32 percent), one of the lowest rates when compared with the black population of surrounding counties like Madison (48 percent), Hamilton (42 percent), and Columbia (39 percent). *Statistical Abstract*.

8. Suwannee History Committee, *Echoes of the Past*, 47.

9. Linton interview.

10. John Evans was killed in 1885 after being accused of rape. Charles Griffin was murdered in 1891 for his role in a murder. On December 15, 1891, two black men, Alfred Jones and Brady Young, were lynched in Suwannee County after being accused of murder. Coot Williams was lynched in 1894 after being accused of murder. Seven years later, on November 6, 1898, Arthur Williams was killed in Welborn, just east

of Live Oak, after being accused of murder. Another black man, Jack Thomas, was lynched on June 27, 1900, having been charged with attempted rape. Edward Dansey was accused of murder in 1919. Tolney and Beck, *Festival of Violence*, 38; NAACP, *Thirty Years of Lynching*, 53–55; Ames, *Changing Character of Lynching*, 2.

11. The Florida Baptist Institute would continue operating in Live Oak until 1941, when the two schools reunified. The school operates today as Florida Memorial University and is located in Miami Gardens, Florida. Scott, *Education of Black People in Florida*, 53.

12. NAACP, *Thirty Years of Lynching*; "Lynchings, by States and Race, 1882–1951," in Guzman et al., *Negro Year Book, 1952*.

13. Florida Department of Agriculture, *Sixth Census of the State of Florida*.

14. DePass interview; Linton interview; Philmore interview; Perry interview; Harry T. Moore to Roy Wilkins, March 15, 1944, NAACP Papers.

15. Reid, "General Characteristics," 281.

16. Daniel, "Responsibility of Education," 388–98.

17. McGovern, *Anatomy of a Lynching*, 6.

18. Mays, *Born to Rebel*, 22.

19. Ellison, *Shadow and Act*, 90.

20. Wright, *Black Boy*, 47–48.

21. Green interview.

22. Robinson interview; Beasley interview.

23. Pinar, *Gender of Racial Politics and Violence*, 67.

24. DePass interview; Philmore interview.

25. Perry interview; Suwannee History Committee, *Echoes of the Past*, 150, 211; Census, Suwannee County, 1935.

26. State Attorney David Lanier to Governor Spessard Holland, February 7, 1944, NAACP Papers. The letter is reprinted from a typewritten copy included with the investigative reports. The reports do not include a copy of the original letter.

27. Linton interview; Hall interview.

28. Subject #2 interview; Philmore interview.

29. Sammy Kahn, Saul Chaplin, Mann Holiner, Alberta Nichols, and L. E. Freeman, "Until the Real Thing Comes Along" lyrics © EMI Music Publishing, Warner/Chappell Music, Inc., Universal Music Publishing Group.

30. Haynes interview.

31. Wood, *Black Scare*; Ferber, *White Man Falling*, 34–43.

32. Brundage, *Lynching in the New South*, 61.

33. Davis, Gardner, and Gardner, *Deep South*; Hall, *Revolt against Chivalry*; Feimster, *Southern Horrors*; Kennedy, *Jim Crow Guide*, 210–11.

34. Census, Suwannee County, 1935. Marriage records also document a marital relationship between Reginald Scott and the McCullers family. Reginald Scott married Jewel McCullers in June 1926. Marriage Records, Suwannee Valley Genealogical Society. Philmore interview.

35. Statement by Lula Howard to Orange County official, March 19, 1944, NAACP Papers; Perry interview.

36. Statement by Lula Howard to Orange County official, March 19, 1944, NAACP Papers.

37. David Lanier to Governor Spessard Holland, "Report of the Death of Willie James Howard," February 7, 1944, NAACP Papers.

38. DePass interview; Linton interview; Philmore interview.

39. Records indicate that the Howards sold their property to a local midwife, Charolette Veasy (Beasley), on January 5, 1944. Deed Records, Suwannee County Courthouse, Live Oak, Florida.

40. Elbert C. Robinson to Walter White, January 4, 1944; Harry T. Moore to Attorney General of the United States, September 16, 1945, both in NAACP Papers; Subject #3 interview; DePass interview.

41. Elbert C. Robinson, Washington, D.C., to Walter White, NAACP, January 4, 1944, NAACP Papers.

42. Robert Jackson to Walter White, NAACP, New York City, January 7, 1944; Edward Davis, Ocala, Florida, to Roy Wilkins, NAACP, January 23, 1944; Edward Dudley, NAACP, to Edward Davis, January 28, 1944; Milton Konvitz, NAACP, to A. L. King, February 14, 1944, all in NAACP Papers.

43. Governor Spessard Holland to Thurgood Marshall, February 14, 1944, NAACP Papers.

44. David Lanier, Acting State Attorney, to the Circuit Court, Third Judicial Circuit of Florida, Suwannee County, May 4, 1944, NAACP Papers.

45. Thurgood Marshall, Special Counsel, NAACP Legal Defense and Education Fund, to Senator Claude Pepper, January 28, 1944, NAACP Papers.

46. Senator Claude Pepper to Milton Konvitz, February 16, 1944, NAACP Papers. It is interesting to note that even though Marshall had written to Pepper, Pepper responded to Milton Konvitz, who served under Marshall as assistant special counsel for the NAACP Legal Defense and Education Fund.

47. "Auto Injury Is Fatal to Live Oak Citizen," *Florida Times Union*, January 5, 1944; Associated Press, "Youth Loses Life in Truck Accident," *Florida Times Union*, January 7, 1944.

48. "17 Year Old Negro Reported Lynched in Live Oak, Florida," January 22, 1944, Tuskegee Institute News Clipping Files, Lynching Files, Tuskegee University.

49. Statement by Phillip Goff, S. B. McCullers, Reginald Scott to Sheriff Tom Henry, Live Oak, Florida, January 2, 1944, NAACP Papers; David Lanier to Governor Spessard Holland, "Report on Death of Willie James Howard, Live Oak, Florida, January 2, 1944," NAACP Papers.

50. Statement by James Howard to Orange County official, March 19, 1944, NAACP Papers; Statement by James Howard to Harry T. Moore, March 19, 1944, DOJ Files.

51. Ibid.

52. According to oral history, while an officer, Wylie Byrd, had shot and killed a black man on the streets of Live Oak in February 1941, no prosecution was ever made in the case. The wife of the victim confirmed this; she was left with two young children to raise on her own. Philmore interview.

53. Statement by James Howard to Harry T. Moore, March 19, 1944, DOJ Files.

54. Ibid.

55. The couple may have fled to Orlando because Lula Figgs Howard's sister, Mamie Figgs Perry, was already living there. Perry interview. Harry T. Moore, Florida State Conference of the NAACP, to Roy Wilkins, President, NAACP, March 25, 1944, NAACP Papers.

56. Harry T. Moore to Roy Wilkins, March 25, 1944, NAACP Papers.

57. James Howard, "Statement of Mr. and Mrs. James Howard of Incidents Attendant to Grand Jury Hearing, May 8, 1944 at Live Oak, Florida," NAACP Papers.

58. Ibid.

59. David Lanier, Madison, Florida, to Governor Spessard Holland, Tallahassee, Florida, May 9, 1944; Harry T. Moore to Thurgood Marshall, June 30, 1944, both in NAACP Papers.

60. Harry T. Moore, President, Florida State Conference of the NAACP, to Thurgood Marshall, Special Counsel, NAACP Legal Defense and Education Fund, June 30, 1944, NAACP Papers.

61. Tom C. Clark, Assistant Attorney General, Department of Justice, to Thurgood Marshall, NAACP Legal Defense and Education Fund, July 11, 1944, NAACP Papers.

62. Harry T. Moore, Mims, Florida, to U.S. Attorney General, Washington, D.C., July 26, 1944, NAACP Papers.

63. Harry T. Moore to U.S. Attorney General, September 16, 1945, NAACP Papers.

64. "IN RE: Death of Sam McFadden Alias Puddin McFadden, in Suwannee County, Florida," n.d., Caldwell Papers; Davis, "'Whitewash' in Florida," 277–98.

65. Edward D. Davis, Ocala, Florida, to Roy Wilkins, New York, January 23, 1944, NAACP Papers; McGovern, Anatomy of a Lynching, 11.

66. Philmore interview.

67. Hall interview.

68. DePass interview.

69. Suwannee Democrat, February 4, 1944.

70. The NAACP had limited success organizing and sustaining branches in Florida, as was the case throughout much of the South. Prior to the mid-twentieth century, those Florida branches existed in major cities in the state such as Key West, Tampa, and Jacksonville. Harry T. Moore to Thurgood Marshall, June 30, 1944, NAACP Papers; Emmons, "Flame of Resistance," 243.

71. DePass interview.

72. Perry interview.

73. Pinar, Gender of Racial Politics and Violence, 66.

74. Harris, Exorcising Blackness, 189.

75. Wiegman, "Anatomy of Lynching," in Hine and Jenkins, Question of Manhood, 350.

76. Bederman, Manliness and Civilization, 48–49. Riche Richardson explores notions of black masculinity through literature and notes not only an intergroup rejection of southern black manhood by southern white men but also an intragroup

tension, wherein northern black men viewed southern black men as cowardly. Richardson, *Black Masculinity and the U.S. South*, 6.

77. *Suwannee Democrat*, January 14, 1944.

78. *Suwannee Democrat*, January 28, 1944.

79. *Suwannee Democrat*, June 9 and September 15, 1944.

80. Feimster, *Southern Horrors*, 62–86; Bederman, *Manliness and Civilization*, 58.

81. Smith, *Killers of the Dream*, 27.

82. Durr, *Outside of the Magic Circle*, 45.

83. The aforementioned behaviors are classified as "racial hoaxes," in which whites falsely claim to be victims of black aggression to hide their own misdeeds. Russell, *Color of Crime*, 65–93; Carter, *Scottsboro*; Jones et al., "Rosewood, Florida"; D'Orso, *Like Judgment Day*.

84. Markovitz, *Legacies of Lynching*, xxvi.

85. Irwin-Zarecka, *Neutralizing Memory*, 104; Irwin-Zarecka, *Frames of Remembrance*; Brundage, *Where These Memories Grow*, 6.

86. Zelizer, *Remembering to Forget*, 3.

87. Evans, *Silencing of Ruby McCollum*, 41–42; Huie, *Ruby McCollum*.

88. Maguire, *At the Dark End of the Street*, xviii–xx; Feimster, *Southern Horrors*, 87–118; Hine, "Rape and the Inner Lives of Black Women," in Hine, *Hine Sight*.

89. Evans, *Silencing of Ruby McCollum*, 27; Bruce E. Baker, "Under the Rope," in Brundage, *Where These Memories Grow*, 336.

90. Sandra Dickson and Churchill Roberts, "Freedom Never Dies: The Legacy of Harry T. Moore" (Watertown, Mass.: Documentary Educational Resources, 2001).

91. Susan K. Lamb, "After 61 Years, a Wrong Is Nearly Righted," *Suwannee Democrat*, January 26, 2005.

Chapter 5. Still at It: The Lynching of Jesse James Payne, Madison County, 1945

1. Madison County also encompasses the towns of Ellaville and Greenville. Rivers, *Slavery in Florida*, 18–19; McCarthy, *Guide to Black Florida*, 165–66.

2. Richardson, *Negro in the Reconstruction of Florida*, 49–50.

3. These men were: Edward I. Alexander Sr. (House, 1877, 1879, 1885); Oliver J. Coleman (House, 1871–72, 1875; Senate, 1874); David Montgomery (House, 1873–75; Senate, Sergeant-at-Arms, 1871); and Alfred Brown Osgood (House, 1868–74, 1879, 1883, 1885; Senate, 1875, 1877). Brown, *Florida's Black Public Officials*, 169–70.

4. Ibid., 120. An excellent summary of race relations in post–Civil War Madison County can be found in Davis, "Shades of Justice," ch. 2.

5. "Florida Census Statistics," *Statistical Abstract*.

6. Sims, *History of Madison County*, 85–89; for more on peonage in Florida, see Shofner, "Postscript to the Martin Tabert Case," 161–73.

7. Shofner, "Postscript to the Martin Tabert Case," 160–63.

8. Pride and Bradley interview.

9. Sims, *History of Madison County*, 112–15.

10. Alexander interview.

11. On January 9, 1894, Samuel Smith was lynched after being accused of murder. The following year, on May 19, 1895, three black men—Samuel Echols, Simeon Crowley, and John Brooks—were accused of rape before they were killed near Ellaville. The following year witnessed three lynchings: Harry Wilson and a man named Murray were killed together on May 11, 1896, for unknown offenses, and on July 6 Jacob Williams was killed for the alleged rape of a white woman. In 1899, Charles Martin and three other black men were killed. On January 7, 1901, whites killed James Denson and his stepson after they were accused of murder. Two years later, Washington Jarvis was killed for the same reason. An unknown black man was lynched after being accused of rape in 1906. Then, in February 1908, murder suspect Charles Pitman was also lynched. Another black man, Theodore "Buckie" Young, met his death on September 11, 1936. After being accused of attacking a white woman, Young was taken from his home by a mob of whites and shot to death in his own yard. The mob kept his body for two days after they killed him. NAACP, *Thirty Years of Lynching*, 53–56; Howard, "Vigilante Justice," 229–31.

12. Fourteenth Census of the United States, 1920.

13. Statement of Jesse James Payne, by O. O. Edwards, Assistant Attorney General for the State of Florida, July 13, 1945, Florida State Prison, Caldwell Papers (hereafter cited as Payne Statement); Davis, "'Whitewash' in Florida," 227–98.

14. Florida Department of Health, Florida Marriage Index, 1927–2001.

15. Affidavit sworn to by Lillie Mae Payne (wife), Lucy Ann Payne (mother), and Lucy Mae Anderson (sister), Sanford, Seminole County, Florida, October 29, 1945, Caldwell Papers (hereafter cited as Family Affidavit).

16. Ibid.; Payne Statement.

17. Florida's allotment system paid farmers the difference between their total acreage and the number of acres they planted. Davis, "Shades of Justice," 278; Family Affidavit; Payne Statement.

18. Family affidavit; Payne Statement.

19. Family affidavit.

20. Ibid.

21. Davis, "Shades of Justice," 17.

22. Ibid.

23. Jones and Sims interview.

24. W. H. Gasque to Governor Millard Caldwell, "Confidential Report," November 7, 1945, Caldwell Papers.

25. Payne statement.

26. Ibid.

27. Davis, "Shades of Justice," 282.

28. *Florida Times-Union*, July 5, 1945; *Daily Democrat*, July 5, 1945; *Richmond Times-Dispatch*, October 13, 1945.

29. *State of Florida v. Jesse James Payne, Millard F. Caldwell v. Crowell-Collier Publishing Company* (1946), Records of the District Courts of the United States, Record Group 21, Boxes 43–44, National Archives and Records Administration at Atlanta (hereafter cited as Caldwell Civil Case Files); Payne Statement.

30. J. Tom Watson, Attorney General for the State of Florida, to Governor Millard Caldwell, October 23, 1945, Caldwell Papers.

31. Ibid.

32. FBI Investigative Report, conducted by Agent James B. Hafley, October 18, 1945, DOJ Files.

33. Ibid.

34. "Verdict of Coroner's Jury," Caldwell Civil Case File.

35. *Jacksonville Journal*, October 12, 1945.

36. *Miami Herald*, October 14, 1945.

37. *St. Petersburg Independent*, October 15, 1945.

38. *St. Petersburg Times*, October 13, 1945.

39. *Lakeland Ledger*, October 14, 1945.

40. In light of his defense of Sheriff Davis, Senator Davis assured the governor that he was no relation to him. W. T. Davis, U.S. Senator, to Governor Millard Caldwell, October 24, 1945, Caldwell Papers.

41. Hatton W. Sumners, U.S. Representative, to Governor Millard Caldwell, October 17, 1945, Caldwell Papers.

42. Rep. Sam Hobbs, Washington, D.C., to Governor Millard Caldwell, February 13, 1946, Caldwell Papers.

43. Edward D. Davis, President, Marion County Branch NAACP, Ocala, Florida, to Governor Millard Caldwell, October 14, 1945, Caldwell Papers.

44. Harry T. Moore, President, Florida Conference of the NAACP, to Governor Millard Caldwell, October 17, 1945, Caldwell Papers.

45. Ibid.; Governor Millard Caldwell to Harry T. Moore, October 22, 1945; Harry T. Moore to Governor Millard Caldwell, October 31, 1945, both in DOJ Files.

46. *Tampa Morning Tribune*, October 14, 1945.

47. *Richmond Times-Dispatch*, October 13, 1945; *Atlanta Daily World*, October 13, 1945.

48. R. E. Sweets, Madison County, to Governor Millard Caldwell, n.d.; Sheriff Lonnie T. Davis to Governor Millard Caldwell, June 26, 1945; John Wigginton, Executive Secretary, Office of the Governor, to Sheriff Lonnie T. Davis, June 28, 1945; Sheriff Lonnie T. Davis to John Wigginton, June 30, 1945; Governor Millard Caldwell to Sheriff Lonnie T. Davis, July 10, 1945; James Vocelle, Director, Beverage Department, State of Florida, to Ed Straughn, Office of the Governor, October 26, 1945, all in Caldwell Papers.

49. *St. Petersburg Independent*, October 15, 1945.

50. Davis, "Shades of Justice," 125.

51. *New York Daily Worker*, October 18, 1945.

52. *New York Daily Worker*, October 22, 1945. Jonathan Rosenberg notes the frequent comparisons in the black and Communist press of Hitler and his treatment of the Jews in Europe to the KKK and segregation in America. Rosenberg, *How Far the Promised Land?*, 112–13.

53. Although Caldwell at times demonstrated a willingness to support equal

opportunities and improved educational resources for African Americans, he was a staunch defender of the color line. He affirmed this stance in 1948 during the Democratic National Convention, where he campaigned against Truman's civil rights plank. Davis, "Shades of Justice," 127, 133; Revels, "Blitzkrieg of Joy," 145, in Wynne, *Florida at War*; *Orlando Reporter-Star*, October 15, 1945.

54. J. Tom Watson, Attorney General, State of Florida, to Governor Millard Caldwell, October 23, 1945, Caldwell Papers.

55. Ibid.; Davis, "Shades of Justice," 31.

56. "Verdict of the Grand Jury," Circuit Court, Third Judicial Circuit of Florida, Madison County, October 27, 1945, Caldwell Civil Case Files, Box 44.

57. *Tampa Morning Tribune*, November 2, 1945.

58. *New York Daily Worker*, November 2, 1945; *Chicago Defender*, October 17, 1945.

59. Watson, a well-known segregationist, seemed particularly perturbed by W. H. Gasque's involvement in the case, complaining to Caldwell that "I do not know, of course, what evidence was given before the grand jury and I do not know what witnesses they summoned before them, and, of course, I have no knowledge of how far they went in their investigations in this case because I had no information of and concerning the time when they were going to be convened and charged with entering upon their investigatory duties." J. Tom Watson to Governor Millard Caldwell, November 1, 1945, Caldwell Papers; *Jacksonville Journal*, November 3, 1945.

60. W. H. Gasque, Special Investigator, to Governor Millard Caldwell, November 7, 1945, Caldwell Papers.

61. Ibid.

62. Capeci, *Lynching of Cleo Wright*; Coleman, "Freedom from Fear," 425–26.

63. Former colleague H. Graham Morison recalled Smith's concern for civil rights violations. "Turner Smith and his staff agreed that when they had a complaint made to the Attorney General or when they read newspaper accounts of violations of all types of civil rights, timely beginning action should be taken after obtaining full information. If such a violation was serious enough, he would . . . ask the aid of the nearest U.S. Attorney in calling those who had been alleged to have violated the civil rights of Negro citizens." H. Graham Morison, interview by Jerry N. Hess, August 8, 1972, Truman Presidential Museum and Library, http://www.trumanlibrary.org.

64. Turner L. Smith, Civil Rights Division, Department of Justice, to Theron L. Caudle, Assistant Attorney General, Criminal Division, October 15, 1945; J. Edgar Hoover to Theron L. Caudle, October 16 and 25, 1945, all in DOJ Files; Cohen, "Screws Case," 94–106.

65. FBI Investigative Report, October 18, 1945; Turner L. Smith to File, November 16, 1945, both in DOJ Files.

66. Frank Baril, Chairman, Executive Board Local 21, International Fur and Leather Workers, to Attorney General Tom Clark, November 26, 1945; Robbie Mae Riddick, President, Braddie Walker, Secretary, Rev. L. V. Freeman, Treasurer, Bea Mc-Crea, Business Agent, Food, Tobacco, Agricultural and Allied Workers Union of America, Suffolk, Virginia, to Attorney General Tom Clark, November 27, 1945; Thomas J.

Fitzpatrick, President, United Electrical, Radio and Machine Workers of America, District Council Number 6, Pittsburgh, to Attorney General Tom Clark, November 28, 1945; Negro Retail Beer Dealers and Merchants of Texas, Sid Hilliard, Chairman, to Attorney General Tom Clark, December 5, 1945; Walter H. Woods, President, Local 137, United Federal Workers of America, Brooklyn, New York, to Attorney General Tom Clark, December 5, 1945; Harry Bridges, President, International Longshoremen's and Warehousemen's Union, San Francisco, to Attorney General Tom Clark, December 12, 1945; Irving Risking, President, United Office and Professional Workers of America, Local 26, Detroit, to Attorney General Tom Clark, December 20, 1945; Paul Schnur, Secretary-Treasurer, San Francisco CIO Council, to Attorney General Tom Clark, December 20, 1945; Louis E. Burham, Organizational Secretary, Southern Negro Youth Congress, Birmingham, Alabama, to Attorney General Tom Clark, December 29, 1945; William B. Stevenson, President, United Electrical, Radio, and Machine Workers of America, Local Union 1412, Oakland, California, to Attorney General Tom Clark, January 8, 1946; Mel J. Heinritz, Secretary-Treasurer, Wisconsin State Industrial Union Council, Milwaukee, Wisconsin, to Attorney General Tom Clark, January 10, 1946; Janet Beyman, Secretary, Local 475, Amalgamated Machine, Instrument, and Metal Workers Association, Brooklyn, New York, to Attorney General Tom Clark, January 17, 1946; John C. Hunt, Food, Tobacco, Agricultural and Allied Workers Union of America, Amalgamated Local, No. 26, Suffolk, Virginia, to Attorney General Tom Clark, February 27, 1946; Wendell B. Phillips Jr., Veteran, Regional Director, Pacific-Northwest Region, Food, Tobacco, Agricultural and Allied Workers Union of America, to Attorney General Tom Clark, February 28, 1946, all in DOJ Files. These represent a sampling of the letters on file.

67. *Chicago Defender*, November 10, 1945, in Davis, "Shades of Justice," 125.

68. "News Release—November 8, 1945," Caldwell Civil Case File.

69. *Lakeland Ledger*, November 9, 1945.

70. *Jacksonville Journal*, November 9, 1945; *Tampa Morning Tribune*, November 19, 1945.

71. Unsigned telegram to Governor Millard Caldwell, November 9, 1945; unsigned letter to Governor Millard Caldwell, November 14, 1945; Bill Bell(?), Mayo, Florida, to Governor Millard Caldwell, October 18, 1945; Vernon L. Tyson, Miami, Florida, to Governor Millard Caldwell, November 9, 1945, all in Caldwell Papers.

72. G. D. Gurley, San Antonio, Texas, to Governor Millard Caldwell, October 14, 1945, Caldwell Papers. Jason Morgan Ward follows this interpretation of white supremacist ideology from the New Deal and into the Cold War. See Ward, *Defending White Democracy*.

73. L. E. Williams, Rocky Mount, North Carolina, to Governor Millard Caldwell, February 24, 1946, Caldwell Papers.

74. J. Clay Murphey, Macon, Georgia, to Governor Millard Caldwell, February 16, 1946, Caldwell Papers.

75. R. B. Eleazer, General Board of Education of the Methodist Church, Nashville, Tennessee, to Governor Millard Caldwell, December 20, 1945, Caldwell Papers.

76. Governor Millard Caldwell to R. B. Eleazer, December 28, 1945, Caldwell Civil Case Files.

77. *St. Petersburg Independent*, January 2, 1946; *Chicago Defender*, January 5, 1946; E. L. Swift, Daytona Beach, Florida, to Governor Millard Caldwell, January 9, 1946, Caldwell Papers.

78. "Two Governors," *Time*, January 7, 1946.

79. *Jacksonville Journal*, January 4, 1946.

80. *Jacksonville Journal*, February 13, 1946.

81. Ibid.

82. *St. Petersburg Independent*, February 14, 1946.

83. Governor Millard Caldwell to Department of Records and Research, Tuskegee Institute, February 14, 1946; Jessie P. Guzman to Governor Millard Caldwell, February 19, 1946, both in Caldwell Papers.

84. Memorandum, "In re: Last draft Tuskegee letter," n.d., Caldwell Papers.

85. The disagreement between the ASWPL, the Tuskegee Institute, and the NAACP over the definition of lynching is described in Waldrep, "War of Words."

86. Governor Millard Caldwell to Jessie P. Guzman, Tuskegee Institute, March 6, 1946, Caldwell Papers.

87. *Collier's*, February 24, 1946.

88. Trial Transcript, Caldwell Civil Case Files, 4–6.

89. *Daily Democrat*, February 28, 1946.

90. Spessard Holland to Millard Caldwell, February 10, 1946, Caldwell Papers.

91. Carl Higginbotham, Orlando, Florida, to Crowell-Collier Publishing Company, New York City, February 16, 1946, copy in Caldwell Papers.

92. *Daily Democrat*, April 22, October 14, December 16, 1947; Trial Transcript, Caldwell Civil Case File.

93. As chairman of the Regional Council for Education for the Southern Governors' Conference, Caldwell was charged with implementing a program "to provide for all their citizens, through cooperative effort, sound, comprehensive, and high-quality educational opportunities." In reality, its purpose was to ease pressure for integrating all-white state colleges by working together with other southern states to provide adequate but separate facilities for blacks. *Administration of Millard F. Caldwell*, 27; Trial Transcript, Caldwell Civil Case File.

94. Trial Transcript, Caldwell Civil Case File.

95. Ibid., 184.

96. Ibid., 370, 409.

97. Ibid., 383.

98. Ibid., 444; Davis, "Shades of Justice," 296.

99. *Tampa Morning Tribune*, March 12, 1948.

100. Harry T. Moore to Governor Millard Caldwell, March 15, 1948, William H. Gray, Jr. Papers, Southeastern Regional Black Archives, Florida A&M University, Tallahassee.

101. "Satisfaction of Judgment," Caldwell Civil Case File.

246 Notes to Pages 188–199

102. Governor Millard Caldwell to R. B. Eleazer, December 28, 1945, Caldwell Civil Case Files.

103. Davis, "Shades of Justice," 153.

Conclusion

1. Zora Neale Hurston, "Crazy for This Democracy," *Negro Digest* (December 1945), reprinted in Walker, *I Love Myself*, 165–68.

2. Rosenberg, *How Far the Promised Land?*, 5.

3. Borstelmann, *Cold War*, 55; Wexler, *Fire in a Canebreak*.

4. John H. Sengstacke, Publisher, *Chicago Defender*, Chicago, to Governor Millard Caldwell, August 14, 1946, Caldwell Papers.

5. Quoted in Anderson, *Eyes Off the Prize*, 16.

6. David Brown, Swarthmore, Pennsylvania, to Attorney General Tom Clark, December 7, 1945, DOJ Files.

7. Shamas O'Sheel, New York City, to Attorney General Tom Clark, December 12, 1945, DOJ Files.

8. William B. Stevenson, President, United Electrical, Radio, and Machine Workers of America, Local Union 1412, Oakland, California, to Attorney General Tom Clark, January 8, 1946, DOJ Files.

9. John Gilman to Attorney General Tom Clark, October 26, 1945, DOJ Files; *Chicago Defender*, December 8, 1945.

10. John J. Kryzak, St. Paul, Minnesota, to Governor Millard Caldwell, November 15, 1945, Caldwell Papers.

11. Cox, *Race Relations*, 579.

12. Coleman, "Freedom from Fear," 415–29.

13. Waldrep, "National Policing," 611–16.

14. Coleman, "Freedom from Fear," 427; Borstelmann, *Cold War*, 56.

15. There is some debate among scholars on the subject about the relative radicalism of the black press. Where Patrick Washburn documents passion and influence, Lee Finkle argues that by the end of 1942, the black newspaper editors began to back away from their heated criticism of the government, fearing prosecution or other forms of retribution. See Washburn, *Question of Sedition*, 66–97; Washburn, *African American Newspaper*, 138–77; Finkle, "Conservative Aims of Militant Rhetoric," 692–713; Finkle, *Forum for Protest*; *Chicago Defender*, July 24, 1943.

16. Mangum, *Legal Status of the Negro*, 305.

17. Florida Voters for Constitutional Government, Orlando Florida—Card and Newsletter, stamped received in Holland Papers, March 20, 1944.

18. J. G. Simpson, Mulberry, Florida, to Governor Spessard Holland, October 26, 1944, Holland Collection, University of Florida.

19. Norrell, *House I Live In*, 146.

20. *Chicago Tribune*, August 25, 1944.

21. *Baltimore Afro-American*, September 2, 1944.

22. Ibid.

23. *New York Daily Worker*, October 10, 1944.

24. For a detailed account of the "Quincy Three" case, see Evans, "Weathering the Storm," 289–302. For a discussion of the rise of lethal executions along with concomitant decline in lynching, see Vandiver, *Lethal Punishment*; Clarke, "'Without Fear or Shame'"; Ogletree and Sarat, *From Lynch Mobs to the Killing State*.

25. *Tampa Times* editorial reprinted in *Tallahassee Daily Democrat*, August 27, 1944.

26. *St. Petersburg Times*, August 27, 1944.

27. Waldrep, "National Policing," 589–93.

28. Mormino, *Land of Sunshine*, 2, 9–10.

29. Dray, *At the Hands of Persons Unknown*, 406–7. Brundage identified four classifications of lynchers: mobs numbering between several dozen and several thousand people, large semilegal posses, gangs acting in defiance of the government or for retribution, and small groups of terrorists. Brundage, *Lynching in the New South*, 21.

30. De la Roche also relates the size of the mob to the social status of the alleged victim; more powerful victims incited larger mobs, while victims with less status attracted the support of small, private mobs. De la Roche, "Why Is Collective Violence Collective?" 126–44.

31. *Baltimore Afro-American*, August 28, 1943; *Chicago Defender*, August 28, 1943. The poll was administered in Florida, Texas, Louisiana, Arkansas, Oklahoma, Georgia, South Carolina, North Carolina, Tennessee, Mississippi, Kentucky, Alabama, and Virginia, asking voters "Do you favor or oppose a Federal anti-lynching law?"

32. Howard, *Lynchings*, 146–48.

33. Rushdy, *End of Lynching*, 95–105.

34. Vandiver, "Race, Clemency, and Executions," 1; Clarke, "Without Fear or Shame," 284–88; Vandiver, *Lethal Punishment*; Ogletree and Sarat, *From Lynch Mobs to the Killing State*.

35. Howard, *Lynchings*, 138–39.

36. Davis, "Shades of Justice," 115.

37. Decker, "Issue in Social Control," 53.

38. Davis, Gardner, and Gardner, *Deep South*, 489.

39. Myrdal, *American Dilemma*, 537, 538; Decker, "Issue in Social Control," 27.

40. Belknap, *Federal Law and Southern Order*, 8, 24; Key, *Southern Politics*, 88.

41. Cohen, "Screws Case," 94–106; Carr, *Federal Protection of Civil Rights*, 107–14.

42. Thurgood Marshall, "The Legal Attack to Secure Civil Rights," an address delivered July 13, 1944, at the NAACP Wartime Conference, in Broderick and Meier, *Negro Protest Thought*.

43. "Whoever, under color of any law, statute, ordinance, regulation, or custom, willfully subjects . . . any inhabitant of any State . . . to the deprivation of any rights, privileges or immunities secured or protected by the constitution and laws of the United States . . . shall be fined not more than $10,000, or imprisonment of not more than one year or both." 18 U.S.C. §§ 52, 88 (1940).

44. Carr, *Federal Protection of Civil Rights*, 174.

45. Emmons, "Striking the First Blow"; Green, *Before His Time*.

46. Communist Party of Jacksonville, "An Appeal to the Negro People," n.d., Caldwell Papers.

47. Green, *Before His Time*.

48. Affidavit by Regina Hadley, January 7, 1946, Caldwell Papers.

49. It was later determined that the note was written by another black man by the name of Parker. Parker was dating Bradwell's ex-girlfriend and apparently was attempting to remove him as a potential threat to his relationship. Orion C. Parker Jr., Tallahassee, Florida, to Governor Millard Caldwell, January 21, 1947, Caldwell Papers.

50. King, *Devil in the Grove*, 74–80; *Chicago Defender*, July 7, 1945, August 3, 1946, February 22, 1947.

51. Green, *Before His Time*, 134–46; Lawson, Colburn, and Paulson, "Groveland," 1–26; King, *Devil in the Grove*.

52. King, *Devil in the Grove*, 98–110.

53. Ibid.; Robinson, "Law and Order."

54. King, *Devil in the Grove*, 202.

55. "What about Harry T. Moore of Mims, Florida, who is the head of the Association for the Advancement of Colored People. He is a Negro, is he not? Give me the dope on him." Ed Straughn to C. Sweet Smith, March 26, 1946, Caldwell Papers.

56. Anderson, *Eyes Off the Prize*, 197–98.

57. Dudziak, *Cold War Civil Rights*, 12.

58. Emmons, "Flame of Resistance," 242–43.

Epilogue. Strange Fruit, Bitter Seeds: The Echoes of Lynching Violence

1. Koritha Mitchell makes this observation in her comparison of two lynching dramas, Angelina Weld Grimké's *Rachel* (1916) and May Miller's *Nails and Thorns* (1936), both of which examine how families were impacted by extralegal violence. Mitchell, "Sisters in Motherhood(?)," in Simien, *Gender and Lynching*, 39.

2. Armstrong, *Mary Turner*.

3. Stephen Payne (also spelled Steven) is listed with the family in the U.S. Censuses of 1920 and 1930, and a death certificate lists his year of death as 1933. According to family members, Stephen was tied to railroad tracks by local whites and left to die. State of Florida, Florida Death Index, 1877–1998, Florida Department of Health, Office of Vital Records; Jones and Sims interview; Worth interview.

4. Wilson interview; FBI Investigation, April 11, 1944, DOJ Files.

5. Family Affidavit.

6. Flipper interview.

7. Ibid.

8. Ben Montgomery, "Spectacle: The Lynching of Claude Neal," *Tampa Bay Times*, October 20, 2011.

9. There are several works that take up the subject of the image and condition of black women in the United States, including Giddings, *When and Where I Enter*; Harley and Terborg-Penn, *Afro-American Woman*; hooks, *Ain't I a Woman*; White, *Too Heavy a Load*.

10. Memories of lynching, he found, were "attached primarily to the families of the victims, lynching victims are more likely to be remembered as part of a genealogical landscape, memories of lynching have a socializing function, and memories of lynching act as covert evidence in private discourse of wrongs that cannot be corrected in public discourse." Baker, "Under the Rope," in Brundage, *Where These Memories Grow*, 334.

11. Hill, "Resisting Lynching," 183–214; Holloway, *Jim Crow Wisdom*, 11.

BIBLIOGRAPHY

Primary Sources

MANUSCRIPT COLLECTIONS

Caldwell, Governor Millard. Papers. Administrative Collection, Florida State Archives, Tallahassee.

Gray, William, Jr. Papers. Southeastern Regional Black Archives, Research Center and Museum, Florida Agricultural and Mechanical University, Tallahassee.

Holland, Governor Spessard L. Papers. Administrative Collection, Florida State Archives, Tallahassee.

NAACP Papers, Manuscript Division, Library of Congress, Washington, D.C. Microfilm.

Suwannee Valley Genealogical Society, Live Oak, Florida. Marriage Records.

Tuskegee Institute News Clipping Files. Lynching Files, Tuskegee University, Tuskegee, Alabama. Microfilm.

Warren, Governor Fuller. Papers. Administrative Collection, Florida State Archives, Tallahassee.

GOVERNMENT DOCUMENTS AND MANUSCRIPTS

Florida Department of Agriculture. *Sixth Census of the State of Florida*. Tallahassee: Department of Agriculture, 1935. Florida State Archives, Tallahassee.

Florida State Planning Board, ed. *Statistical Abstract of Florida Counties*. Jacksonville: Florida State Chamber of Commerce, 1944.

Live Oak, Florida. Suwannee County Courthouse. Circuit Court Records.

———. Suwannee County Courthouse. Deed Records.

———. Suwannee County Courthouse. Marriage Records.

Marianna, Florida. City Hall. Municipal Court Records.

———. Jackson County Courthouse. Court Records.

————. Jackson County Courthouse. Deed Records.
Records of the Florida Supreme Court. Florida State Archives, Tallahassee.
Records of the United States District Courts, Record Group 21, National Archives and
    Records Administration, East Point, Ga.
U.S. Congressional Record. 75th Congress, 1st Session, 1937.
U.S. Department of Commerce. *Statistical Abstract of the United States.* Washington,
    D.C.: U.S. Government Printing Office, 1954.
U.S. Department of Justice, Record Group 60, National Archives and Records Admin-
    istration II, College Park, Md.

INTERVIEWS

Alexander, Marie Bell. Interview with the author, Madison, Fla., December 15, 2003.
Beasley, Samuel. Interview with the author, Live Oak, Fla., June 7, 2013.
Bryant, Elmore. Interview with the author, Marianna, Fla., October 18, 2003.
Daniels, Carl. Interview with the author, Quincy, Fla., November 9, 1999.
DePass, Dorothy. Interview with the author, Live Oak, Fla., February 28, 1999.
Dixie, A. I. Interview with the author, Quincy, Fla., March 21, 1998.
Flipper, Ann. Interview with the author, Indian Springs, Nev. (via telephone), March
    31, 1998.
Green, Robert. Interview with the author, Quincy, Fla., August 13, 2003.
Hall, Louise Hicks. Interview with the author, Live Oak, Fla., July 11, 2003.
Haynes, Detta B. Interview with the author, Live Oak, Fla., June 11, 2013
Jones, Shirley, and Fannie Sims. Interview with the author, Sanford, Fla., September
    9, 2013.
Kelley, Vivian. Interview with the author, Quincy, Fla., December 16, 1999.
Kinsolving, Ruth Barnes. Interview with author, Marianna, Fla., May 7, 2013.
Linton, Ruth. Interview with the author, McAlpin, Fla., July 13, 2003.
Morison, H. Graham. Interview by Jerry N. Hess, August 8, 1972, Truman Presiden-
    tial Museum and Library, http://www.trumanlibrary.org.
Pender, Sarah Speights. Interview with the author, Marianna, Fla., May 8, 2013.
Perry, Mamie. Interviewed by Marvin Dunn, Orlando, Fla., June 2007.
Philmore, Walter Mae. Interview with the author, Live Oak, Fla., July 19, 2003.
Pittman, Eva. Interview with the author, Marianna, Fla., January 6, 2004.
Pittman, Richard. Interview with author, Miami, Fla., May 26, 2013.
Pride, Ellen and Lucille Bradley. Interview with the author, Madison, Fla., April 11,
    2004.
Robinson, Earnest. Interview with the author, Marianna, Fla., May 8, 2013.
Singleton, Frank. Interview with the author, Tallahassee, Fla., December 7, 1999.
Subject #2. Interview with the author, Live Oak, Fla., December 25, 1995.
Subject #3. Interview with the author, Live Oak, Fla., December 25, 1995.
Summers, Ronald. Interview with the author, Quincy, Fla., March 9, 1999.
Wilson, Nellie. Interview with the author, Marianna, Fla., October 18, 2003.
Worth, Rosa Payne. Interview with author, Troy, Mich. (via telephone), September
    9, 2013.

Secondary Sources

Adams, Maurianne, and John Bracey, eds. *Strangers and Neighbors: Relations between Blacks and Jews in the United States.* Amherst: University of Massachusetts Press, 1999.

The Administration of Millard F. Caldwell as Governor of Florida, 1945–1949. n.p. n.d. Florida A&M University, Black Archives, Research Center and Museum, Tallahassee, Fla. .

Allen, James, Hilton Als, John Lewis, and Leon F. Litwack. *Without Sanctuary: Lynching Photography in America.* Santa Fe, N.Mex.: Twin Palms, 2000.

Ames, Jessie Daniel. *The Changing Character of Lynching, Review of Lynching, 1931–1941.* Atlanta: Commission on Interracial Cooperation, 1942.

Anderson, Carol. *Eyes Off the Prize: The United Nations and the African American Struggle for Human Rights, 1944–1955.* Cambridge: Cambridge University Press, 2003.

Armstrong, Julie Buckner. *Mary Turner and the Memory of Lynching.* Athens: University of Georgia Press, 2011.

Arsenault, Raymond. *St. Petersburg and the Florida Dream, 1888–1950.* Gainesville: University Press of Florida, 1996.

Avant, David A. *Illustrated Index: J. Randall Stanley's History of Gadsden County.* Tallahassee, Fla.: L'Avant Studios, 1948.

Ayers, Edward L. *Vengeance and Justice: Crime and Punishment in the Nineteenth Century South.* New York: Oxford University Press, 1984.

Baptist, Edward E. *Creating an Old South: Middle Florida's Plantation Frontier before the Civil War.* Chapel Hill: University of North Carolina Press, 2002.

Bederman, Gail, *Manliness and Civilization: A Cultural History of Gender and Race in the United States, 1880–1917.* Chicago: University of Chicago Press, 2008.

Belknap, Michael R. *Federal Law and Southern Order: Racial Violence and Constitutional Conflict in the Post-Brown South.* Athens: University of Georgia Press, 1987.

Borstelmann, Thomas. *Cold War and the Color Line: American Race Relations in the Global Arena.* Cambridge, Mass.: Harvard University Press, 2009.

Broderick, Francis L., and August Meier, eds. *Negro Protest Thought in the Twentieth Century.* Indianapolis: Bobbs-Merrill, 1965.

Brown, Canter, Jr. *Florida's Black Public Officials.* Tuscaloosa: University of Alabama Press, 1998.

Brown, Richard M., ed. *American Violence.* Englewood Cliffs, N.J.: Prentice-Hall, 1970.

Brundage, W. Fitzhugh. *Lynching in the New South: Georgia and Virginia, 1880–1930.* Urbana: University of Illinois Press, 1993.

———, ed. *Under Sentence of Death: Lynching in the South.* Chapel Hill: University of North Carolina Press, 1997.

———, ed. *Where These Memories Grow: History, Memory, and Southern Identity.* Chapel Hill: University of North Carolina Press, 2000.

Burran, James A. "Violence in an 'Arsenal of Democracy.'" *East Texas Historical Journal* 14 (Spring 1976): 39–52.

Capeci, Dominic J., Jr. *The Lynching of Cleo Wright*. Lexington: University Press of Kentucky, 1998.

Capeci, Dominic J., Jr. and Martha Wilkerson. *Layered Violence: The Detroit Rioters of 1943*. Jackson: University Press of Mississippi, 1991.

Carr, Robert K. *Federal Protection of Civil Rights: Quest for a Sword*. Ithaca, N.Y.: Cornell University Press, 1947.

Carrigan, William D., and Christopher Waldrep, eds. *Swift to Wrath: Lynching in a Global Historical Perspective*. Charlottesville: University of Virginia Press, 2013.

Carter, Dan T. *Scottsboro: A Tragedy of the American South*. Baton Rouge: Louisiana State University Press, 1979.

Cash, W. J. *The Mind of the South*. New York: Alfred A. Knopf, 1941.

Cassanello, Robert, and Melanie Shell-Weiss, eds. *Florida's Working-Class Past: Current Perspectives on Labor, Race, and Gender from Spanish Florida to the New Immigration*. Gainesville: University Press of Florida, 2009.

Chafe, William H., ed. *The Achievement of American Liberalism: The New Deal and Its Legacies*. New York: Columbia University Press, 2003.

Chamberlain, Charles D. *Victory at Home: Manpower and Race in the American South during World War II*. Athens: University of Georgia Press, 2003.

Chestang, Ennis Lee. "The Shade-Grown Cigar Wrapper Tobacco District of Gadsden County, Florida." Ph.D. diss., Indiana University, 1965.

Clark, James C. *Red Pepper and Gorgeous George: Claude Pepper's Epic Defeat in the 1950 Democratic Primary*. Gainesville: University of Press of Florida, 2011.

Clarke, James W. "'Without Fear or Shame': Lynching, Capital Punishment and the Subculture of Violence in the American South." *British Journal of Political Science* 28 (1998): 269–89.

Cobb, James, and Charles Wilson, eds. *Perspectives on the American South: An Annual Review of American Society, Politics, and Culture*. Vol. 4. Jackson: University Press of Mississippi, 1997.

Cohen, Julius. "The Screws Case: Federal Protection of Negro Rights." *Columbia Law Review* 46 (January 1946): 94–106.

Colburn, David R., and Jane Landers, eds. *The African American Heritage of Florida*. Gainesville: University Press of Florida, 1995.

Colburn, David R., and Richard K. Scher. *Florida's Gubernatorial Politics in the Twentieth Century*. Gainesville: University Press of Florida, 1980.

Coleman, Frank. "Freedom from Fear on the Home Front." *Iowa Law Review* 29 (March 1944): 415–29.

Cortner, Richard C. *A Mob Intent on Death: The NAACP and the Arkansas Riot Cases*. Lebanon, N.H.: University Press of New England, 1988.

Cox, Oliver C. "Lynching and the Status Quo." *Journal of Negro Education* 14, no. 4 (Fall 1945): 576–88.

———. *Race Relations: Elements and Social Dynamics*. Detroit: Wayne State University Press, 1976.

Cronon, David. *Black Moses: The Story of Marcus Garvey and the Universal Negro Improvement Association.* Madison: University of Wisconsin Press, 1955.

Curry, Chestine Epps. "History of Suwannee County and Its Black Settlers." n.d. Unpublished paper in author's possession.

Daniel, Pete. "Going among Strangers: Southern Reactions to World War II." *Journal of American History* 77 (1990): 886–911.

Daniel, Walter G. "The Responsibility of Education for the Preparation of Children and Youth to Live in a Multi-Racial Society." *Journal of Negro Education* 19, no. 3 (Summer 1950): 388–98.

Davis, Allison, Bureleigh B. Gardner, and Mary R. Gardner. *Deep South: A Social Anthropology Study of Cast and Class.* Chicago: University of Chicago Press, 1941.

Davis, Jack E. "Shades of Justice: The Lynching of Jesse James Payne and Its Aftermath." Master's thesis, University of South Florida, 1989.

———. "'Whitewash' in Florida: The Lynching of Jesse James Payne and Its Aftermath." *Florida Historical Quarterly* 68, no. 3 (January 1990): 277–98.

Decker, Scott H. "An Issue in Social Control: The Case of Putnam County Sheriff's Department." Master's thesis, Florida State University, 1974.

de la Roche, Roberta Senechal. "Why Is Collective Violence Collective?" *Sociological Theory* 19, no. 2 (July 2001): 126–44.

Dickson, Sandra, and Churchill Roberts. "Freedom Never Dies: The Legacy of Harry T. Moore." Watertown, Mass.: Documentary Educational Resources, 2001.

D'Orso, Michael. *Like Judgment Day: The Ruin and Redemption of a Town Called Rosewood.* New York: G. P. Putnam's Sons, 1996.

Dray, Philip. *At the Hands of Persons Unknown: The Lynching of Black America.* New York: Random House, 2002.

Dudziak, Mary L. *Cold War Civil Rights: Race and the Image of American Democracy.* Princeton, N.J.: Princeton University Press, 2000.

Dunn, James William. "The New Deal and Florida Politics." Ph.D. diss., Florida State University, 1971.

Dunn, Marvin. *Black Miami in the Twentieth Century.* Gainesville: University Press of Florida, 1997.

Durr, Virginia. *Outside of the Magic Circle: The Autobiography of Virginia Foster Durr.* 1985. Reprint, Tuscaloosa: University of Alabama Press, 1994.

Egerton, John. *Speak Now against the Day: The Generation Before the Civil Rights Movement in the South.* Chapel Hill: University of North Carolina Press, 1994.

Ellis, Mary Louise. "'Rain Down Fire': The Lynching of Sam Hose." Ph.D. diss., Florida State University, 1992.

Ellison, Ralph. *Shadow and Act.* New York: Vintage, 1964.

Emmons, Caroline S. "Flame of Resistance: The NAACP in Florida, 1910–1960." Ph.D. diss., Florida State University, 1998.

———. "Striking the First Blow: Harry T. Moore and the Fight for Black Equality in Florida." Master's thesis, Florida State University, 1992.

Escobar, Edward J. *Race, Police, and the Making of Political Identities: Mexican Americans and the Los Angeles Police Department, 1900–1945*. Berkeley: University of California Press, 1999.

Evans, Jon S. "Weathering the Storm: Florida Politics during the Administration of Spessard L. Holland in World War II." Ph.D. diss., Florida State University, 2011.

Evans, Tammy. *The Silencing of Ruby McCollum: Race, Class, and Gender in the South*. Gainesville: University Press of Florida, 2006.

Feimster, Crystal. *Southern Horrors: Women and the Politics of Rape and Lynching*. Cambridge, Mass.: Harvard University Press, 2009.

Feldman, Glenn, ed. *Before Brown: Civil Rights and White Backlash in the Modern South*. Tuscaloosa: University of Alabama Press, 2004.

Ferber, Abby L. *White Man Falling: Race, Gender, and White Supremacy*. Lanham: Rowman & Littlefield, 1998.

Finkle, Lee. "The Conservative Aims of Militant Rhetoric: Black Protest during World War II." *Journal of American History* 60, no. 3 (December 1970): 692–713.

———. *Forum for Protest: The Black Press during World War II*. Madison, N.J.: Fairleigh Dickinson University Press, 1975.

Fox, Stephen. *The Guardian of Boston: William Monroe Trotter*. New York: Atheneum Press, 1970.

Franklin, John Hope, and August Meier, eds. *Black Leaders of the Twentieth Century*. Urbana: University of Illinois Press, 1982.

Fredrickson, George M. *The Black Image in the White Mind: The Debate on Afro-American Character and Destiny, 1817–1914*. New York: Harper and Row, 1971.

Gallicchio, Marc S. *The African American Encounter with Japan and China: Black Internationalism in Asia, 1895–1945*. Chapel Hill: University of North Carolina Press, 2000.

Gannon, Michael, ed. *The New History of Florida*. Gainesville: University Press of Florida, 1996.

Garfinkel, Herbert. *When Negroes March: The March on Washington Movement in the Organizational Politics of FEPC*. Glencoe, Ill.: Free Press, 1959.

Giddings, Paula. *When and Where I Enter: The Impact of Black Women on Race and Sex in America*. New York: William Morrow Press, 1984.

Gill, Johnpeter H., and Robert L. Jenkins. "The Nazis and the American South in the 1930s: A Mirror Image?" *Journal of Southern History* 58 (November 1992): 667–94.

Gilmore, Glenda. *Defying Dixie: The Radical Roots of Civil Rights, 1919–1950*. New York: W. W. Norton, 2008.

———. *Gender and Jim Crow, Women and the Politics of White Supremacy in North Carolina, 1896–1920*. Chapel Hill: University of North Carolina Press, 1996.

Ginzburg, Ralph. *100 Years of Lynching*. New York: Lancer Books, 1962.

Gonzales-Day, Ken. *Lynching in the West: 1850–1935*. Durham, N.C.: Duke University Press, 2006.

Green, Ben. *Before His Time: The Untold Story of Harry T. Moore, America's First Civil Rights Martyr*. New York: Free Press, 1999.

Greenberg, Mark I., William Warren Rogers, and Canter Brown Jr., eds. *Florida's Heritage of Diversity*. Tallahassee, Fla.: Sentry Press, 1997.

Guthrie, John, Jr. *Keepers of the Spirits: The Judicial Response to Prohibition Enforcement in Florida, 1885-1935*. Westport, Conn.: Praeger, 1998.

Guzman, Jessie Parkhurst, Lewis W. Jones, and Woodrow Hall, eds. *Negro Year Book, 1952: A Review of the Events Affecting Negro Life*. New York: Wm. H. Wise, 1952.

Hackney, Sheldon. "Southern Violence." *American Historical Review* 74 (1969): 906–25.

Hadden, Sally E. *Slave Patrols: Law and Violence in Virginia and the Carolinas*. Cambridge, Mass.: Harvard University Press, 2001.

Hall, Jacquelyn Dowd. *Revolt against Chivalry: Jessie Daniel Ames and the Women's Campaign against Lynching*. New York: Columbia University Press, 1993.

Harley, Sharon, and Rosalyn Terborg-Penn, eds. *The Afro-American Woman: Struggles and Images*. New York: Kennikat Press, 1978.

Harris, Trudier. *Exorcising Blackness: Historical and Literary Lynching and Burning Rituals*. Bloomington: Indiana University Press, 1984.

Harrison, Alferdteen, ed. *Black Exodus: The Great Migration from the American South*. Jackson: University Press of Mississippi, 1992.

Hart, Justin. "Making Democracy Safe for the World: Race, Propaganda, and the Transformation of the U.S. Foreign Policy during World War II." *Pacific Historical Review* 73 (2004): 49–84.

Hill, Karlos. "Resisting Lynching: Black Grassroots Responses to Lynching in the Mississippi and Arkansas Deltas, 1882–1938." Ph.D. diss., University of Illinois at Urbana-Champaign, 2009.

Hill, Robert A., ed. *The FBI's RACON: Racial Conditions in the United States during World War II*. Boston: Northeastern University Press, 1995.

Hine, Darlene Clark. *Hine Sight: Black Women and the Re-construction of American History*. Bloomington: Indiana University Press, 1994.

Hine, Darlene Clark, and Earnestine Jenkins, eds. *A Question of Manhood: A Reader in U.S. Black Men's History of Masculinity*. Vol. 2. Bloomington: Indiana University Press, 2001.

Holloway, Jonathan Scott. *Jim Crow Wisdom: Memory and Identity in Black America since 1940*. Chapel Hill: University of North Carolina Press, 2013.

hooks, bell. *Ain't I a Woman: Black Women and Feminism*. Boston: South End Press, 1981.

Horne, Gerald. "Race from Power: U.S. Foreign Policy and the General Crisis of 'White Supremacy.'" *Diplomatic History* 23, no. 3 (Summer 1999): 437–61.

Hovland, C. I., and R. R. Sears. "Minor Studies of Aggression: Correlations of Economic Indices with Lynching." *Journal of Psychology* 9 (1940): 301–10.

Howard, Walter T. *Lynchings: Extralegal Violence in Florida during the 1930s*. Selinsgrove, Pa.: Susquehanna University Press, 1995.

———. "Vigilante Justice: Extra-Legal Executions in Florida, 1930–1940." Ph.D. diss., Florida State University, 1987.

"How Secure Is the Right to Safety of the Person?" *New South* 4, no. 3 (March 1949): 1–5.

Huie, William Bradford. *Ruby McCollum: Woman in the Suwannee Jail.* New York: E. P. Dutton, 1956.

Ifill, Sherrilyn A. *On the Courthouse Lawn: Confronting the Legacy of Lynching in the Twenty-First Century.* Boston: Beacon Press, 2007.

Ingalls, Robert P. *Urban Vigilantes in the New South: Tampa, 1882–1936.* Knoxville: University of Tennessee Press, 1988. Reprint, Gainesville: University Press of Florida, 1993.

Irwin-Zarecka, Iwona. *Frames of Remembrance: The Dynamics of Collective Memory.* New Brunswick, N.J.: Transaction Publishers, 1994.

———. *Neutralizing Memory: The Jew in Contemporary Poland.* New Brunswick, N.J.: Transaction Publishers, 1989.

Johns, Claude J., Jr. "A Case Study of the Sheriff's Office in Three Florida Counties." Master's thesis, Florida State University, 1953.

Johnson, Charles. *To Stem This Tide: A Survey of Racial Tension Areas in the United States.* Boston: Pilgrim Press, 1943.

Johnson, Kimberley. *Reforming Jim Crow: Southern Politics and the State in the Age Before Brown.* New York: Oxford University Press, 2010.

Johnson, Marilynn S. "Gender, Race, and Rumours: Re-examining the 1943 Race Riots." *Gender and History* 10, no. 2 (August 1998): 252–77.

Jones, Maxine D. "'Without Compromise or Fear': Florida's African American Female Activists." *Florida Historical Quarterly* 77, no. 4 (Spring 1999): 475–502.

Jones, Maxine D., and Kevin M. McCarthy. *African Americans in Florida.* Sarasota, Fla.: Pineapple Press, 1993.

Jones, Maxine D., Larry E. Rivers, David R. Colburn, R. Tom Dye, and William W. Rogers. "A Documented History of the Incident Which Occurred at Rosewood, Florida in January 1923." Submitted to the Florida Legislature, December 22, 1993.

Jordan, Winthrop D. *White Over Black: American Attitudes toward the Negro, 1550–1812.* Chapel Hill: University of North Carolina Press, 1968.

Kapur, Sudarshan. *Raising Up a Prophet: The African-American Encounter with Gandhi.* Boston: Beacon Press, 1992.

Katznelson, Ira. *When Affirmative Action Was White: An Untold History of Racial Inequality in Twentieth-Century America.* New York: W. W. Norton, 2005.

Kearney, Reginald. *African American Views of the Japanese: Solidarity or Sedition?* Albany: State University of New York Press, 1998.

———. "Japan: Ally in the Struggle against Racism, 1919–1927." *Contributions in Black Studies* 12 (1994): 117–28.

Kennedy, David M. *Freedom from Fear: The American People in Depression and War, 1929–1945.* New York: Oxford University Press, 1999.

Kennedy, Stetson. *Jim Crow Guide: The Way It Was.* 1959. Reprint, Boca Raton: Florida Atlantic University Press, 1990.

Kessleman, Louis Coleridge. *The Social Politics of FEPC: A Study in Reform Pressure Movements.* Chapel Hill: University of North Carolina Press, 1948.

Key, V. O. *Southern Politics: In State and Nation.* New York: Alfred A. Knopf, 1949.

Kharif, Wali R. "Refinement of Racial Segregation in Florida." Ph.D. diss., Florida State University, 1983.

King, Gilbert. *Devil in the Grove: Thurgood Marshall, the Groveland Boys, and the Dawn of a New America*. New York: Harper Collins, 2013.

Kirby, Jack Temple. *Rural Worlds Lost: The American South, 1920–1960*. Baton Rouge: Louisiana State University Press, 1987.

Kneebone, John T. *Southern Liberal Journalists and the Issue of Race, 1920–1944*. Chapel Hill: University of North Carolina Press, 1985.

Kruse, Kevin, ed. *Fog of War: The Second World War and the Civil Rights Movement*. New York: Oxford University Press, 2012.

Kryder, Daniel. *Divided Arsenal: Race and the American State during World War II*. New York: Cambridge University Press, 2000.

Lawson, Steven, David Colburn, and Darryl Paulson. "Groveland: Florida's Little Scottsboro." *Florida Historical Quarterly* 65 (July 1986): 1–26.

Layton, Azza Salam. *International Politics and Civil Rights Policies in the United States, 1941–1960*. New York: Cambridge University Press, 2000.

The Legacy: African Americans of Jackson County, Florida. Clanton, Ala.: Heritage Publishing Consultants, 2006.

Lerner, Gerda, ed. *Black Women in White America: A Documentary History*. New York: Vintage Books, 1972.

Lewis, David Levering. *When Harlem Was in Vogue*. New York: Knopf, 1981.

Litwack, Leon F. *Been in the Storm So Long: The Aftermath of Slavery*. New York: Alfred A. Knopf, 1979.

———. *Trouble in Mind: Black Southerners in the Age of Jim Crow*. New York: Vintage Books, 1998.

Logan, Rayford. *What the Negro Wants*. Chapel Hill: University of North Carolina Press, 1944.

Maguire, Danielle. *At the Dark End of the Street: Black Women, Rape, and Resistance— A New History of the Civil Rights Movement from Rosa Parks to the Rise of Black Power*. New York: Alfred A. Knopf, 2010.

Mangum, Charles S., Jr. *The Legal Status of the Negro*. Chapel Hill: University of North Carolina Press, 1940.

Manley, Walter W., II, and Canter Brown Jr. *The Supreme Court of Florida, 1917–1972*. Gainesville: University Press of Florida, 2006.

Markovitz, Jonathan. *Legacies of Lynching: Racial Violence and Memory*. Minneapolis: University of Minnesota Press, 2004.

Marks, Carole. *Farewell—We're Good and Gone: The Great Black Migration*. Bloomington: Indiana University Press, 1989.

Mays, Benjamin E. *Born to Rebel: An Autobiography*. New York: Scribner, 1971.

Mazón, Mauricio. *The Zoot-Suit Riots: The Psychology of Symbolic Annihilation*. Austin: University of Texas Press, 1984.

McCarthy, Kevin M. *The Hippocrene U.S.A. Guide to Black Florida*. New York: Hippocrene Books, 1995.

McGovern, James. *Anatomy of a Lynching: The Killing of Claude Neal.* Baton Rouge: Louisiana State University Press, 1982.

McGuire, Phillip. *Taps for a Jim Crow Army: Letters from Black Soldiers in World War II.* Santa Barbara, Calif.: ABC-Clio, 1983.

McMillen, Neil. *Remaking Dixie: The Impact of World War II on the American South.* Jackson: University Press of Mississippi, 1997.

Mormino, Gary R. "GI Joe Meets Jim Crow: Racial Violence and Reform in World War II Florida." *Florida Historical Quarterly* 73 (July 1994): 23–42.

———. *Land of Sunshine, State of Dreams: A Social History of Modern Florida.* Gainesville: University Press of Florida, 2005.

Muhammad, Khalil Gibran. *The Condemnation of Blackness: Race, Crime, and the Making of Modern Urban America.* Cambridge, Mass.: Harvard University Press, 2010.

Muhammad, Salahuddin. "Justified Southern Punishment: The Florida Lynching of Will Larkins." Unpublished paper in author's possession. n.d.

Myrdal, Gunnar. *An American Dilemma: The Negro Social Structure.* 1944. Reprint, New York: McGraw-Hill, 1964.

Nalty, Bernard C. *Strength for the Fight: A History of Black Americans in the Military.* 1986. Reprint, New York: Free Press, 1989.

National Association for the Advancement of Colored People. *Thirty Years of Lynching in the United States, 1889–1918.* New York: Negro Universities Press, 1919.

Newby, I. A., ed. *The Development of Segregationist Thought.* Homewood, Ill.: Dorsey Press, 1968.

Newton, Michael. *The Invisible Empire: The Ku Klux Klan in Florida.* Gainesville: University Press of Florida, 2001.

Norrell, Robert J. *The House I Live In: Race in the American Century.* New York: Oxford University Press, 2005.

O'Brien, Gail Williams. *The Color of the Law: Race, Violence, and Justice in the Post–World War II South.* Chapel Hill: University of North Carolina Press, 1999.

Odum, Howard W. "Lynchings, Fears, and Folkways." *Nation* 133, no. 3469 (December 30, 1931): 719–20.

Ogletree, Charles J., and Austin Sarat. *From Lynch Mobs to the Killing State: Race and the Death Penalty in America.* New York: NYU Press, 2006.

Olson, James S., and Sharon Phair. "Anatomy of a Race Riot: Beaumont, Texas, 1943." *Texana* 11 (1973): 64–72.

Ortiz, Paul. *Emancipation Betrayed: The Hidden History of Black Organizing and White Violence from Reconstruction to the Bloody Election of 1920.* Berkeley: University of California Press, 2005.

Pando, Robert T. "Shrouded in Cheesecloth: The Demise of Shade Tobacco in Florida and Georgia." Master's thesis, Florida State University, 2004.

Patterson, Orlando. *Rituals of Blood: Consequences of Slavery in Two American Centuries.* New York: Basic Books, 1998.

Patton, Gerald W. *War and Race: The Black Officer in the American Military, 1915–1941.* Westport, Conn.: Greenwood Press, 1981.

Peek, Ralph L. "Aftermath of Military Reconstruction, 1868–1869." *Florida Historical Quarterly* 43 (October 1964): 123–41.

———. "Lawlessness in Florida, 1868–1871." *Florida Historical Quarterly* 40 (October 1961): 164–85.

Pfeffer, Paula F. *A. Philip Randolph, Pioneer of the Civil Rights Movement.* Baton Rouge: Louisiana State University Press, 1990.

Pfeifer, Michael J. *Rough Justice: Lynching and American Society, 1847–1947.* Urbana: University of Illinois Press, 2004.

Pilkington, Charles K. "The Trials of Brotherhood: The Founding of the Commission on Interracial Cooperation." *Georgia Historical Quarterly* 69, no. 1 (Spring 1985): 55–80.

Pinar, William F. *The Gender of Racial Politics and Violence in America: Lynching, Prison Rape, and the Crisis of Masculinity.* Ann Arbor: University of Michigan Press, 2008.

Platt, Oliver. *Pegler: Angry Man of the Press.* Boston: Beacon Press, 1963.

Plummer, Brenda Gayle. *Rising Wind: Black Americans and U.S. Foreign Affairs, 1935–1960.* Chapel Hill: University of North Carolina Press, 1996.

Porter, Gilbert, and Leedell W. Neyland. *History of the Florida State Teachers Association.* Washington, D.C.: National Education Association, 1977.

Rabinowitz, Howard. *Race Relations in the Urban South, 1865–1890.* New York: Oxford University Press, 1978.

Raper, Arthur. *The Tragedy of Lynching.* Chapel Hill: University of North Carolina Press, 1933.

Reid, Ira De A. "General Characteristics of the Negro Youth Population." *Journal of Negro Education* 9, no. 3 (July 1940): 278–89.

Richardson, Joe M. *The Negro in the Reconstruction of Florida, 1865–1877.* Tallahassee: Florida State University, 1965.

Richardson, Riche. *Black Masculinity and the U.S. South.* Athens: University of Georgia Press, 2007.

Rivers, Larry E. *Slavery in Florida: Territorial Days to Emancipation.* Gainesville: University Press of Florida, 2000.

Robinson, Timothy Brandt. "Law and Order, By Any Means Necessary: The Life and Times of Willis V. McCall, Sheriff of Lake County, Florida." Master's thesis, Florida State University, 1997.

Roman, Meredith L. *Opposing Jim Crow: African Americans and the Soviet Indictment of U.S. Racism, 1928–1937.* Lincoln: University of Nebraska Press, 2012.

Rosenberg, Jonathan. *How Far the Promised Land? World Affairs and the American Civil Rights Movement from the First World War to Vietnam.* Princeton, N.J.: Princeton University Press, 2006.

Royster, Jacqueline Jones, ed. *Southern Horrors and Other Writings: The Anti-Lynching Campaign of Ida B. Wells, 1892–1900.* Boston: Bedford/St. Martin's, 1997.

Ruchames, Louis. *Race, Jobs, and Politics: The Story of the FEPC.* New York: Columbia University Press, 1953.

Rushdy, Ashraf H. A. *The End of Lynching in America*. New Brunswick, N.J.: Rutgers University Press, 2012.

Russell, Katheryn K. *The Color of Crime: Racial Hoaxes, White Fear, Black Protectionism, Police Harassment, and Other Macroaggressions*. New York: New York University Press, 1998.

Schechter, Patricia A. *Ida B. Wells-Barnett and American Reform, 1880–1930*. Chapel Hill: University of North Carolina Press, 2001.

Schneider, Mark Robert. *"We Return Fighting": The Civil Rights Movement in the Jazz Age*. Lebanon, N.H.: University Press of New England, 2002.

Scott, J. Irving E. *The Education of Black People in Florida*. Philadelphia: Dorrance, 1974.

Sherman, Richard. *The Case of Odell Waller and Virginia Justice*. Knoxville: University of Tennessee Press, 1992.

Shofner, Jerrell H. "Custom, Law and History: The Enduring Influence of Florida's 'Black Codes.'" *Florida Historical Quarterly* 55 (January 1977): 277–98.

———. *Jackson County, Florida—A History*. Marianna, Fla.: Jackson County Heritage Association, 1985.

———. "The Legacy of Racial Slavery: Free Enterprise and Forced Labor in Florida in the 1940s." *Journal of Southern History* 47 (August 1981): 411–26.

———. *Nor Is It Over Yet: Florida in the Era of Reconstruction*. Gainesville: University Press of Florida, 1974.

———. "Postscript to the Martin Tabert Case: Peonage as Usual in the Florida Turpentine Camps." *Florida Historical Quarterly* 60, no. 2 (October 1981): 161–73.

Simien, Evelyn M., ed. *Gender and Lynching: The Politics of Memory*. New York: Palgrave Macmillan, 2011.

Sims, Elizabeth H. *A History of Madison County, Florida*. Madison, Fla.: Madison County Historical Society, 1986.

Sitkoff, Harvard. *A New Deal for Blacks*. New York: Oxford University Press, 1978.

Smith, Lillian. *Killers of the Dream*. 1949. Reprint, New York: W. W. Norton, 1994.

Snitow, Ann B., Christine Stansell, and Sharon Thompson, eds. *Powers of Desire: The Politics of Sexuality*. New York: Monthly Review Press, 1983.

Solomon, Marc. *The Cry Was Unity: Communists and African Americans, 1917–1936*. Jackson: University Press of Mississippi, 1998.

Southern Commission on the Study of Lynching. *Lynchings and What They Mean*. Atlanta: Southern Commission on the Study of Lynching, 1931.

Stampp, Kenneth. *The Era of Reconstruction, 1865–1877*. New York: Vintage Books, 1965.

Stanley, J. Randall. *History of Jackson County*. Marianna, Fla.: Jackson County Historical Society, 1950.

Stein, Judith. *The World of Marcus Garvey: Race and Class in Modern Society*. Baton Rouge: Louisiana State University Press, 1986.

Stoutamire, Ralph C., P. Helfenstein, and S. C Kierce. *Tobacco Growing in Florida*. Tallahassee: State of Florida, Department of Agriculture, 1946.

Sullivan, Patricia. *Days of Hope: Race and Democracy in the New Deal Era*. Chapel Hill: University of North Carolina Press, 1996.

Suwannee History Committee. *Echoes of the Past: A History of Suwannee County, 1858–2000*. St. Petersburg, Fla.: Southern Heritage Press, 2000.

Sydnor, Charles S. "The Southerners and the Laws." *Journal of Southern History* 6, no. 1 (February 1940): 3–23.

Tannebaum, Frank. *Darker Phases of the South*. New York: G. P. Putnam's Sons, 1924.

Tebeau, Charlton W. *A History of Florida*. Coral Gables, Fla.: University of Miami Press, 1971.

Thompson, Sharyn, and Gwendolyn Waldorf. *Historical and Architectural Survey: Quincy, Florida's African-American Resources*. Quincy, Fla.: City of Quincy, 1996.

Tisdale, W. B. *Tobacco Diseases in Gadsden County in 1922 with Suggestions for Their Prevention and Control*. Gainesville: University of Florida Agricultural Experiment Station, 1922.

Tolnay Stewart E., and E. M. Beck, *A Festival of Violence*. Chicago: University of Illinois Press, 1995.

Tonry, Michael. *Punishing Race: A Continuing American Dilemma*. New York: Oxford University Press, 2011.

Vandiver, Margaret. *Lethal Punishment: Lynchings and Legal Executions in the South*. New Brunswick, N.J.: Rutgers University Press, 2005.

———. "Race, Clemency, and Executions in Florida, 1924–1966." Master's thesis, Florida State University, 1983.

Vital Speeches of the Day: 1941. New York: City News Publishing, 1941.

Voogd, Jan. *Race Riots and Resistance: The Red Summer of 1919*. New York: Peter Lang, 2008.

Waldrep, Christopher. *The Many Faces of Judge Lynch: Extralegal Violence and Punishment in America*. New York: Palgrave Macmillan, 2002.

———. "National Policing, Lynching, and Constitutional Change." *Journal of Southern History* 74 (August 2008): 589–626.

———. "War of Words: The Controversy over the Definition of Lynching, 1899–1940." *Journal of Southern History* 66, no. 1 (2000): 75–100.

Walker, Alice, ed. *I Love Myself When I Am Laughing . . . and Then Again When I Am Looking Mean and Impressive: A Zora Neale Hurston Reader*. New York: Feminist Press at CUNY, 1979.

Ward, Jason Morgan. *Defending White Democracy: The Making of a Segregationist Movement and the Remaking of Racial Politics, 1936–1965*. Chapel Hill: University of North Carolina Press, 2011.

Washburn, Patrick S. *The African American Newspaper: Voice of Freedom*. Evanston, Ill.: Northwestern University Press, 2006.

———. *A Question of Sedition: The Federal Government's Investigation of the Black Press during World War II*. New York: Oxford University Press, 1986.

Weinfeld, Daniel R. *The Jackson County War: Reconstruction and Resistance in Post–Civil War Florida*. Tuscaloosa: University of Alabama Press, 2012.

Wells-Barnett, Ida B. *Crusade for Justice: The Autobiography of Ida B. Wells.* Ed. Alfreda Duster. Chicago: University of Chicago Press, 1970.

———. *Southern Horrors (1892). A Red Record (1894). Mob Rule in New Orleans (1900).* New York: Arno Press, 1969.

Wexler, Laura. *Fire in a Canebreak: The Last Mass Lynching in America.* New York: Scribner, 2003.

White, Deborah Gray. *Too Heavy a Load: Black Women in Defense of Themselves, 1894–1994.* New York: W. W. Norton, 1999.

White, Walter. *A Man Called White: The Autobiography of Walter White.* New York: Viking Press, 1948.

———. *Rope and Faggot.* New York: Arno Press and the New York Times, 1929.

———. "What the Negro Thinks of the Army." *Annals of Social and Political Science* 223 (September 1942): 67–71.

Whitfield, Stephen J. *Death in the Delta: The Story of Emmett Till.* Baltimore: Johns Hopkins University Press, 1991.

Wilkins, Roy. "Now Is the Time Not to Be Silent." *Crisis* (January 1942): 7.

Winsboro, Irvin D. S., ed. *Old South, New South, or Down South? Florida and the Modern Civil Rights Movement.* Morgantown: West Virginia University Press, 2009.

Wood, Forrest G. *Black Scare: The Racist Response to Emancipation and Reconstruction.* Berkeley: University of California Press, 1968.

Wright, Richard. *Black Boy.* New York: Harper and Brothers, 1945.

Wyatt-Brown, Bertram. *Honor and Violence in the Old South.* New York: Oxford University Press, 1986.

Wynne, Lewis N., ed., *Florida at War.* Saint Leo, Fla.: Saint Leo College Press, 1993.

Zangrando, Robert L. *The NAACP Crusade against Lynching, 1909–1950.* Philadelphia: Temple University Press, 1980.

Zelizer, Barbie. *Remembering to Forget: Holocaust Memory through the Camera's Eye.* Chicago: University of Chicago Press, 1998.

INDEX

Page numbers in *italics* refer to illustrations.

Adams, Alto, 92, 94

Adams, Leroy, 152

African American business owners: Live Oak, 124; Marianna, 72; Quincy, 44

African American elected officials, 157

African American land owners, 71

African American press, 17, 19, 38, 103–5, 195–96

African Americans in the military: World War I, 15; World War II, 23, 24, 39–40, 105–7, 210

Agricultural Adjustment Act, 21

Alachua County, 125

Alexander, Will W., 11

Allied Forces, 39

American Civil Liberties Union (ACLU), 20, 106, 120

Ames, Jessie Daniel, 12, 13, 59, 182

Amsterdam News, 195

Anderson, Edwin, 160, 168

Anderson, Lucy Mae Payne, 159–62, 168, 214

Andrews, Charlie, 35

Anti-Lynching Crusaders, 10

Antilynching legislation, 8, 36, 38, 54, 58–59, 106, 167, 170, 202; Dyer Antilynching Bill, 10, 11, 103–4; Wagner-Van Nuys Bill, 35

Apalachicola River, 42, 69

Anti-Mob and Lynch Club (Marion County), 6

Apopka (Orange County, Fla.), 24

Associated Press, 102

Association of Southern Women for the Prevention of Lynching (ASWPL), 12–15, 36, 54, 59, 120, 182–83, 202, 203

Atkinson, Clyde "Gus," 92, 97

Atlanta Constitution, 11

Atlanta Daily World, 102, 103, 104

Atwater, Maggie Pinder, 72

Axis Powers, 39, 69, 95

Baker, Bruce E., 153, 218

Baker, Dick, 72

Baltimore Afro-American, 60, 64–65, 193, 195

Barnes, Benjamin F., Jr., 83, 84, 85, 86, 87, 88, 89, 90, 91, 92, 117

Bartow, 6

Bates, Ruby, 147

Batesburg, S.C., 190

Beasley, Samuel, 128

Beaumont, Tex., race riot, 102, 104, 107

Beck, E. M., 28–29

Belcher, Tom, 98, 99, 101, 115, 116

Bell, Annie, 47, 48, 62, 63

Bell, Maria, 47, 62, 63

Bell, Thelma, 46, 47, 48, 62, 63

Bell, William, 46, 47, 62, 63

Belle Glade, Fla., 1–4
Berge, Wendell, 52, 107, 108
Bethune, Mary McLeod, 10, 21
Bethune-Cookman College (Daytona Beach),
    10, 21
Biddle, Francis, 107, 108, 195
Black, Hugo, 89
"Black Belt" counties, 41, 69, 123
Black Codes, 5
Blanding, Albert, 199
Blankenship, Homer, 146
Blue Front (Marianna), 72
Bolita, 109
Bond-Howell Lumber Company (Live Oak),
    126, 134, 149
Bootlegging, 74, 84, 169
Borstelmann, Thomas, 39
Bradwell, Leroy, 207–8
Brookland (Marianna), 72
Broward County, 89
Brown, Ansel, 135
Brown, Armstead, 92, 94
Brown, Miles, 36
Brundage, W. Fitzhugh, 27, 67, 119, 132, 150,
    201
Bryant, Ben, 208
Buck, Pearl S., 105
Buford, Rivers, 90, 92, 93–95
Butler, W. E., 99
Byrd, Wylie, 139

Caldwell, Millard, 31, 156, 196, 197, 201, 210;
    libel suit, 178–87; reaction to Payne lynch-
    ing, 166–77, 188, 190
Camp Gordon Johnston (Carrabelle), 24
Cannady, Lola, 73
Carlen, John, 160
Carr, T. C., 83
Catts, Sidney J., 8, 35
Caudle, Theron L., 173
Cawthon, L. F., 109
Chambers, Isiah, 89
Chambers v. Florida, 89–90, 93, 94
Cherry, Gregg, 181, 183
Chambliss, W. F. "Flake," 73
Chapman, Roy, 90, 92, 93, 94, 101
Chattahoochee, Fla., 83, 153

Chattahoochee River, 69
Chattanooga News, 11
Chenery, William L., 183
Chicago Defender, 40, 174, 190, 192, 195
Chipola River, 69
Civilian Conservation Corps (CCC), 22, 37
Civil Rights Congress, 210
Civil War, U.S., 5, 7, 12, 41, 69–70, 123, 157
Clark, Tom, 117, 142, 173–74, 176, 191
Clifton, Reid, 99–100, 114
Cohen, Harold, 3
Cold War, 189, 198
Colee, Harold, 56
Coleman, Frank, 194
Coleman, Luke, 84
Collier's Magazine, 180, 183–87
Collins, Vivien, 199
Columbia, Tenn., 190
Columbia County, Fla., 7, 125
Committee for Interracial Cooperation (CIC),
    11–12, 52, 202
Committee for the Defense of Civil Rights,
    20
Communism/Communists, 17, 157, 170,
    207–8
Cone, Fred, 20, 21, 34, 77–78, 109
Congress of Industrial Organization (CIO),
    170
Cook, Plessie, 72
Cotton Club (Marianna), 72
Courtney, Horace, 50
Crews, Tom, 206
Crowell-Colliers Publishing Company, 184

Dale Mabry Air Field (Tallahassee), 24
Damascus Baptist Church (Madison), 159
Daniels, Earl, 79–80
Daniels, Jonathan, 14
Davis, Charlie, 89
Davis, Dan, 45–48, 50
Davis, Edward, 136, 168
Davis, Essex, 96
Davis, James, 164, 171
Davis, James ("Quincy Three"), 198–200
Davis, Lonnie T., 161–62, 167, 169–78, 185,
    187, 204
Davis, W. R., 110

Davis, W. T., 167
Daytona, Fla., 9, 10
De la Roche, Roberta, 202
Democrats, 5
Department of Justice (DOJ). *See* U.S. Department of Justice
Department of State. *See* U.S. Department of State
DePass, Dorothy, 143–44
Detroit, Mich., race riot, 103–4, 108
Devane, Dozier, 184, 187
DeVaughn, Edna, 72
DeVaughn, E. E., 72
"Double V" (Victory), 23, 69, 137, 193, 195
Douglass School (Live Oak), 124, 126, 129, 135
Dray, Philip, 201
DuBois, W. E. B., 8, 16–17, 19
Dudley, Edward R., 136
Dudziak, Mary, 210
Dunbar, Corrine, 134
Dunnellon, Fla., 6
Durr, Virginia, 147
Dyer, Leonidas, 8, 103
Dykes, Joe, 109

Edwards, O. O., 164
Eleazer, R. B., 178
Ellison, Ralph, 127
Ethiopia, 18
Evans, J. C., 36
Evans, Tammy, 152–53

Fair Employment Practices Commission (FEPC), 22–24, 198
Federal Bureau of Investigation (FBI), 31, 108, 109, 110, 111, 112, 115, 116, 117, 118, 142, 170, 173, 174, 194
Figgs, Lula. *See* Howard, Lula Figgs
Flipper, Ann, 66, 216
Florida, economy of, 10, 28–29, 36, 41, 42, 43, 71, 124, 158, 201; New Deal changes to, 24–25
Florida Agricultural and Mechanical College (FAMC), 49, 184, 186, 187
Florida Baptist Academy, 125
Florida constitution (1885), 6
Florida Highway Patrol, 98, 114

Florida House of Representatives, 70, 129, 170
Florida Industrial School for Boys (Marianna), 74, 79
Florida State Hospital for the Insane (Chattahoochee), 153
Florida State Prison at Raiford, 95, 96, 163, 164, 165, 188, 199, 209
Florida State Teachers Association, 206
Florida Sumatra Leaf Tobacco Company (Madison), 158
Florida Supreme Court, 20, 32, 68, 88, 90, 91, 92, 93, 94, 95, 97, 101, 112, 115, 117, 118, 199, 209
Florida Tattler (Jacksonville), 138, 195
Florida Times Union (Jacksonville), 138
Florida Voters for Constitution Government, 196–97
Foote, L. H. B., 49
Forrest, Charles, 71–72
Forrest, Cynthia, 72
Fort Benning, Ga., 40
Fort Lauderdale (Broward County), 12
Fortune, T. Thomas, 8
Foster, Leo L., 184
Franklin County, Fla., 34
Friedman-Goldberg Leaf Tobacco Company (Madison), 158
Fryar, Mack, 208

Gadsden County, Fla., 9, 29, 33, 40, 79–80, 123, 128; case of Leroy Bradwell, 207–8; history of race relations in, 41–44; response to Arthur C. Williams's lynching, 53, 57, 61, 66
Gadsden County Times (Quincy), 45
Garret, Zannie, 72
Garvey, Marcus, 16
Gasque, William "Buddy," 79–86, 80, 102; Payne investigation, 172
Gatlin, Cecil, 82, 84
Gause, Addis, 77, 113
Gause, Barkley, arrest and conviction of Cellos Harrison, 77–79, 81–82, 85–86; kidnapping and lynching of Harrison, 88, 90, 93, 97, 112–15, 204
Gause, J. P., 77–78

Gause, J. P., Jr., 77
Germany, 39, 58, 90, 95, 174, 200
Gilliam, J. J., 199
Goff, Alex Phillmore, Jr., 146
Goff, Alex Phillmore, Sr., 144–46, 149;
    kidnapping and murder of Willie James
    Howard, 129–30, 133–34, 138–42
Goff, Cynthia, 129–31, 134, 146–47, 152
Golden, Bernice, 1
Golden, Feraris "Ray," 1–4, 220
Goodman, Arch, 161
Goodman, Daniel Levy, 160, 161, 162, 163,
    164, 168, 188, 214, 215
Goodman, David, 161
Goodman, Lavone, 162–63
Goodman, Robert, 161
Granberry, Henry, 72
Granberry, Lemuel, 72, 101
Grant, Dallas
Grant, Doc, 74
Great Depression, 10, 37, 42, 129
Great Migration, 16, 37
Green, Ernest, 121
Green, James, 109
Green, Robert, 128
Greene, Moses, 174–76
Greenlee, Charlie, 208
Greenville, Fla., 160, 177
Gregory, G. Scott, 44–45
Groveland, Fla., 208
"Groveland Boys," 208–9
Guyton, Charles, 112
Guzman, Jessie, 182

Hadley, Robert, 113
Hafley, James B., 174
Hair, H. H., Jr., 140
Hall, Felix, 40
Hall, J. Lewis, 184
Hall, Jacquelyn Dowd, 12
Hall, Robert, 173, 205
Hambrey, Willard, 160
Harlem Peoples Club (New York), 59
Harris, Julian, 11
Harris, Thomas, 124
Harris, Trudier, 145
Harris, Pvt. Wilbur, 24

Harrison, Bessie (née McClinton), 79, 92,
    117, 215, 217
Harrison, Cellos, 4, 29, 31, 68–69, 198,
    122, 140–41, 164, 193, 201, 204, 211, 213,
    215, 217, 219; arrest and trials of, 73–92,
    95–96; coroner's inquest, 101; discovery
    of body, 100; investigation into lynch-
    ing of, 102, 104, 108, 110–12, 114–20;
    kidnapping of, 97–100, 204
Harrison, Leverett, 74
Harrison, Mary, 74, 117
Harrison, Pete, 72
Harrison, Theresa, 74, 117
Harrison, Willie, 72
Hastie, William H., 190
Havens, Jane, 59
Hawkins, Ernest, 35
Haynes, Detta, 131–32
Haynes, George, 107
Henry, Tom, 134–35, 139–42, 146
Hicks, William "Red," 75–76, 83
Hill, Jesse Lee, 50
Hinds, Robert, 34
Hitler, Adolf, rhetoric of Jim Crow policies
    and lynching, 19, 20, 34, 38, 40, 54, 58,
    60, 106, 170, 189–90, 192–93, 201
Hobbs, Sam, 168
Hoffman, George Earl, 108
Holden, William, 72
Holiday Inn Café (Marianna), 72
Holland, Porter, 82
Holland, Spessard, 69, 188, 196, 197, 198,
    199, 201; response to lynching of Cellos
    Harrison, 105–6, 115; response to the
    lynching of Willie James Howard, 130,
    137–38, 140–42; response to lynching of
    Arthur C. Williams, 29, 31, 36–37, 51–52,
    59
Holloway, Jonathan, 219
Holmes, Eddie, 124
Holocaust (World War II), 19
Hoover, J. Edgar, 108, 117, 173, 195–96
Hope, John, 11
Hopps Building (Live Oak), 124
Horne, Aggie Bell, 72
Horne, Willie, 71
Hornsby, J. C., 78

Howard, James, 126, 131; kidnapping and lynching of Willie James Howard, 134–35; impact of lynching upon, 149–50, 152, 154–55, 215, 217; investigation of lynching, 136–37, 138–46

Howard, Lula Figgs, 126; impact of son's lynching upon, 150, 151, 215, 217; investigation of lynching, 138–42, 144; kidnapping and lynching of Willie James Howard, 131–35

Howard, Walter, 27, 29, 119, 202, 204

Howard, Willie James, 4, 29, 31, 122, 126, 128–29, 130–32, 138, 139, 141–49, 198, 201, 206, 211, 213, 215, 217, 220; kidnapping of, 133, 134, 136, 151, 152, 153, 154, 155; lynching of, 134–35

Howell, R. L., 139

Hunter, William, 139

Hurston, Zora Neale, 189–90

Ingalls, Robert, 26–27

International Labor Defense (ILD), 17, 20, 171, 174, 175, 176

International League of Darker People, 16

Irvin, Walter, 208–10

Jackson, James, 60

Jackson, Robert, 136

Jackson County, Fla., 6, 28–29, 41; arrest and trials of Cellos Harrison, 74, 78–83; history of race relations, 68–73; kidnapping and lynching of Cellos Harrison, 90–93, 96–97; lynching investigation, 101, 110, 112, 114, 115, 117, 118, 119, 128, 211, 215

Jackson County Floridan, 72, 82, 88, 96–97

Jackson County Training School, 78, 84

Jacksonville, 9, 123, 195

Jacksonville Journal, 166, 181

Japan, rhetoric of Jim Crow policies and lynching, 16–19, 39, 90, 95, 106, 137, 166, 174, 200

Jefferson County, Fla., 41, 160, 163

Jim Crow laws, 6, 37, 39–41, 44, 49, 71, 78, 94, 126–27, 128–29, 150, 158–59, 204–5, 218–19; compared to laws against Jews, 19

Johnson, Charles S., 11

Johnson, James Weldon, 8

Johnson, R. H., 19

Jordan, E. B., 98, 99, 116

Kelley, J. R., 164

Key West, 8

Kilgore, John, 182–83

King, A. L., 136

King, Martin Luther, III, 2

King, Martin Luther, Jr., 3, 127

Kirkland, Leo, 100

Konvitz, Milton, 137

Ku Klux Klan (KKK), 9, 19, 24–26, 140, 143–44, 199, 210

LaCossit, Henry, 186, 187

Lafayette County, Fla., 125

La Guardia, Fiorello, 21

Lakeland Ledger, 166

Lane, Fred, 198–200

Lang, Charles, 121

Lanier, David, 135, 137, 140, 141

Larkins, Will "Bull," 44, 45, 219

Law enforcement, 38, 109, 196, 205, 207; failure to protect prisoners, 61, 67, 114, 169, 172–73, 204; suspected complicity in lynching, 112–13, 114, 115, 118, 204

League of Nations, 18

Lee, Frank, 74, 109, 110, 118

Leon County, Fla., 41, 44, 123

Levy County, Fla., 9

Lewis, Amos, 57, 116

Live Oak, Fla., 9, 29; history of race relations, 123–26; lynching of Willie James Howard, 129–30; lynching investigation, 135–38, 150–55, 220

Livingston, Lonnie, 160, 161

Logan, Rayford, 22

Los Angeles, Calif., race riot, 102–3

Love, Edgar C., 49

Luten, Morgan P., 46–50, 52, 60, 61, 204

Lynching, 38; changing form, 27, 28, 57, 58, 119, 120, 122, 188, 201; decreasing frequency, 53, 118, 203; definition, 15; dispute of definition, 179–82; "legal lynching," 118, 119, 164, 203; statistics, 25, 29, 125, 203

MacDill Air Field, 24

Mackay, Cliff, 105

Madison, Fla., 4, 29, 165–66, 172, 181, 183, 211

Madison County, Fla., 7, 9, 29, 41, 44, 123, 125, 143; lynching of Jesse James Payne, 156–58, 160, 163–71, 174, 177, 179–80, 207–8

Malloy, Hershel, 80

March on Washington Movement, 23

Marianna, Fla., 4, 29, 56, 68, 70, 71, 72, 73, 74, 78, 79, 80, 81, 83, 84, 90, 92, 96, 98, 99, 104, 105, 107, 109, 112, 113, 114, 117, 119, 193, 217, 219

Marianna Peanut Plant, 71

Marion County, Fla., 6, 7, 125, 136

Markovitz, Jonathan, 148

Marshall, Thurgood, 136–37, 142, 206

May, Sanford, 59

Mayo, Frank, 111

Mayo, Johnnie: investigation, 76–83, 86; lynching of Cellos Harrison, 88, 90, 100, 108–11, 117; murder, 74–76

Mayo, Milton, 111

Mayo, Nella, 74–76, 78, 83, 88, 109–11

Mayo, Roy, 111

Mayo, Wilbur, 111

Mays, Benjamin, 127

McCall, Willis, 208–9

McClinton, Bessie, 79

McCollum, Ruby, 152–53

McCray, John, 104

McCullers, Seldon "Mack," 133–34, 139–42, 144–46, 149

McFadden, Sam, 143, 174–76, 206–7

McGovern, James, 28, 127

McGuire, Phillip, 40

McKenzie, Marjorie, 103–4

McMullian, Jack, 81, 82, 84–85, 97, 99

McNutt, Paul, 195

McPherson, Edward, 133

McRae, LeRoy D., 82, 86, 101

Meeks, James, 109

Meeks, Jess, 109

Miami, 108, 195; Coconut Grove, 9

Miami Herald, 20, 166

Miami Negro Youth Council, 59

Mills, Henry, 99

Milton, George Fort, 11

Milton, John, 70

Miranda v. Arizona, 89

Monroe, Ga., 190

Monticello, Fla., 162, 163, 165, 188

Moore, Harriette, 210

Moore, Harry T., 106; lynching of Willie James Howard, 140–43, 154; lynching of Jesse James Payne, 168–69, 186–87; response to the lynching of Jesse James Payne, 206–7, 209–10

Moore, Simeon H. "Simmie," 162–63, 187

Moore, Tom, 113–14

Moore v. Dempsey, 91

Morehouse College (Atlanta, Ga.), 127

Mormino, Gary, 24

Moton, R. R., 11

Mussolini, Benito, 20, 38, 54

Myers, James, 107

Nation, 14

National Anti-Mob and Lynch Law Association, 6

National Association for the Advancement of Colored People (NAACP), 2, 8, 10–11, 14–16, 20, 54, 60, 69, 103, 118, 120, 136, 142–44, 150, 178, 202–3, 206, 210; Florida State Conference, 106, 140–41, 168, 209; Legal Defense and Education Fund, 136–37; Marion County, 136, 168; Orange County, 138, 140

National Labor Relations Act, 22, 37

National Labor Relations Board, 24

National Socialist Party (also Nazis), 19, 39, 41, 58, 60, 89, 105, 166, 170, 192

Neal, Allie Mae, 216–17

Neal, Claude, lynching of, 27–29, 30, 33, 65, 68, 72–73, 81–82, 88, 90, 104, 117–19, 217, 219

New Deal, 4, 21, 24–25, 37, 137, 211

New York Age, 105

New York Daily Worker, 170

New York Herald Tribune, 55

New York Times, 19, 55
New Zion Baptist Church, 159
Nuremberg Laws, 19, 170

Ochlockonee River, 42
Ocoee, Fla., 9
Odum, Howard, 11
Oral history or tradition, 65, 66, 99–100, 122,
    150–53, 214–20
Orange County, Fla., 9
Orlando, Fla., 138–41
Orlando Reporter-Star, 170
Ortiz, Paul, 6, 9

Padgett, Norma Lee, 208
Palm Beach County, Fla., 2
Paris Peace Conference, 16
Parker, Julius F., 184
Parker, Orion, 47–48, 50–51
Payne, Amos, 214
Payne, Jesse James, 4, 26, 29, 31, 143,
    156, 159, 160, 197, 204, 207, 211, 213–15;
    kidnapping and lynching of, 161–65, 204;
    reaction to lynching of, 166–88, 190–91,
    201, 209
Payne, Leroy, 214
Payne, Lillie Mae Wiley, 160–62, 168, 187,
    214–15
Payne, Lucy Ann, 160–62, 168, 187, 214
Payne, Lucy Mae. *See* Anderson, Lucy Mae
    Payne
Payne, Ruby, 215
Payne, Stephen, 214
Payne, William, 159
Pegler, Westbrook, 34, 55–57
Pensacola Colored Citizen, 195
Pensacola Journal, 108
People's Funeral Home (Marianna), 72
Pepper, Claude, 35, 137–38, 198
Perry, John "Bubba," 162–63
Perry, July, 9
Perry, Mamie, 145
Perry, Susie, 162
Pfeifer, Michael J., 28
Phillips Citrus, 24

Pinar, William F., 128, 145
Pittman, William "Jabo," 47, 50, 78–81,
    83–84, 117
Pittsburgh Courier, 18, 23, 60, 63, 103, 195
Polk County, Fla., 6, 36
Ponder, Richard, 34–35
Pope, Washington, 70
Powell v. Alabama, 91
Price, Otis, 36
Price, Victoria, 147
Progressive Voters League, 207
Purdee, Armstrong, 72

Quincy (Gadsden County, Fla.), 4, 29, 79,
    80, 85, 93, 114–15, 198, 216, 219; African
    Americans in, 44; lynching of Arthur C.
    Williams, 41–67
"Quincy Three," 198–99

Racial etiquette, 12, 63, 75, 126–27, 132–33,
    153, 159, 184
Raiford. *See* Florida State Prison at
    Raiford
Randolph, A. Philip, 22-23, 37
Rape, allegations of, 34, 44–45, 46–48, 54,
    61–63, 67, 73, 132, 147, 179; insinuations
    of, 184; against Jesse James Payne, 156,
    164, 169; in the Scottsboro case, 91
Raper, Arthur R., 11
Reconstruction, 5, 9, 35–36, 41, 70, 124,
    194
Red Bird Café (Marianna), 72
Red Cross, 40
Reddick, Tink, 100
Red Summer (1919), 8, 16
Reid, Ira De A., 126
Reid, T. R., 142
Reiff, Charlie, 75–76, 83
Republicans, 5, 9, 70, 157
Riley, John Gilmore, 59
River Junction Tribune (Chattahoochee),
    57
Robinson, Abraham, 84
Robinson, Elbert C., 136
Rogers, J. A., 18

Rogers, Lewis, 98–99, 101, 116

Roman, Meredith, 17

Roosevelt, Eleanor, 21, 178; fears of "Eleanor Clubs," 22

Roosevelt, Franklin D., 21–22, 31, 35, 37, 38, 60, 69, 94, 173, 178, 189; policy toward lynching, 107–8, 194–96

Rosewood, Fla., 9, 147

Rowe, R. H., 171

Rushdy, Ashraf, 203

Russia (also U.S.S.R.), 178, 192, 210; use of lynching as propaganda, 17–18, 20

Scott, Reginald H., Sr., 133–34, 141–42, 144, 149

Scottsboro Boys, 17, 91

Screws, Claude, 173, 205–6

Screws v. United States, 173, 205–6

Sebring, Harold L., 93–95

Sengstacke, John, 190

Shepard, Sammy, 208–10

Shoemaker, Joseph, 20

Shofner, Jerrell, 70

Sikeston, Mo., lynching, 107

Sims, Bunny, 99

Sims, Joe, 98, 100, 101, 113–14

Singleton, Sam, 50

Sixth World Comintern Congress, 18

Slavery, 41, 69–70, 123, 157

Smith, Ben, 72

Smith, Lillian, 147

Smith, T. R., 56

Smith, Turner L., 173–74

Smith v. Allwright, 207

Snell, Lee, 36

Solomon, Gertrude, 124

Southern Christian Leadership Conference (SCLC), 2

Southern Commission for the Study of Lynching (SCSL), 11

Southern Negro Youth Congress, 60, 171, 174

Spanish-American War, 7

Speights, Jim, 72

Speights, Raymond, 75–76, 83

Springfield Missionary Baptist Church, 126, 154

St. Augustine, 8

St. Petersburg Independent, 166, 179, 181

St. Petersburg Times, 54–55, 166, 182, 200

Stacey, Rubin, 12

Stambaugh, Judi, 1

Standland, Charles, 81, 84

Starry, Weldon G., 97, 114

Stevens, William Spencer, 44

Stinson, R. T., 72

Sumatra Tobacco Corporation (Quincy), 42

Sumners, Hatton W., 167–68

Suwannee County, Fla., 9, 29; history of race relations, 123–25; lynching of Willie James Howard, 131, 134, 136–41, 142–44, 150, 174, 206–7, 211

Suwannee Democrat, 138, 144, 146, 154–55

Suwannee High School, 129, 146

Suwannee River, 121–23, 134, 141, 148–49, 158

Swilley, Alphonso, 72

Swilley, Alvin, Jr., 72

Swilley, Alvin, Sr., 72

Swilley, Earnest, 72

Swilley, Lawrence, 72, 84

Talbert, Mary, 10

Tallahassee, Fla., 24, 35, 123; Millard Caldwell's libel case, 183–84; lynching of Cellos Harrison, 81–82, 85, 90, 95, 112, 114; lynching of Arthur C. Williams, 44, 49–50, 52, 59, 61, 64; "the Quincy Three," 198

Tallahassee Daily Democrat, 55, 56, 101

Tampa, Fla., 8, 20, 24–27, 109, 181–82, 195

Tampa Morning Tribune, 102, 169

Tampa Star Cigar Company (Madison), 158

Tampa Tribune, 54, 186

Taylor, Fannie, 147

Taylor County, Fla., 125

Taylor's Restaurant (Marianna), 72

Terrell, William Glenn, 35, 92, 94

Thomas, Elwyn, 92, 93

Thomas, Ernest, 208

Thompson, James G., 23

Till, Emmett, 2, 64, 121–22, 147–48

Till, Mamie, 2

Time Magazine, 181, 183

Times Courier (Marianna), 71

Tobacco, 43, 158, 160–61; black shank disease, 42; shade-grown, 42

Tolnay, Stewart E., 28–29

Trammell, Park, 35
Tripp, Maurice, 51, 52
Trotter, William Monroe, 8, 16
Trueblood, Wyatt, 208
Truman, Harry S., 94, 194, 210
Turner, Guy, 100
Turner, Mary, 214
Tuskegee Institute, 15, 36, 179, 182–83
Tyson, Vernon L., 178

Udell, Douglas, 154
United Citrus Workers, 24
Universal Negro Improvement Association, 16
U.S. Army Air Corps, 24
U.S. Department of Justice, 31, 52, 69; response to Jesse James Payne's lynching, 174–76, 191–94; response to Cleo Wright's lynching, 107–8, 116, 173
U.S. Department of State, 39
U.S. House of Representatives, antilynching legislation, 21, 103, 167
U.S. Senate, 39
U.S. Supreme Court, 89–90, 209

Van Nuys, Frederick, 35
Van Priest's Store, 129

Wade, Alexander, 164, 165, 188
Wagner, Robert, 35
Waldrep, Christopher, 194
Walker, Madame C. J., 16
Walker, Thomas, 116
Walker, W. May, 199
Wallace, Henry, 195
Walls, Lonnie, 110–10
Warren, Fuller, 209
Wash, Howard, 116, 194
Washington Tribune, 19
Watford, Walter, 76, 112
Watson, J. Tom, 95, 170–72, 178
Webb, Will, 49–52, 64
Welch, Ernest C., 83, 85, 87–88, 90, 96, 117
Wells, D. W. "Red," 98, 100, 114
Wells, Ida B., 7, 10–11, 16, 146
West Florida Bugle (Marianna), 72
Whitaker, C. D., 76, 83

Whitaker, Pat, 57, 184, 186
White, Curly, 72
White, Eartha M. M., 10
White, John, 83
White, Sam, 72
White, Walter, 19, 136
White, W. C., 72
Whitfield, James B., 92, 94
Wiegman, Robyn, 145
Wigginton, John T., 174, 184, 186, 187
Wiley, Lillie Mae. *See* Payne, Lillie Mae Wiley
Wilhoit, Sterling E., 48–50, 52, 64–65
Wilkins, Roy, 60, 140
Williams, Arthur C., 4, 29, 31, 33–34, 36, 40; arrest, kidnapping, and murder of, 45–50; coroner's jury, 50–51; investigation of lynching, 52–55, 60–82, 93, 122, 198, 201–2, 204, 213, 216, 219
Williams, Eddie, 216
Williams, Frank, 216
Williams, Frank, Jr., 216
Williams, Freddie, 216
Williams, Hattie, 47, 49, 66, 215–16
Williams, Jack, 89
Williams, James, 198–200
Williams, Rufus, 50
Wilson, Christopher, 3
Wing, John D., 58–59
Withlacoochee River, 50
Woodward, Isaac, 190
Woodward, Walter, 89
Work, Monroe N., 11
Workers' Defense League, 208
Works Progress Administration (WPA), 22, 37
World War I, 15–16, 94, 143, 192
World War II, 4, 26, 31–32, 34, 38–39, 42, 66, 119–20, 129, 148, 157, 168, 178, 188–94, 200–201, 206, 210–11; bombing of Pearl Harbor, 23; mobilization in Florida, 23–24, 37
Wright, Cleo, 107, 173, 194
Wright, Richard, 127–28
Wynn, "Bunk," 72
Wynn, Ed, 49–50, 52, 61

Zelizer, Barbie, 151

TAMEKA BRADLEY HOBBS is assistant professor of history at Florida Memorial University in Miami Gardens, Florida.

CPSIA information can be obtained at www.ICGtesting.com
Printed in the USA
LVOW11*2309080116

469508LV00006B/42/P

9 780813 061047